Kent McCray:
The Man Behind the Most Beloved Television Shows

Marianne Rittner-Holmes & Kent McCray

Ten-K AlphaDox Publishing

BELEN, NEW MEXICO U.S.A.

Ten-K AlphaDox Publishing
Belen, New Mexico USA 87002
www.kentmccray.com

Publisher's Note: This book is based upon the experience and recollections of Kent McCray. It is Mr. McCray's intent to represent events as he remembers, understanding that memories are fallible. The conversations in the book come from Mr. McCray and those interviewed based on their recollections, and are not written to represent word-for-word transcripts. Rather, Mr. McCray and the others have retold them in a way that evokes the feeling and meaning of what was said in order to capture the essence of the dialogue, which is accurate to the best of their knowledge. All photos are taken from Kent and Susan McCray's personal collection.

Book Layout © 2014 BookDesignTemplates.com

KENT McCRAY: The Man Behind the Most Beloved Television Shows/Marianne Rittner-Holmes & Kent McCray. -- 1st ed.
ISBN 978-0-9982960-0-5 52995

Dedications

To my husband Dave, whose fathomless patience reinforces my belief that I married well; and to my parents, Dr. James and Bernice Rittner, who taught me to love God.

Marianne Rittner-Holmes

This book is in memory of my parents Dorothy and Tom McCray and my close friend Michael Landon.

It is dedicated to my four children, my grandchildren, to those who have been members of my crew whom I consider my special family and to my beloved wife, Susan. Without her love, insight, vision and encouragement, I probably would not have pursued writing this book about my life and career.

Kent McCray

To my husband: I am very proud of your life, your successful career and who you are as a human being. Most of all I am proud to be your wife, soul-mate, partner and best friend. You bring joy and laughter into my life and into the lives of all who have the pleasure of knowing you.

Susan McCray

Notes & Acknowledgements

I first met Kent and Susan McCray in 2013 at a public gathering related to *The High Chaparral*. This late-60s television series played a huge role in my life growing up, and the idea of meeting some of those involved in making this historic show was like a young girl's dream-come-true.

Kent and Susan, for all their tremendous television and movie work, were not initially well-known to me. This is really not surprising because Kent is a very humble man. Susan, who is much more outgoing, focuses on her husband, their life together, their charities, and her various successful business endeavors.

Kent and Susan entered the main room. I greeted them and said to Kent, "Sir, I have a question for you that I'd like to ask once you and your wife are settled, if that's okay." He said, "Ask me now." I looked at Susan and back at Kent. "Sir, it can wait until you get into the room and get settled." "No," he said. "Ask me now. That's what I'm here for."

I asked my question and got the answer. I also got my first glimpse into the amazing mind and the spellbinding storytelling skills of production manager/producer Kent McCray.

Kent's narrative style is strong and his stories are mesmerizing. These were shared with me through audio recordings he made in 2012 and interviews we had in person from 2014 to 2017. The voice you hear in this work is his. If other quotes are interjected, those speakers are identified at that time.

This book attempts to capture Kent's historic career in television and his early life as well. To know Kent is to know where he came from, because he surely has never forgotten.

My immense thanks and appreciation to Kent & Susan McCray; Mallory Furnier of The Autry Museum for her research; Don Rittner, Ray Collins, Jan Pippins & Wendy St. Germain for their authors' insight; Sandi Bachom for memories of her dad, Jack; Doris Long (Ni Langain) and Diann L. Reed for their help on Facebook while this work was written; Ray "George" Marin for his research materials; all those quoted within the book who allowed me to interview them; brother Jay Rittner; and to special friends Don Collier, the late Kiva Lawrence-Hoy, Marc Mitzell, Michele Simmons, Genevieve Rafter Keddy, MJ Muller, Sherrod Baden, Ruth Diehl, Angela & Mark Norman, Andrew & Dorothy Barreras, Deacon Lorenzo & Gloria Castillo, and Father José A. Hernández y Cosme for their encouragement and support.

Marianne Rittner-Holmes
New Mexico, USA
February 22, 2017

Acknowledgement

Many thanks to Marianne Rittner-Holmes, a gifted writer and friend, for without her talent and dedication there would be no book. A special thank you to those special friends who were interviewed for this book.

Hire the best, get out of their way, and let them do their job.

Kent McCray

CONTENTS

Dedications III

Notes & Acknowledgements i

Acknowledgement iii

The Roots of the Tree Run Deep 1

The Doctor from Yale 17

"Never Say No to a Job" or "If You See Me, You Don't Know Me" ...27

"Everything Was Live!"..31

My Life with Ralph Edwards...39

The Production Supervisor Takes a Wife 47

Big Brother...53

Uncle Miltie's Whistle..55

Hope Springs Eternal in Alaska 63

Bob Hope & the One-Star General Explore the Orient....................69

The Road to Europe 85

Forging Friendships with *Outlaws* 93

Someone's in Denmark with Dinah… 97

Riding with *Outlaws* Again..107

A *Bonanza* of Color 113

A Production Manager Keeps It All Going...............................117

Tales from the Ponderosa...129

The High Chaparral..133

Mr. Burris' Homestead 139

"*Chaparral* Was My Baby" 143

Tales from the Sonoran Desert..149

Consolidating Resources..155

Introducing Susan Sukman 159

Ending an Era: Cancellation of *Chaparral* and *Bonanza*......................167

Little House on the Prairie...173

Walnut Grove Comes to Life 181

Casting the Casting Director 185

Prairie Companions..191

Changes, New Productions & MGM 200

Killing Stone & Father Murphy 207

Little House with a New Perspective 211

Tales from the Prairie..217

Introducing Susan Sukman McCray 223

Highway to Heaven..231

Tales from the Highway...239

Where Pigeons Go to Die...247

Us 251

Us Minus One 255

With Laughter & Love..261

Bonanza Movies: This Ain't No Music Video 264

It's Not Where You Start; It's Where You Finish 273

My Work..283

CHAPTER ONE

The Roots of the Tree Run Deep

My mother, Dode McCray, was shopping in downtown Hartford, Conn., when the elevator she was in quickly dropped three floors before it stopped. Rescuers came to her aid and she was liberated from the tiny car by climbing a ladder to one of the floors. I don't know if it was the excitement of the mishap or the actual free fall, but the event caused her to be rushed to the hospital where she soon gave birth to me, weighing in at all of four pounds-four ounces. Me is Kent Baldwin McCray. It was June 7, 1928.

While my family's roots can be traced back to Europe in the 1400s, I'll just share that my dad's side was Scottish and my mom's side was English. Some ancestors came over on the *Mayflower* or in that time period. Dode, a nickname for Dorothy, was born January 4, 1900 in Northampton, Mass. Her dad, my grandfather, Ralph Lyman Baldwin, moved to Hartford, Conn., where he became the Supervisor of Music for all Hartford's public schools from the turn of the century until 1936 when he retired. He improved music instruction by the standards he set, plus he raised money for music students to study outside the classroom. He also directed the Men's Choral Club of Hartford for thirty years until his death in 1937.

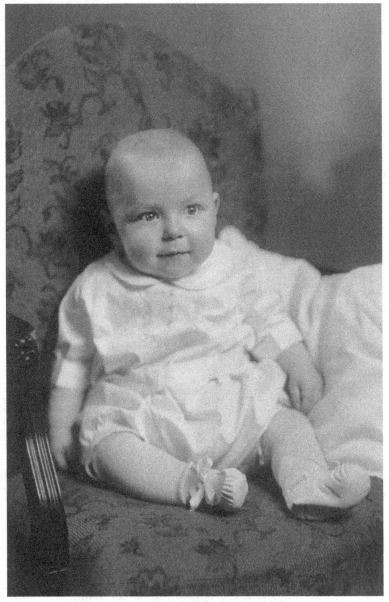

Me: Kent Baldwin McCray

Grandfather Baldwin taught at Smith College in Northampton, Mass. during the summers. My mother's side of the family grew up only nine miles away on a farm in

Williamsburg, Mass. The farm, which was started in 1868, was originally owned by mother's family. They kept it until the early '30s then sold it to W.E. Kellogg. My grandfather bought an acre of land on the edge of the farm around 1907 and built a summer house.

I just loved that house. It didn't have a cellar or heat or insulation, but it had a kitchen, a living room that went the whole length of the house, and a back room that grandfather used as an office. Later on we called that the "crying room" because that's where my brother Alden and I were sent when we acted up, returning to be with the family when we found a better attitude.

My family's summer house near Williamsburg, Mass.

The upstairs had six bedrooms because my mother's family had six children. It had one bath. The house was built out over the porch that ran on three sides. When the weather was good, we lived on that porch. We slept out there. We ate out there. We sat out there on big rockers. Ever been to a Cracker Barrel

Restaurant? Those big rockers they have? Those are the kind of rockers we sat in.

We had large gatherings there on the weekends, maybe thirty people. Family members came in for different holidays or events. We always had a crowd. I loved it. There were two big trunks in the attic that had old clothes in them dating back to the 1800s. We all dressed up in different costumes, which was fun to do. We also had sporting events. Our family gatherings were great. Being around so many people most of the time, I learned to be tolerant and to accept others, which were great childhood lessons. Plus, I always liked being in the midst of all that action. I wanted to see something happen; I wanted to be part of *making* something happen.

My father, Thomas Chapman McCray

My dad, Thomas Chapman McCray, was born in Hartford, Conn. on April 18, 1901. His family also had a history of music and singing. My great-great grandfather Calvin Curtis McCray was a noted singer prior to the Civil War.[1] Dad developed his baritone voice at school in Philadelphia and sang on weekends back in Hartford, where he met fellow singer Dorothy Spelman Baldwin. On June 23, 1923 they married, and by the mid-1920s, he worked as an underwriter for Travelers Insurance in his hometown. Travelers Insurance was the original owner of radio station WTIC in Hartford. The TIC stands for Travelers Insurance Company.[2]

In 1926, a memorandum came through dad's office posting an opening for a part time announcer at WTIC. A co-worker in the office bet my dad five dollars that he wouldn't get the job. Dad tried out for it and did get the job. He also took the five dollars which was a good sum of money in 1926. However, the job cost him a little money, too, because he had to go downtown and buy a tuxedo. Even though it was radio, WTIC wanted all its announcers to portray a dignified and prestigious image.

Dad started as a part time announcer, became a full time announcer and later, became program manager for the station. Mother and he had done concerts at church and small gatherings, so he hired her to work on commercials because she played piano and sang. They also did a talk show together on radio. Dad hired Ed Begley to read the funny papers on Sunday morning and he also hired Moshe Paranov, who was head of the Hartt School of Music. Dad had the Hartt orchestra perform on radio, which began a long lasting association with that institution.

Every night after dinner, my dad listened to the radio to make sure the right show was on at the right time. In those days, they recorded what aired on huge, thick discs like an Edison phonograph record. I sprawled on the floor and listened to the shows, imagining in my own head what the scene or action looked like. You did that with radio. Without realizing it, I think that's why I was drawn to theatrics. It was instilled in me early on.

My dad in hat and overcoat next to the column far right. This is an actual picture of WTIC's coverage of the 1938 hurricane in Hartford.

In 1938, we had a huge hurricane in Hartford. I was in grade school at the time, about ten years old. I remember walking home from school, stepping over wires and debris. I got back to the house nearby when all of a sudden, the roof blew off. Mother was there and we moved mattresses downstairs to sleep on the floor. Dad was at the radio station, which became a liaison to the outside world because they had a shortwave set up and they contacted other cities. They reported on people who were safe, relaying the information so loved ones outside the area didn't worry. Those reports went on twenty-four hours a day. Dad stayed at the studio over two straight weeks until the crisis was over.[3]

In the meantime, mother went out and found a three-story house to rent. My dad's mother moved in with us along with her sister, and they lived with us for a long, long time. My grandmother was a great cook.

My dad had a lot of talents. I remember working with him as he re-finished furniture. He loved to do that. I scraped down the old wood and he created a design and painted it like gold leaf. He took up artistic painting in his later life. He also had a wonderful sense of humor and he used it when he wrote, which was often.

In the early days of the Hartt School, students put on a musical play. My dad wrote a parody of it and the faculty played all the parts. For instance, in one of the student plays, there was a moose over the mantle. In my dad's version, instead of a moose, the Dean of the Hartt School was on a ladder in back of the wall with his head sticking out of a hole, rolling his eyes back and forth at the audience.

During holidays, we went to grandmother's house for the whole day while she cooked and we visited. The house had a big room, an addition that used to be a store. My dad wrote plays and all of us were in it. About thirty people and everybody had a part. We performed in that big room. Dad always made fun of somebody or some activity, but never to be hurtful. Just to have a good-natured laugh. My dad was very witty but very kind, too.

My mother also had a good sense of humor and she was very kind. I worked better with my father because he was very calm and quiet. My mother was a lot like me. She had little patience and would fly off the handle. She and I bickered a lot. Not fights, but she'd say, "Why don't you do it this way?" I'd say, "No, I'm not going to do it that way!"

My mother, Dorothy "Dode" Baldwin McCray

When I was really young, she gave me a dime to go to the movies on Saturday afternoons. I sat through them a second time because the films were so enjoyable. I had no idea I would be working in them one day. If there was a double feature, I sat there for four or five hours. Mother had to come to the theater to collect me for dinner.

My mom and dad had big hearts. They had a positive attitude in everything they did, and that rubbed off on me. I learned to see value in things many people didn't. For instance, when I got older, I took a job on the Kellogg farm near the summer house.

My pay was three dollars a week plus meals. I worked from five in the morning until eight o'clock at night. Sundays were a bit lighter. While there I learned to work for people not related to me, which was quite different than working for family. I loved it!

I never minded work. In fact, I liked working with my hands. It seemed the thing for me. I wasn't very studious. I was not a good student at all. Just hated English. Hated it. Today, I spell phonetically, but that ain't right. Rather than memorize a lot of rules, I loved to work things out by myself because it felt like I accomplished something.

When I was in prep school, I did most of the solos for the congregational church because I had a pretty good voice. I was lucky to be in outside activities because they were tied to school grades. I was the lead singer in the choir, the glee club and the church, and I did pretty well at football and lacrosse. A lot of my professors were also on the activities eligibility committee, and I think they kind of slid me through.

I grew up in the Depression era, but my parents maintained as much of a normal life as possible. We were fortunate enough in Hartford that, while the Depression was bad, it never hit our city as hard as it did other cities because Hartford was the insurance capital of the world. Everyone paid their insurance premiums, even if they were only a dime. They paid them because they were afraid to lose them. The city also had Colt Firearms and Underwood Typewriters as well as the Pratt/Whitney Airplane Motor Factory and Fuller Brush. These were very prosperous businesses that kept the city afloat.

In seventh grade, I got a job at a grocery store. It was a meat market that also sold vegetables. I cleaned meat, I cleaned vegetables, I kept the aisles neat and clean. I did anything, even delivered groceries on my bicycle. I worked afternoons and all day Saturday. Then they went out of business. My brother

Alden had gotten a job at a florist company in West Hartford. At Christmas one year they were looking for a gofer, and he let me know, so I got hired there, too. I continued working there for many, many years, all through high school and college.

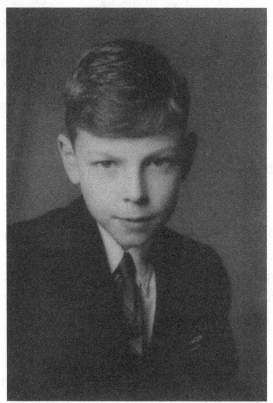

Me about the age I started working

When I was thirteen, I remember one day coming in from playing outside. I started to say something but my dad harshly told me to be quiet, which hurt my feelings. I realized he was listening to the radio and the announcers were informing us that the Japanese had bombed Pearl Harbor. That day changed our whole family's life. Everything and everybody became part of the War. The park where I used to play football turned into a battery of anti-aircraft guns. Alden, who was four years older, was drafted right away and sent to England. He spent his entire War years there working at a big supply depot in the Quartermaster division, even during the Nazi blitzkrieg. Later, he came home and went to college.

Dad was now program manager of WTIC. In 1943, the U.S. government's Office of Censorship asked him to work for their broadcasting division. Dad arranged radio shows to be transcribed and sent overseas for the troops.[4] His new role came with a transfer to New York. During dad's time there, my mother decided to work on behalf of the War effort, too. She took a job at Fuller Brush making brushes to clean guns. Fuller Brush was running double shifts then. With this exception, mom was home all during the time I was growing up. My grandmother and her sister took care of me when she wasn't home.

During the War, our house had black-out curtains. We had one room we called my grandmother's "hot box." We didn't have much heat in the house because fuel was rationed and we had to conserve it for our oil furnace. However, we got my grandmother a two-burner kerosene stove for this particular room in the house. She loved it because it was like going into a steam bath. We went in there every night and played checkers and other games. During the day, my aunt made the beds and did other house chores with gloves on because it was so cold.

When my dad worked in New York during the War years, I used to catch the train and visit him there. I was probably about fourteen or fifteen years old. By then he had an apartment where I stayed with him. He took me to Yankee Stadium and Dodger Stadium. He took me to Radio City Music Hall. That's where I saw *Gunga Din* and that's why it's a favorite movie and memory for me, because of time spent with my dad.

Eventually, my parents decided to move permanently to New York when dad was made program manager for NBC's Eastern

Region in 1944.[5] In August 1944, I went to New York to live with my parents and to start my second year of high school.

Living in New York was a new experience. My parents had a two-bedroom apartment on Forty-seventh and Third. It was very hot, muggy and sticky with no air conditioning in the apartment. We sat in front of the refrigerator and tried to get a little cool air to keep from sweating so much. After two weeks, it wasn't a happy arrangement for any of us, and we all agreed that I would attend a boys' prep school in New Hampshire. I enrolled in Kimball Union Academy in Meriden, N.H., about fourteen miles south of Dartmouth College. Best thing that ever happened to me and my parents, sanity-wise.

My early years meant a lot to me because my parents and I were always close. They were always there. However, the War changed a lot of my upbringing from being together as a family to being spread out all over. I have to admit I was on my own a lot during that time. Mother wrote me letters, but I hardly wrote her back because, yes, I hated English. When I went away to prep school, I didn't see my parents until Christmas time. Every summer, I worked at the florist's or the Kellogg farm and I sent my trunk from Kimball Academy with all my things in it to mother in New York. She stored it in a locker in the basement. Never unpacked it. In the fall of the year, she sent it back to me. A far cry from our summer house gatherings.

During my time at Kimball, I made three special friends there: Tony Colby from California, Bill Boyton from Vermont, and David Batchelder from Connecticut. We became known as The Big Four. We were very close friends through the three years at Kimball and for our whole adult lives. It was a great association.

I had little side jobs at Kimball. I worked in the kitchen, and by senior year, I was a head waiter and ran part of the dining room. While at school, I tried to make a little extra money. I went to the seniors and bought chairs, rugs, lamps, basically anything that didn't belong to the school, and then sold them to incoming classmates the next year.

One year Tony Colby and I bought the tuxedo concession from a senior. Kimball let us have two dances a year during which girls were allowed on campus. We emptied one dorm for the girls, who stayed over the weekend with a dance on Saturday night. Tony and I provided tuxedos for these dances. The two of us went to Manchester, N.H., and made a deal with a tuxedo rental house. We added a dollar to that fee, so we made more than a buck per tux.

We took measurements in the evenings in my dorm room. Tony measured and I wrote the names and numbers down. One night, I looked up to see Tony measuring someone using a six-inch ruler, a straight-edge, coming down the guy's bent arm end-over-end. I said, "Tony, geez, where's your tape measure?" He said, "I can't find it. This is the only thing I have." We took all the measurements that night with a six-inch ruler.

Needless to say, some of the tuxedos were a little ill-fitting when the guys tried them on. We had somebody make last minute adjustments, but if it was too short, well, that's all we could do. For some, their shirts popped up when they sat down because of the bad fit. No one took it too seriously because it was only for one night. We heard a few grumpy words, but no one held any grudges. We also had the flower concession. We always looked for ways to make a dollar.

Kimball was a great, great experience growing up. I went out for basketball and played for three years. Our coach was an ex-Army officer. Everything by the book. It was a twelve-man squad. I was the twelfth man. I worked my tail off in the scrimmages when we practiced. He alternated the two centers, but I stayed in the whole damn time and ran back and forth.

If we went away to play another school, the coach sat everybody down on the bench and said, "Those making the trip to…" whatever school we were going to, and he read off the names of the players. He took all twelve players anyway, but in his mind he had to read it off because that was his Army background. Then he came to me and said, "We'll take McCray along because he's good for a laugh whether we win or lose."

When we made these trips, especially in the cold weather, the two best forwards sat in the front seat of coach's car because it had a heater. The three other first-string players were in the back seat of his car so they could get the heat. I was in the back of a station wagon with the luggage and no seat, sprawled out on the equipment. That's how I went to all the games.

Me (left) as the villain in *Love Rides the Rails*

I also discovered the stage at Kimball Academy. In my senior year, I did a play when one of my teachers asked me to try out for it. It was a good lead part in a melodrama called *Love Rides the Rails*. I played a very devious villain trying to convince the girl she should marry me. However, since it was an all-boys school, the girl was played by a boy. That was a challenge.

The performance took place during what was called "Dads Weekend." Every February, dads from all over came on the campus. We moved out of one dorm and the dads moved in. We students slept in bunk beds in the basement. Of course, in the middle of the night, we got up, rang the bell and woke everybody up.

Dad came to see the play. It was well-received and he asked me, "Do you like doing that?" I said, "Yes, I do." He asked, "What do you think you want to do after high school?" I said, "Something to do with the stage, although I don't know specifically. I'd like to consider going to Yale." At the time they had the best theater department that I knew of.

CHAPTER TWO

The Doctor from Yale

Mother saw the play, too, and she and dad discussed my desire to study drama at Yale. They agreed it would be a great path for me to take. My parents were champions on my side. They supported my decisions.

Like any father guiding his son to success, dad suggested I speak to an expert in the field prior to making a commitment at Yale. Since he had connections at the Hartt School having worked with Moshe Paranov on WTIC, dad sent me off to discuss the matter with Dr. Elemer Nagy.[6] Dr. Nagy joined the Hartt School in 1942 and headed the Opera Department there. He was a former Yale professor.

During the Easter break while working in the flower shop, I called Dr. Nagy and asked if I could talk to him. In our meeting, he told me what I could anticipate in going to Yale, and he mentioned some books to get to explore different studies and topics. I thanked him and went back to work at the flower shop.

Dr. Nagy called me a few days later and said, "I'd like to talk to you again. I have a deal for you that you will not refuse." That sparked my interest and I immediately got off work early to talk to him again. He said, "I will teach you for free the course that I taught at Yale *but* you'll have to work for me for as many hours as I want you to." This appealed greatly to me and my parents. After graduating from Kimball Union Academy in June 1947, I planned to start working with Dr. Nagy in the fall at the Hartt School.

When my parents moved to New York with dad's promotion, they left my furniture with our neighbors who offered to keep it on the third floor of their home. They said, "If anybody comes to town, they have a place to stay." When I went to Hartt I stayed there, which was awfully nice of them. I was pretty well settled when the fall semester began: a place to stay, at least one job at the florist, and a plan to shadow and work for a highly-accomplished theater expert/musician who was about to give me a very comprehensive, well-rounded education.

Dr. Nagy directed and designed the sets for all the operas the Hartt School put on. He was very creative. A clever, clever man. We did two new operas a year, one repeat, and always *Hansel and Gretel* at Christmas. For new operas, he drew a water-color sketch for each scene. His sketches were beautiful. They still exist somewhere at the University of Hartford. We took his sketches and made a model of each set piece. We had a permanent stage model at scale.

Dr. Nagy played with these model set pieces to see how they worked visually and practically. He sat and studied them, sat and studied them. He was very particular, not finicky, but particular. Had it in his head things had to be just so. For instance, in the opera *Don Pasquale*, the character is a big, robust fat guy who wants a girl. Dr. Nagy wanted the buttons on this character's wardrobe to be in perspective, starting small and getting bigger. He had that much detail in his head.

I guess you could say Dr. Nagy was a genius and, like most of us, had his own quirks, too. One of them had to do with his driving. I forget what kind of car he had, but the front seat on the passenger side folded over and into the dashboard so you could get into the back seat. There was a gentleman who came out from New York to teach a special singing class one day every two weeks. He stayed at Dr. Nagy's house, so he hung around the stage while we rehearsed. He rode home with Dr. Nagy, who often dropped me off afterwards.

This singer-teacher was about three-hundred pounds. Big tenor. No neck. With Doc, when you got in the car, you better be ready because once he got in, he hit the gas pedal. He didn't wait around while you messed with shutting the door. The tenor got into the car and Doc pulled out. The singer went backwards from the force and ripped the bolt out of the seat. I was behind the driver and the singer was lying on his back with his feet up on the dashboard. Doc leaned over and said, "Don't worry, I'll take you home by Pullman!" which was an old railroad term. Never a dull moment.

Once Dr. Nagy okayed the set models, we made blueprints of them. "We" was me and his assistant; I was the only student in this course. I never made a blueprint in my life until then. We took the blueprints down to the basement and built the actual sets. We made the frame and put canvas on it. We sized the canvas, which means we stretched it so we could paint it without bleeding through. We painted it and took it up on the stage to set it up. Dr. Nagy told me where to put the lights. In my final year, he told me, "You put the lights where you think they should be." I did and he critiqued it.

In later years, I also coached some of the understudies and I sang in the chorus for a lot of the operas. Actually, one year we did a show called *White Wings*, which was about street cleaners in New York City. I became the front end of a horse for that show. Trying to find a partner to be in the back end was a little difficult. Finally, a friend of mine at the school decided she would do the rear end. Once we got into the outfit, she poked me in the ribs and said, "You make one mistake and I'm outta here." It was very close quarters, but we had a lot of fun.

When I started working with Dr. Nagy, my first thought was to become a stage director. After coaching the actors/singers, I realized I loved doing the backstage tasks more than the acting/directing part of it. Up in the lighting booth, I took my music score and marked in all the movements so I knew what cues were coming up. With Dr. Nagy, you brought the lights in over so many measures of music. Since I knew how to read music, I changed the lights that way.

It was fine while they were singing, and I kept up with the dialogue since most of the shows we did were in English. On the opening Overtures or the long passages of music, I counted measures and then threw switches. I worked one of the three dimmer boards along with two other guys. The boards were small and a lot of times we unplugged and re-plugged other lights as the opera went on. I cued the two guys to re-plug where needed and when needed in the music. It was all very exciting.

One night we started a dress rehearsal and I counted out music measures as described. My foot tapped on the floor to keep the tempo going when all of a sudden the orchestra stopped. They started again. Then they stopped. Then they started again. Shortly after, Moshe Paranov, who was directing the orchestra, flew into the room where we were working the lights and accused me of sabotaging the whole rehearsal. He was very upset and I really didn't understand what he was talking about until he said, "You're flashing the lights."

Come to find out that while I kept tempo, my foot hit the electrical cord of the lights on all the music stands so they went on/off, on/off. I assured him I didn't do it on purpose, but he was convinced I did. All I could think to ask was, "Was I in tempo?" He didn't like that question, but we got on with the practice to everyone's satisfaction.

My interactive coursework with Dr. Nagy was supplemented with formal courses in music, singing and composition. You guessed it. I spent more time doing my hands-on school work and paid jobs rather than my studies.

I took a course in Italian diction. The course required us to come to class each week with a different opera song in Italian that we had to sing in front of our fellow students. The teacher critiqued our pronunciation and such. I worked nights doing all the scenery, setting up everything for Dr. Nagy's operas, and I neglected to practice or to even get a new song each week.

The Italian lady who came from New York to teach said, "We've heard this song before, Mr. McCray." Always very dignified. "Mr. McCray." I said, "Yes, that's true, but it's still voted as Number One on *Your Hit Parade*, so I'm compelled to sing it again." She said, "That's a clever answer, but next week have a new song." I did, but I was never a great person with Italian diction.

As for my many jobs, I worked at the school as a part time janitor. They needed one and I said, "I'll take it." I did anything for money because you didn't get paid to go to college. My education was basically free per Dr. Nagy's agreement, but dad still had to pay for a few special courses. I took a lunch time job at a restaurant next door that paid seventy-five cents and a free lunch, however that work caused me grief with one of my professors.

It was the college English teacher, my first class after lunch. He insisted I be in the room by the first bell. There were two bells. As long as we were in class by the second bell, we weren't late. He wanted me to be there before the first bell. Working next door bussing dishes, I couldn't make it by the first bell. I worked until one o'clock, ran down the street and hurried to his classroom. I was always there before the second bell. He said, "You have to be here by the first bell." I said, "That's impossible." I went to the Dean and told him my problem. He said he'd take care of it, but nothing ever happened.

One day I walked into the room once again after the first bell but before the second bell. The teacher said, "That's an 'F' for McCray." I got up to leave. He asked, "Where are you going?" I said, "If I already have an 'F' for the day, why should I sit around and listen to you?" I walked out.

Later, this same teacher, who had a nice tenor voice, was doing the lead in one of our operas, the one about street cleaners in New York. There was one scene where he had to pick up a pigeon and sing to it. The first night, he picked up the prop pigeon and cradled it in his hands as he sang to it, mugging to the audience for all it was worth. He had a big ego. The next night, he bent down to scoop up the pigeon prop. He couldn't because I nailed that sucker to the floor! He had to get down on his knees and sing to the pigeon with his head facing the stage floor.

I still had my job at the florist shop during holidays. I decorated the entire store at night for sales the next day. Put bows on plants, put arrangements into vases, plus anything else that needed to be done. In later years, I ran the wholesale department there.

I was good with organizational tasks. I remember setting up a schedule for the floral employees to avoid them going from one end of town to another and back again when making flower deliveries. Now, at the college level, I was able to expand this skill thanks to one of Dr. Nagy's dreams.

As I said, every year Dr. Nagy put on *Hansel and Gretel* at Christmas time. He thought many schools around New England would love to have us perform for them at their site. This had never been done before, and he wasn't sure where to begin. I said, "That's no problem. We have boxes with the wardrobe already stored in them. I can take some of those boxes and put lights in them. I'll rent a truck. I'll get a couple of guys to go with me, and we'll travel anywhere." We ended up with twelve boxes that I lugged on my back and loaded on the truck. Away we went. During Christmas for my last two years at Hartt, we travelled to many schools around New England performing *Hansel and Gretel*.

Dr. Nagy also introduced me to an early managerial opportunity that would lead to even more organizing and logistics experience. During the summertime, Dr. Nagy was asked to direct the operas for the Central City Opera Association in Colorado.

This was a town up in the mountains over nine thousand feet high and forty miles outside of Denver. The business manager who ran the Association came to Hartford to talk with Dr. Nagy. I met him and he asked me to join him as the assistant manager. I was to run the opera house in Central City while he was to stay in Denver to do his work there. Our schedule included a month of opera in July and a week of no performances followed by a play.

Me in a white jacket at the far right door. Ushers march in prior to our performance of *Madame Butterfly* in Central City.

Central City, Colorado is a very small town. The opera house was built during the 1860s and 70s when it was a big mining town. The opera house itself had over seven hundred seats with very hard wood chairs, but they were the original chairs at the time it was built. Still a very historic site today.

I was in the town and my boss was in Denver trying to raise money. I was in my early twenties then and oversaw seventeen ushers and box office folks. A lot of the old mining houses had been converted to housing for the cast members who came out from New York. That meant I had a lot of cleaning people to supervise. I was also in contact with everything that came in through a trucking line that was our only access to get supplies out of Denver.

While I was in Colorado, my dad called me one day in 1948 to let me know NBC transferred him to California to become director of AM network radio operations, all affiliates west of the Mississippi.[7] My parents moved to Hollywood where they remained until dad's retirement in 1966, and for the rest of their lives.

My college graduation photo

As my college graduation date neared in 1951, dad called to tell me about some crew openings at TV station Channel 9 in Los Angeles. I hadn't really considered working in television up to that point, but I was interested in the opportunity my dad mentioned because of my theater background. Dad gave me the man's name and I wrote to him. I got a letter back that said if I was in Los Angeles by the fifteenth of September, I would have a job at Channel 9 as a stage manager.

That sounded pretty good to me. At the end of that summer, I drove back to Connecticut from Colorado and said good-bye to everyone. I couldn't have had a better mentor than Dr. Nagy. He was the best. I packed up my belongings and drove to California.

My mother and dad rented a house in California and I lived with them. I went to Channel 9 and presented the gal at the desk with my job offer from the gentleman I had written earlier.

They ushered me into another office to a different gentleman who informed me that the man who wrote my offer letter was no longer with Channel 9.[8] The man told me the station's ownership changed and Channel 9 was restructuring, not hiring. The gentleman did say, however, that when they were hiring, he would give me a job as a stage manager per the offer letter. But at that point, I was out of work.

CHAPTER THREE

"Never Say No to a Job" or "If You See Me, You Don't Know Me"

After the disappointment of the Channel 9 job falling through, I continued to stay with my parents in their Hollywood home as I looked for other opportunities. My dad always told me, "Never say no to a job." His point was that you can never know what an opportunity may lead to if you don't try. With that thought in mind, I accepted a position at a California theater as a stage hand.

It was a small theater in Hollywood that had three union stage hands and three non-union stage hands. I was a non-union stage hand and I worked that show every night for six weeks. The three union guys told me, "You're fun to work with. We can get you into the IA Union."[9] I said I'd think about it, but I didn't want that because I didn't like the idea of working for somebody else. I liked being my own boss.

When the play ended, the group prepared to do another show. They asked me to stay on for another six weeks, which I said I would do. However, I got my draft notice for the Korean War. I went for my physical and they said I was 4-F. I had a hernia from playing football in prep school. I figured they were going to say, "You fix it or we fix it, and you're in," because the rest of me was in pretty good shape. Instead, they gave me a 4-F card.

Fate has its way of working out. I'm not saying I'm sorry I didn't go to the Korean War. If I had had to go, I would've gone. I'm just glad I didn't. By the time the Korean War was over, the television business was getting very sophisticated.

I didn't get drafted and I couldn't go back as a stage hand because they already replaced me. I bummed around for a while and even went back to work in the flower shop in Hartford, running the wholesale department. I picked up other work back in Connecticut. Then I returned to California to stay with my parents. One day, we were invited to a barbecue at the home of NBC executive John West.

John happened to be a little higher in rank than my father because John came up through the ranks of RCA. They both had vice president titles, but this gentleman had a little more seniority. We went to his house in Encino, which was quite a trek because there were no freeways then. We spent a very nice Sunday afternoon there.

John West was a big man, about 6'7" or so. Quite a stature. I had never met him until that day. As we talked, he asked me what my background was and I told him about my stage work and studies. He asked, "Why aren't you working for us? We just opened up the coaxial cable. We're getting very busy and we need people. It sounds like you have experience that could be very useful." I said, "My dad won't allow it." He asked, "What do you mean he won't allow it?" I said, "He doesn't want people to think I got a job because of him. Nepotism."

The coaxial cable that John West mentioned was one of the key technological developments that literally changed how television conducted business in its early years. It played a large part in my career.[10] In essence, the coaxial cable let shows be broadcast live over a phone line from L.A. to New York. Most of the big name stars were in California. Before coaxial, they had to fly back to New York which disrupted them for two or three weeks just to do one show. Now, the actors had an outlet that let them stay in L.A.

and still do TV appearances. All of a sudden, television took off. It was a zoo. There weren't that many people in the business when the explosion hit.

John West told me General David Sarnoff, chairman of RCA Corporation and founder of the National Broadcasting Corporation, had two sons in the business. Robert was RCA chairman and Thomas worked for NBC. He said, "One more son shouldn't hurt." He asked me to call him the following week and advised me, "Don't say anything to your father."

I called John West on Monday afternoon and he directed me to meet with Director of Television Operations Earl Rettig on Friday. I talked with Mr. Rettig. He had me meet with Fenton Coe and Dick Welch. Those two gentlemen were unit managers. I met with the art department. I met with a lot of people.

My background and education gave me knowledge and experience in about every department I visited. This was 1951 and I was 23 years old. I did stage work at Hartt, and if you think about it, that's what it takes to put on a live television show. I had that kind of background. I knew the nuts and bolts of putting on a show.

At seven o'clock that night, I was back at Mr. Rettig's office. He said, "Everybody says they like what you say, and you look good on paper. However, since we know nothing about you, we'll put you on at a week-to-week basis." I said, "I couldn't ask for anything more."

I was hired. It was seven o'clock Friday night and I figured I had the weekend off before starting. Then Mr. Rettig ordered, "At five o'clock tomorrow morning, you report to Dick Welch at the El Capitan Theater on Vine Street." That was the name of the theater that was right across the street from the Capitol Records building. It's now called the Palace Theater.

I went home and found my mother and dad having dinner. I sat down and dad asked what I had done during the day. I said, "I got a job." He said, "Fine! Where?" I said, "NBC." He stood up and said, "The hell you do!" Oh, he was mad. He said, "I told you you're never going to work at NBC." I said, "John West says" and he cut me off saying, "I don't care what John West says. You're not working for NBC." He was strong about nepotism. He wanted me to work, but I had to get the job myself. I did, but with him as vice president it might look like he helped.

He left the table, hadn't finished his dinner yet, and called Mr. West. They were hollering at each other over the phone. I heard my father. He was very agitated. He came back to the table and said, "They're trying you out on a week-to-week basis." I said, "Yes, that's correct." He said, "If you ever see me in the parking lot, you don't know me." I said, "If that's the way you want it, that's the way it'll be."

I know that sounds harsh of my dad, but he wasn't working against me. He's the one who got me the interview at Channel 9. He was happy to help me, but at NBC, he didn't want it to look like he got me a job. Any position I did get he wanted it to be because of my work and not because of his name. Any upset we had over my being hired blew over once I lasted long enough for him to get feedback that I was doing my job well and that they were pleased with my work and my talents. I never went to him for a favor because I didn't have to. He was proud of me as time went on, especially when I worked for Bob Hope, among others.

CHAPTER FOUR

"Everything Was Live!"

When I entered the business in the fall of 1951, programming demands jumped to an incredible height. People were buying television sets. I already mentioned how the coaxial cable opened up the industry. Ever see the movie *My Favorite Year*[11] starring Peter O'Toole? It re-creates somewhat of a sense of the chaos of those early days of live television. Many obstacles stood in the way of meeting the tremendous amount of deadlines to produce just one live variety television show, not to mention all the programs and commercials needed for one network for one week. And the overnight boom was not just at NBC. It was at CBS, ABC and DuMont,[12] as well.

You can imagine office space was very critical. Our main office building was an old converted radio station at Sunset and Vine. We moved to another building that was originally the J. Walter Thompson Agency over Thrifty Drugstore on Vine and Selma. We had four people to an office with one light overhead. It was crowded and everybody was cramped in their quarters.

One day I came to work and got in the elevator. Two writers for one of the shows were sitting on camp stools with a typewriter on a table. They said, "We don't have an office," and all day long they rode up and down in the elevator to do their work. One of the secretaries complained about the lighting in her office, so every morning she wheeled her typewriter down to the lady's room and sat in there all day typing scripts because she could see better.

It was an unbelievable display of the dedication of our people. They were glad to be employed. This television thing had just started and everybody worked their tails off. I walked in at the time we laid the basis for what television is today. We couldn't say we'll do the work tomorrow. There was no tomorrow. It was now.

We also didn't have enough equipment. I borrowed a zoom lens on the day of some shows from an independent local television station that wasn't even an NBC affiliate. They used it for sporting matches. We scrambled to get all kinds of equipment. It was that fast, believe me.

That was the chaos I walked into that following Saturday morning. I met with Dick Welch at five o'clock in the morning at the Capitan Theater for my first assignment: a variety show on Sunday night called the *Colgate Comedy Hour*.[13] It was a comedy/music series with different performers each week. Hosts included Jimmy Durante, Eddie Cantor, Ed Wynn and Martin & Lewis to name a few.

Regarding Martin & Lewis, my dad actually played a role in their careers, if you want to call it that. When dad was an executive in New York radio, their contract came up for renewal. He actually was *not* going to sign it, but because the legal department didn't cancel it in the timeframe specified, the comic team was automatically given a new contract. By then, television was on the rise and their careers are, of course, well known.

I never knew if Martin & Lewis ever found out that my dad didn't want to renew them. I never brought it up. On *Colgate Comedy Hour,* I was introduced to them but they didn't connect the name at all. They were bigger stars by then and my dad's name didn't mean anything to them at that point. I was very shy at meeting actors. I felt intimidated, and they could intimidate you pretty easily. I backed off. It wasn't my job to know them or associate or socialize with them.

As for Jimmy Durante, he walked around to everybody and gave them a twenty dollar bill. He had rolls of them. I said, "I can't take that." He said, "You take it. I've always given everybody on a stage show a twenty dollar bill and I'm doing it now." I don't know if NBC ever knew about it or not, but he made you take it. He appreciated what the crew did. I don't know many people who did what he did.

Back to my first day on the job. We were getting ready for production of the *Colgate Comedy Hour*, which aired live Sunday nights at six o'clock on the West Coast. Dick Welch said, "Follow me around and pick up on what's going on. If you have questions, ask. We'll go from there." I agreed. Not too long after that a gentleman came up to him and said the flip stand on stage right was broken and we needed to get a new one. Dick Welch turned to me and said, "Go down to Studio F and get a new flip stand."

Not wanting to sound ignorant, I said to the stage hand, "Let me look at the flip stand to see if we can fix it." I had a background in stage building and thought maybe I could save some time, and buy some time, because, frankly, I didn't know where Studio F was nor did I know what a flip stand was. I learned that day.

A flip stand was a three-ring binder mounted on a big easel that was on wheels so it could be moved around easily. In those days, the only television graphics were done on black cards with white lettering. We had one flip stand on stage right and one on stage left. The camera came over to photograph those cards alternately. We'd shoot a card on stage left, and then the director would cut to the camera on stage right for that flip stand. While they were shooting the stage right stand, a crew member flipped a new card down on the left one for the next shot. The director went back and forth in that manner for whatever graphics were being broadcast.

I looked at the broken flip stand; it had seen better days. There was nothing to do but go to Studio F like Dick Welch said. I went to the parking lot and found a driver assigned to a pickup truck and said, "I need to go down to Studio F, but I'm not sure where it is." He said, "I'll take you down there." The driver who took me to Studio F was Wynn Hainey. He ended up being our Chapman boom operator on *Little House on the Prairie* many years later. I went to Studio F, got a new flip stand and took it to the stage.

If office space was an issue for employees, imagine the scheduling conflicts that existed for the very limited stage and rehearsal space. Dinah Shore had a fifteen-minute show and we shot her car commercials live in a hallway.

The hallway opened up into a kind of vestibule at the end, which is where we put the car. We dollied down the hall to get close-ups; however, the lighting was very difficult to do. We put lights in specific spots because if we moved them, the car picked up reflections from them. We sprayed the car with PET milk because that was the only thing that dulled it without hurting the finish. This was before dulling spray.

NBC had only one facility large enough to rehearse and perform the *Colgate Comedy Hour*. We had to share that stage with another show called *The All Star Revue*.[14] On Thursdays, we moved in sets for *The All Star Revue* and rehearsed all day with the camera and the set crew. Thursday nights we moved out that scenery and brought in the *Colgate Comedy Hour* scenery. We set that up and lit it, and Friday we rehearsed the *Colgate Comedy Hour*.

After rehearsal, we took out the scenery from the *Colgate Hour* and brought back the scenery for *The All Star Revue*, which aired live Saturday nights. After *All Star Revue* was over, we struck that set and sent it down to the dock. We brought back the *Colgate Comedy Hour* sets and re-set the stage for the Sunday night show. This became the routine and I was later in charge of coordinating all the set changes for both shows. We worked all night.

Everything was live! We went on the air at six o'clock at night for a nine o'clock New York air time, and we went off in one hour. We were cut off. We had to back-time to make sure we ended correctly. A lot of the comedy acts like Martin & Lewis got on stage and started ad-libbing. They didn't stick to the script completely, so we never knew what time a skit would finish. I'm not faulting them because the show was better the way it went on the air, but we had to get off the air on time. If we ran long, we had to figure out what to cut. Often it was the credits. The script supervisor kept track of that.

Behind the scenes, the assistant director could talk to the floor manager and both had communication with the orchestra, but often they couldn't get a hold of the backstage folks. I found myself going outside, running down the alley and going in the backstage door to relay messages to the backstage guys. "Don't put up this set. Don't put up this drop. It's being cut." It was a hectic time. It was great and I loved it!

I was the production supervisor and the production supervisor at that particular time had to work with directors and producers and whoever the ad agency was. Let me explain a little bit about the mechanics of early television shows. Most of the writers, directors and cast were considered what we call "above the line." That is, all the creative people. The "above the line" in many cases on the early shows was controlled by the stars and/or ad agency. NBC owned the studios and employed the crews who were all on NBC's payroll. These people, the network employees, were "below the line."[15] My job was "below the line," meaning I worked for the network.

However, as the production supervisor, I had to work with the producers and directors "above the line" to find out how much rehearsal was needed, how big a rehearsal, how big a crew, what engineering crew was needed as well as the number of stage people. I ordered the crews accordingly with NBC. At the end of each show, I reported the hours people actually worked for billing purposes.

On one show with Eddie Cantor hosting the *Colgate Comedy Hour*, there was a scene where a goat was supposed to come in and chew a deck of cards. The question came up, "Who pays for the goat?" Is it a prop? Or is it part of a creative segment of the show?

NBC said the goat was creative and the producer should pay for it. The argument went on all week, and finally Eddie Cantor said, "No, I don't want a live goat to come in and chew the cards. I want a mechanical goat. Therefore, it's definitely a prop and NBC, you have to pay for it!" That ended the argument and NBC paid for the live goat.

During this time the industry was in a constant state of change. Networks and ad agencies vied for talent and personnel, trying to lure people away to gain a bigger share of the growing viewer market. When someone moved on, opportunities opened for others. Like when Fenton Coe, a fellow production supervisor, left NBC for other ventures.

In January 1952, I was asked to do *The Red Skelton Show*[16] because Fenton went to work for the talent agency that handled Mr. Skelton. Fenton had been the production supervisor on Skelton's TV show, so I fell into working with another great comic. This was the first show I worked on as a production supervisor that featured one main star as opposed to all the different hosts of the *Colgate Comedy Hour* and *The All-Star Revue*. I was only in the company a few months when I switched over to Skelton's show, so Fenton helped me. Even though he worked for the talent agency, he coached me as I transitioned into the new assignment.

Red Skelton was a very funny man. I enjoyed working with him. He audio taped his rehearsals on Saturday nights and after the show, he did a lot of ad lib jokes he knew weren't going to be on the show. He did it just to irritate the NBC Broadcast Standards censor, who couldn't keep up writing down the jokes he wanted taken out because they were too dirty. Red did that just to agitate him. He had a great sense of humor.

After the rehearsal on Saturday night, we sat down in the control room and listened to the audio tape. Red was very critical of his work. In many cases he said, "I don't like the way that plays. It's not good." When we came in the next day, Sunday morning, Mr. Skelton would hand us a whole new scene or a whole new set which required a crew to build, paint and get ready to go on the air live that night at seven.

Many times, the art director was distracted working on the new sets and controlling the artists who were painting, so he sent me to the prop house to pick out set pieces. In the early days, we did everything. Anything that had to be done, anything that somebody needed, we production supervisors were the ones they looked to and said, "Get it done." And it got done.

In addition to *The Red Skelton Show* that aired live on Sunday, I had a daytime show I did five times a week, and I did commercials on Saturday and Sunday. In fact, once I started to work that first September Saturday morning in the fall of 1951, I never got a day off until the following May. We worked seven days a week and all hours of the day and night you can imagine. I had many weeks where I worked over a hundred hours because I also covered for other people.

CHAPTER FIVE

My Life with Ralph Edwards

Red Skelton eventually moved over to the CBS network, so my next assignment was *The Ralph Edwards Show* which made its debut in January 1952. Ralph was quite a history-making radio personality. He brought the game show *Truth or Consequences* to radio and eventually to television. That was later on. His first television series was *The Ralph Edwards Show*.[17]

I remember the show having lots of gags and activities. One time, Ralph set up the wife of a man who had just bought a brand new car. This was the first time the wife had driven it. In the gag, the car comes into the parking lot where the attendant gives the wife a voucher ticket. She goes up the street to do some shopping or whatever. When she returns, she gives the attendant the voucher for the car. As the attendant drives the car around the corner, he crashes into three other cars.

The lady was fit to be tied. The attendant was Cal Howard, one of the writers on the camp stools inside the NBC elevator riding up and down all day. He told the woman, "You know it says on the ticket we're not responsible for anything." She said, "But it's a brand new car. This is the first time I've driven it. My husband's going to kill me!" It was all phony of course. It wasn't her car at all. It was a car that looked like hers.

Another time we were out on Sunset Boulevard trying to get somebody to ride a camel. All of a sudden, the animal trainer got sick. Who led the camel down Sunset Boulevard? Me. I put on a crazy hat and away we went. Ever lead a camel before? They're dirty, they smell and they spit.

When we weren't pulling pranks outside the studio, we were playing games with the live studio audience. Our audience was made up of a lot of folks we called "regulars." "Regulars" were a group of people who went up and down Sunset Boulevard from CBS to NBC to ABC to watch radio shows as they were performed. The group's behavior carried over into television. We tried to keep them out but there was no way. We couldn't control it because they always got tickets somehow.

Every Friday on the show, we featured a game which displayed ten pictures facing the wall. Most of the pictures were things like washing machines, dryers, trips down Hollywood Boulevard or up to the Hollywood sign. Our biggest item was a trip to Paris. Members of the audience had a number and we chose the winner by drawing. Whoever was selected came on stage and turned one of the pictures around. That was the prize they won.

Lo and behold, one of the "regulars," a lady I'll call "Mrs. Johnson," had her number chosen. She walked on stage and picked the picture that said a trip to Paris. You have to remember in 1952, a trip to New York and a trip to Paris were difficult to arrange. Plane flights took longer and they were not as accessible. We got "Mrs. Johnson" to New York and had somebody meet her at her hotel where she stayed overnight. Someone took her to the airport the next day to make sure she got on the airplane. A few hours later, she showed up at Rockefeller Center in the lobby of the NBC building and told somebody at the front desk she missed the plane.

An employee in the office knew Ralph Edwards, and when "Mrs. Johnson" mentioned Mr. Edwards' name, the employee called him. No one could ever figure out how she missed the plane, by the way. Ralph put her up at a hotel in New York for a week while we arranged another flight to Paris. He had somebody take her out to the airport again, and make sure she got on the plane this time.

A week later as she was about to get on the plane, an FBI agent cuffed her. There was a lot of publicity about this trip and someone checked up on the woman. She was leaving the country but owed back taxes. Apparently she was released and went back to the hotel. Ralph paid for her to stay *another* week in New York until she finally got on the plane for France. And that was the end of "Mrs. Johnson's" trip to Paris.

One thing with Ralph, he was a sincere and caring man known for his extreme generosity. When radio petered out and he didn't have a show for a while, there were about nine people on his staff he kept on payroll for two years. He said, "You were with me through the good days and you're with me through the bad." They all took turns being the receptionist or the secretary. They didn't have big titles anymore. They helped each other through two years until they got into television. How many people would do that in today's market?

Ralph Edwards cared about people. We did a lot of gags, but he always said that when he joked with people, they had to leave with a laugh. They had to know it was a joke, like the lady whose car was smashed.

After *The Ralph Edwards Show* and *The Red Skelton Show* finished in the May/June timeframe, I was assigned to *The Johnny Dugan Show*[18] over the summer of 1952. It was a five-day-a-week, one hour show that consisted of singer/entertainer Johnny Dugan in an interview format. His set included a café with tables for people from the audience to join him. Johnny was a nice guy to work with, but the show didn't last long.

By the fall of 1952, I paired up with Ralph Edwards again, this time for two years on *This is Your Life*.[19] The idea of the show was that Ralph surprised celebrities or everyday people by bringing their family, friends, co-workers or guest stars on stage to talk about the subject's life. This was done at the El Capitan Theater on Vine Street.

The subjects never knew they were going to be on live television, so their unpredictable reactions kind of scared us when Ralph revealed what he was doing. A couple of times, Ralph interviewed someone and asked, "You remember your Uncle Harry?" and the guest said, "Yeah. Uncle Harry? I never liked him, and anyway, he's dead." Well, out through the curtain came Uncle Harry. Ralph always had a few problems with the surprise format.

Over time, people got suspicious when they saw Ralph, but he arranged for friends or co-workers of the guest-of-honor to set them up. Lots of times, the guests would think they were going to a show at the Pantages Theater, which still exists today. They had to park in a nearby lot and walk a block over to the theater. Ralph approached them as they walked down the street.

The parking lot bordered the Knickerbocker Hotel and lots of times we had people meet at the hotel for some made up reason. Ralph surprised them that way. Or, we ran cable from the NBC studio on Vine Street up to the Brown Derby restaurant, and Ralph walked into the Brown Derby to surprise a guest that way.

Remember in those days, we were tied by cable. We didn't have a satellite feed. That didn't exist. The equipment was bulky and heavy. We had to stretch cable. If we worked at the El Capitan Theater, we stretched cable over to the lobby of the Knickerbocker, which was time consuming. If we went to the Brown Derby, we ran a cable out of the main plant at Sunset and Vine, up the street, blocked off one street with cable guards which people could drive over, and sneaked him in that way. Lots of chores to pull these surprises off.

As mentioned, one of the most important aspects of the show was the secrecy of the guest. Secret from the audience and secret from the subject, especially. However, Ralph broke his own rule for one show. He wanted to surprise Eddie Cantor, who through the years suffered several heart attacks. Ralph called Eddie Cantor's doctor because Ralph didn't want to hurt anybody. The doctor said a surprise like Ralph was planning *would* be detrimental to Mr. Cantor's health. Ralph opted to call Mr. Cantor and inform him he was going to be the guest on *This is Your Life* for a certain week. Eddie Cantor was very thrilled and thought it would be great because they all knew the show.

We were sitting in the office and the phone conversation ended. Ralph said, "Well, he's set. We'll move forward." About five minutes later, the secretary said, "Mr. Cantor wants to speak to you again, Ralph." Ralph took the call and said, "Uh-huh. Uh-huh." Well, the gist of the conversation was that Mr. Cantor told Ralph, "You know, I've had *such* a wonderful life, don't you think we should do it in two installments?" We did it in one.

One week we had Victor McLaglen who was a well-known actor.[20] He had six brothers who we flew in from South Africa. They stayed in town for a week and had a big party. After the show was over, one of the brothers came into the office and asked Ralph, "Who's gonna pay our salary? We left work to be here and we haven't been paid in a week, so who's going to pay our salary while we've been here?" There again, Ralph paid their salary and everybody was happy.

As I said, Ralph was a very caring person. Just wonderful. We also did a lot of shows with every day exceptional people, like Dr. Kate Pelham Newcomb.[21] She was a Midwest country doctor who drove an old Model T. It was one of my favorites and I thought it was so wonderful for this lady to be honored in such a way. She really worked hard to help other people.

We also did a show on Billie Clevenger.[22] Billie was the head NBC phone operator for many, many years and she knew everybody. She worked with Ralph in radio and did all the shows that he did. She was always on the set when Ralph asked her to place a call if he needed to get someone on the phone to honor his weekly guest.

We did one rehearsal of the episode without Billie knowing it was about her. When we rehearsed with her, Ralph gave her a false phone number to call. When we went on the air for the real thing, Ralph gave her the real number. It was actually Billie Clevenger's brother's number. We were live and she said, "That's not the number you want to call. That's not the number we rehearsed." He said, "You call that number." She did, and her brother surprised her and we did, "This Is Your Life, Billie Clevenger."

Ralph Edwards was one of the dearest, sweetest men you could ever talk to. When I started with him on both shows, we met in his office and he said, "I want a list of everybody on the crew by name." I gave it to him and from day one when he came on set, he knew the crew members by first name. He always said, "Hello," and always said, "Thank you" at the end of the show. That was quite nice. Made you feel part of it. I mean, we got paid, but he made us feel that he liked what we did.

The performers in that era, I can't say one was a better comic than another, like Milton Berle or Bob Hope or Red Skelton. They were all different, but they had a certain persona, they knew what they were doing and what they were about.

Other live shows I worked on in the early 50s include the Rose Bowl Parade and football game. For the parade, we went out the day before and laid cable. On New Year's Day at three o'clock in the morning, the crew and I took all the trucks to set up for live coverage of the parade, which was scheduled to be aired at eight o'clock in the morning Pacific Time.

After the parade was over, all the equipment was broken down, put back in the trucks and moved to the Rose Bowl to cover the football game. We had a police escort to get us to the stadium, but it didn't mean much because there was such a crowd that we only moved at a snail's pace. We covered the game. After it was over, we broke everything down and got home about midnight. It was a long day, but quite an exciting one.

In October 1952, I began working on *Hollywood Opening Night*[23] in the new NBC West Coast television studio in Burbank. The early complex consisted of two soundstages, Stages 1 and 3, and a small workshop. They later added Stages 2 and 4. *Hollywood Opening Night* was one of the first shows out of Studio 3, which was a dramatic show with host Jimmy Fidler. We did that for a year. Then I was assigned to work with Bob Hope in 1954 along with "Mr. Television" himself, Milton Berle. But first, I took a little time for myself.

CHAPTER SIX

The Production Supervisor
Takes a Wife

I met Ruth Senkel when we were both students at the Hartt School. She graduated in 1952, which is the year we married. The marriage was good for about the first ten years. It's hard for me to talk about it because I don't want to sound like she was all bad and I was all good. It's not that way at all. She had her good and bad points and I had my good and bad points like we all do.

My parents rented a home on Hollywood Boulevard from the finance minister of Mexico who bought one city block with two houses on it. It was a few blocks from Grauman's Theater. Behind their place was a guest house, a two-room bungalow which Ruth and I rented when we first married. Our rent was fifty dollars a month, which was good because I was just starting out in my new career. Ruth took a job as a music teacher at a local school.

In 1954, Ruth informed me she was pregnant. We realized the bungalow was not going to be big enough, so we found a new home in Van Nuys on a very quiet street. A small house with two bedrooms and two baths. We set up everything for the baby's arrival. The crib we used was Ruth's crib that her father made. Her parents sent it to us and I re-assembled it. It had a lot of sentimental meaning.

Knowing you're having a baby for the first time is overwhelming. You don't know what to expect. At least I didn't. I had no concept of what it would be like to take care of a child of that age. Deborah was born in May 1955. Our first born. We came home from the hospital and Ruth's mother was there to help because I worked different hours.

The first night the baby was home, naturally she pooped her diaper. We arranged a little foam pad in the bathroom with a towel so the baby wasn't on the tile. We used diapers because there were no such things as Pampers then. I changed her that night and many, many times after. In my thoughts, if something had to be cleaned, you just cleaned it. I shoveled enough horse and cow manure on the farm, what was the difference? I got up in the middle of the night and fed the baby, too. None of those things bothered me.

I looked at Deborah and pondered at the marvel of it all. You look at the hands; you look at the feet. You put your finger out to see if she'll grab it. Things like that don't happen right away but you want them to. It's a very caring experience.

Our son Scott was born two years later in June 1957. He had a digestive problem and an allergy to milk which gave him very bad gas cramps. Many nights I got up and rocked him in a big rocking chair in the living room. I put him on my shoulder. It's a wonderful feeling to hold a baby, someone you created who is a very close part of you.

I was also happy, of course, that I had a son to carry on my side of the McCray family. Scott has a son, so the McCray family will continue. In later years, I gave Scott my dad's onyx ring because I wanted to pass it down. It's not an expensive ring, but it's something that my dad had and I had. Scott has it and so will my grandson, Spencer. Those things are important to me. It gives me a nice feeling. It may go on even further.

Ruth and I added on a bigger master bedroom for ourselves at the Van Nuys house when Scott was born. When Kristen arrived in February 1960, we decided to find a bigger home. We bought one in Northridge where we lived for the rest of our married lives.

I admit that Kristen was a surprise. We went to Las Vegas for a holiday and I said she was my jackpot baby. Carolyn was also a surprise. She was born in August 1967.

I was present for the births of all my children but not like today. I was never in the delivery room because that wasn't allowed in those days. I went to the hospital waiting room where we dads sat and twiddled our thumbs. Carolyn's birth was in the middle of the night. We had the same doctor for all the kids and he told me it was going to be a while. He said, "Come with me. Why don't you lie down in the doctor's lounge and take a nap?" I crawled into bed and slept through the whole thing.

All the kids were healthy, strong babies, much bigger than I was, certainly. I picked them up gently and put them over my shoulder and held them. I think they bonded to the strength they felt by my touch. I watched them grow. It was heartwarming. You can't be overjoyed too much, but you are.

We attended the kids' activities, their games and their plays. I worked hard but made time to be with them. I took them out for Halloween so they didn't go alone. Ruth stayed at the house and handed out candy to the neighborhood kids.

One time, we returned to our house when two adults in costume came toward us shouting, "We want candy. We want candy." They started badgering my kids. I told them, "Get the hell out of here!" "No, we want candy!" They wouldn't let up and they wouldn't leave. I got really angry because they were annoying my kids and I wasn't going to allow it.

Turns out the two adults were my mother and father! They both dressed up in costume and drove out to the house to pull a gag on us. Afterwards, we all went inside and had a great time.

Each Christmas, we went to my mother and dad's house. All the kids slept in one room with twin beds pushed together. My dad read them "The Night Before Christmas." As he did, the kids slowly pushed the beds apart so he fell down in the middle. Boy, did they all laugh. It became a Christmas ritual.

Ruth raised the kids very well. They were brought up Lutheran because Ruth's family members were staunch Lutherans. I never objected to that. I went to her church and I had the kids go to the Lutheran school because I thought it was a good education for them. I never balked at that.

None of the kids were on drugs; none of them smoked; none of them had any vices that kids have today. They were all good. I respected the fact that Ruth was the one who did that through her guidance in their home life.

Our kids are great and have done well for themselves. Deborah was a school teacher. She wanted to teach, even as a child. She set up her dolls like a classroom and pretended they were her students. She has three children. Scott has a doctorate in chemical and thermal engineering from UCLA. His work includes developing membranes for water purification as well as materials for medical pharmaceuticals. He has three kids.

Kristen entered my world of television as a film editor, but over time she found she didn't like the working environment. She married and moved to England. My daughter Carolyn is a very caring person. Even when she was in first or second grade, the teacher wrote a note to Ruth and me about how nice she was to a special child in the class who had troubles.

Carolyn is a therapist and has worked in hospitals. Now she works at a state prison for women counseling in group therapy and one-on-one. She carried that sense of caring through her whole life. That's Carolyn's nature. She has two children.

Only Deborah's son has followed my path. He went through film school and worked in video productions in underprivileged nations as part of a research project. Now, he works for a company in Seattle doing documentaries.

I am proud to say I have four wonderful children, eight grandchildren and, yes, eight great-grandchildren. I love it. I love all the kids. It's a great family.

As for married life with Ruth, that became rocky over time. Her father was a school teacher and her mother was an accountant. Since her early years, her family sat down for dinner at five o'clock each night. That was their life. When she and I came out to California, I had a job in television and at five o'clock in the evening, I was starting my day, so to speak. There were many nights I didn't get home until late. Sometimes I invited Ruth to the show I was doing and took her to dinner if it was early enough. Over time she became resentful of my hours.

For dinner, my colleagues and I frequented a restaurant near the studio. Our orders were phoned in so they were ready when we showed up. We ate and then went straight back to work. After rehearsal, I often got together with the writers. The man that owned this restaurant told us, "If you work late, if you missed dinner, or if you want to relax a minute and have a drink, buzz me and I'll let you in." He stayed there into the early morning hours doing his books. Many, many nights the writers and I went there to work through the material and the production logistics. It was two or three o'clock in the morning before I got home.

When I was associate producer for Bob Hope, we worked until one or two in the morning. Hope often called me during the night, too. That bothered Ruth. I also missed three Christmases in a row while the kids were growing up because of my work.

Bonanza wasn't a nine-to-five job. I went in before six in the morning and many times left at nine or ten o'clock at night. For *High Chaparral*, we were in Tucson for a month at a time doing location work.

Ruth's anger and bitterness about my work hours grew over time and extended into other areas. She complained about everything, even the kids. She destroyed some religious books I inherited from my parents. I put them in a hallway bookcase and when I came home one day, they were gone. She had burned them. Why? Why would she burn something that was left to me?

It hurt me and she knew it. That kind of bitterness. We got into a big argument over that.

I also brought home some of my parents' furniture, meaningful things that were left to me after their passing, but Ruth didn't want them in the house. Why, I don't know but I brought them in anyhow. More bad feelings on top of the ones about my work hours. It got to the point I was nervous going home because I knew she would be angry. It took a toll on both of us.

I separated from Ruth[24] in the 1970s about twenty years after our marriage. As to the actual divorce date, I put it out of my mind. Those things were difficult. That life was not good any more.

CHAPTER SEVEN

Big Brother

I had a big brother named Alden. We got along but our four-year age gap made a big difference when we were young. I already mentioned that he was drafted right away at the start of World War II when I was an early teen.

As he served out his duties in England, he grew to really love the place. After the War, he came home and attended college at Connecticut University. He married, and he and his wife spent his third year as an exchange student at a college outside London. After he returned for graduation, he took a job with the Navy Department in Washington. Eventually, he joined the FBI.

Alden wanted to work as an attaché at a foreign embassy, and he finally arranged to get an overseas appointment to England where he worked at the American Embassy for twenty years. Normally, they don't let agents stay in one spot that long but he pulled it off. Eventually, the home office informed him they were going to bring him back, but he didn't want to leave. He and his family had a house there, his three kids had all gone through school there, and they had jobs there. He took early retirement instead because he didn't want to disrupt the whole family.

Meanwhile, Alden got a job with an investment company out of Phoenix, Ariz. He travelled all over Europe doing surveillance and background checks on people making large investments. One morning, he came down for breakfast and then went back upstairs to change his clothes. His wife went upstairs and found him dead.

Heart attack. He was 54. Our father passed away at age 74 followed by our mother at age 75.

CHAPTER EIGHT

Uncle Miltie's Whistle

To go back a bit, after World War II the networks picked up where they left off in developing television for commercial use. Radio had already proven its worth but television was an unknown factor at the time. Many top radio performers hesitated to appear on television because they didn't know what effect it might have on their career. In the fall of 1948, NBC made an offer to Milton Berle, or rather Texaco did, to be the host of the New York-based *Texaco Star Theater.*[25] Berle accepted and "Mr. Tuesday Night" was born.[26] His success lured other stars to join him under the lights.

In the fall of 1953, Texaco dropped its sponsorship and the show was re-titled *The Buick-Berle Show.* The format changed so that Berle performed three weeks in a row with the fourth week being filled by golf club-wielding comedian Bob Hope. By 1955, the show included Hollywood as one of its locations. At that point I was a unit manager on staff with NBC assigned to both shows.

Milton Berle loved to be in control, and he was. He knew what he wanted and he was generally right. Milton wasn't nasty about anything, but the comedians of that era all came out of vaudeville and they knew timing. They envisioned a sketch or a scene and how it would play out with the audience because they'd done it so much. Berle envisioned it better than the director. He knew where the cameras should be.

The studio was configured with the stage down and the audience up on a diagonal. The control room where the director and technicians sat was on the second floor looking out over the stage. The orchestra was on the main level. Berle talked to the director because the microphones were open, and the director talked back to him. Berle would say, "I think the camera should be here for this and that, and move this one back," or whatever. If it got to be a heated argument, the director came out of the booth and talked to Berle face-to-face off to the side without everybody listening in.

Berle was a character, a perfectionist. We rehearsed for two days, blocked the on-stage movements and by Tuesday, we did a dress rehearsal. Most other dress rehearsals finished within one hour or one hour and fifteen minutes. Milton's lasted three hours. He never wore his wardrobe for dress rehearsal. Instead, he wore a sweatshirt with a towel around his neck and a whistle. Anytime he blew the whistle, everybody and everything stopped. He told the director what changes he wanted. We set up a pool and bet on how many times in the three hours he would blow that whistle. Many times it was well over a hundred. It could even go as high as one-hundred-thirty.

When Milton wasn't performing, I worked with Bob Hope. At that point, I interacted with Jack Hope, Bob's brother who was the producer. I coordinated as I did on every show for NBC, but not directly with Bob. That came later.

The Berle and Hope shows were live. However, NBC was positioning itself to replace live television with filmed shows. NBC realized that live television had no residual value. Once the show was over it couldn't be aired again.[27] Filmed shows could be replayed and resold, plus filmed shows freed up limited stage space. NBC wanted more film to fill in the hours because it was cheaper in the long run. We unit managers assigned to live TV worried about losing our jobs if live TV was replaced by film shows. This was before video tape was invented.

We sat down with Fenton Coe. As I said, Fenton left the network to work for the agency representing Red Skelton. When *The Red Skelton Show* went to CBS, Fenton stayed with it until Red retired. Then Fenton came back to NBC as a unit manager. Fenton had a film background. He was a prop man for many years at RKO Studios. One of the movies he did was *Gunga Din.* When we unit managers expressed concern about the network switching to film, Fenton volunteered to teach us what he knew.

We met once a week in the conference room. There were four of us. Three backed out of the training and I was the only one who stayed with it. The other three ended up working for NBC in managerial capacities, running different departments. It got so big, NBC had to departmentalize and they used these men in those areas. I'm not saying the men were wrong for taking those jobs, but it would have been boring for me. I stayed with Fenton's film training.

We went to the lab. We went to different studios where they shot film. I took scripts and broke them down by scene and location, for instance. Fenton critiqued them for me and let me know what I was doing right and what I was doing wrong. Gradually, I learned how to put together a film script and schedule it along with all those tasks associated with film production. He really laid it out for me and I soon found out what it was like to be a film production manager.

I did the film training while working my full time hours. Between 1954 and 1956, I did three live daytime shows through the summer. Fifteen shows a week, so it was kind of hectic. Among them were *The Pinky Lee Show*[28] and *Queen for a Day*[29].

I was then assigned to the *Lux Video Theatre*.[30] This was originally a radio show hosted by Cecil B. DeMille, which re-created the story of a film on radio. It went to CBS television but the agency moved it to NBC. Every week we went live with the re-creation of a film show. It was very exciting, very demanding, and quite an experience.

Also in that year, we started working with film on a game show called *You Bet Your Life* with Groucho Marx.[31] Marx's people were unhappy with the facilities they were working in, so NBC converted another radio studio to a film studio at Sunset and Vine. This consisted of gutting the studio and making a different stage with a grid to hang lights. We also changed the audience configuration so we had more room to work the cameras and more room for the orchestra. I was in charge of following through on all of that.

The project was completed and we started working on *You Bet Your Life*. Groucho Marx was a very, very talented man. I remember the day we met because it was odd. He walked in the first day of shooting while I was standing with NBC executive Jerry Stanley. Mr. Marx asked, "Are you the NBC representative?" and I said, "Yes, sir." He said, "There's no hot water in my dressing room." Okay, well, we goofed there. I sent some men to take care of it. The next week, he came back in and walked by us. All he said was, "Very funny." We found out the workmen had put hot water in both his faucets.

You Bet Your Life's format had Mr. Marx interviewing different contestants who were pre-selected and interviewed by the writers and directors. The staff prepared questions ahead of time for Groucho to ask. In those days we didn't have a teleprompter. We used a machine similar to those used in bowling alleys where you put a piece of paper on a flat area and it was projected on a screen.

Mr. Marx questioned each contestant so the audience got to know a bit about him or her. From there on, it was all ad-lib. Groucho ad-libbed like you wouldn't believe. It was a very dramatic show and a lot of fun. If someone said the secret word for the day, a fake duck came down from the ceiling and that contestant won a one-hundred dollar prize. George Fenneman was the announcer. He was a very generous man and a great man to work with, too.

My exposure to film production on *You Bet Your Life* along with my studies with Fenton Coe allowed me to capitalize on NBC's business decision to expand into film. Once again, the timing was right because NBC's film production exploded.[32]

Initially, NBC used us film unit managers as liaisons between NBC and the outside film companies who were contracted to shoot the shows. I was associated with *Dragnet*[33] and other series that we rotated daily. I met Jack Webb twice but we never got to know each other. He was suspicious of me because NBC representatives were seen as snoops and people presumed we were on site to see if the network's money was being spent wisely. It did give me a chance to be on a film stage, though, and I learned more about what it took to do a film show.

At the same time, *Matinee Theatre*[34] was being produced by Albert McCleery. This live dramatic show was done five days a week out of the Burbank Studios. NBC realized they had problems with space with other shows coming in so they wanted to film *Matinee Theatre*. I was asked to do twenty-six filmed shows. We had to film according to Mr. McCleery's direction, which meant we never shot below the waist. There was no set design, no scenery, since each show was done against set pieces already there. These set pieces were raised so the audience never saw the whole person, plus everything was shot against a black curtain.[35]

Matinee Theatre was one of the first shows I ever did by myself. We shot it on film similar to how they performed it live. The technique was a little different so I made a point to get the directors in ahead of time and show them what was new. Some of them had never done film. Boris Sagal, a well-known director. Lamont Johnson. It was a matter of teaching the directors, showing them how to work in film because in live television the action was continuous. In film, we stopped to re-load the film canister. The directors had to pace themselves, which Mr. McCleery never understood. Argued with me tooth and nail. "Why do we have to stop?" "The film magazine is only so big."

"Well, make them bigger." "That's impractical." "Why?" And so on. My training with script breakdowns became invaluable. It's what I shared with the directors.

On the filmed *Matinee Theatre*, we used an editing firm called Jacmar. Fenton Coe knew this company which was staffed by Jack Bachom and Marvin Coil. Their facility was in Hollywood. Marvin Coil had been in the editing business for years. He started out working in the lab, so he knew everything about a lot of things. He taught me more than you can imagine about post-production. Through his association with Bob Hope, he became the editor for all the Bob Hope shows that we did, and in later years also controlled Mr. Hope's film vault. Bob had five vaults full of films that he had done and Marvin catalogued everything for him.

When we started doing *Bonanza*, Marvin became one of the editors. In later life, Marvin became a post-production supervisor on *Bonanza, High Chaparral*, and then *Little House on the Prairie* and *Highway to Heaven*. My association with Marvin Coil lasted well over forty years. I couldn't have been happier with him. He was a character, a lovable man who really knew his craft. Marvin won many awards from NBC plus an Emmy because he delivered everything on time. There was never a glitch in any of the editing. He was a gem. I respected him and loved working with him.

In addition to *Matinee Theatre* being filmed, it was also credited with being one of the first Monday through Friday daytime color broadcasts in the United States.[36] When color was first being developed for television around 1953, all the production and engineering people had to take a color test. Most of us failed it and no one could figure out why. Someone decided to give the test proctor his own test, and he failed. Turns out *he* was color blind. They had to find someone else to conduct the test.

NBC had us set up a series of little bays to encourage people from the ad agencies who were enthusiastic about color. The bays held up to twenty people and each room had a black and white television set and a color television set. The agency people came in and watched continuously-running commercials so they could see the difference in the value of color as compared to black and white.

Agencies were in a quandary back then and didn't know what to do with the technology crossover. Should they order color commercials or black and white? These booth demos were NBC's way of telling them it didn't cost anything to come in and look. RCA was promoting color; NBC was owned by RCA. RCA said, "We have to get the advertisers on board. We can't have a color show with black and white commercials." I coordinated getting those demos together. That was my first exposure to color. I can't remember when *This is Your Life* went to color, but Hope was in color.

Hope Springs Eternal in Alaska

Bob Hope was a comedian, an actor, a vaudevillian and a humanitarian. In the mid-1950s, he was in his prime. Of particular importance to Hope and his team was the Christmas entertainment he provided U.S. troops all over the world through the USO beginning in the World War II years.[37]

When I was 28 years old in the fall of 1956, I finished filming my final episode of *Matinee Theatre*. NBC told me Hope wanted to film a Christmas show in Alaska. Bob had filmed a USO show in Thule, Greenland, either a year or two before this. He filmed it with military personnel doing the production work, but it was not very good. He wanted it to have better quality. Fenton Coe asked if I would put together a unit and go to Alaska. I said, "Sure."

I flew up to a base outside of Seattle and took a military DC-3 up to Elmendorf Air Force Base. When we came in for the landing, it was snowing so hard we couldn't see anything. The pilot told me to come up to the cockpit and gave me a headset to hear what the approach people instructed him to do. It was quite a thrill, the first time I'd ever done that. We landed and I didn't even know we hit the ground, it was just that smooth. The military really knew what they were doing.

I went up in advance to do a survey, as we called them. Basically, that means I coordinated with the military person assigned to me at each location to arrange stages, set up housing, organize transportation and the like.

In one location, my survey team and I had lunch with a general who greeted us. First, he took us through the kitchen on the way to the dining room. Soldiers dropped things lining up at attention. That's the way he ran his base.

During lunch, he got a phone call and left the table. He came back a little mad, yet he was smiling. One of his recruits was learning how to shoot a bazooka when an elk ran across the firing range. The guy nailed it. Of course, everybody was upset because he killed the elk. The general said, "If I have a guy who can kill an elk with a bazooka running across open range, I sure want him on my side."

I came home to California and put a crew together, and we flew back to Alaska over Christmas to film the shows. We did four or five shows, mostly in Anchorage and Fairbanks. The locations were pretty well contained with the shows performed inside. It was dark and cold every day, at times about forty-four-below zero with the wind chill, so we didn't hang around outside too much.

Ginger Rogers was one of Bob's guests on this trip.[38] We rehearsed the first show in Anchorage, a saloon set. Bob said, "I think I should come through the swinging doors into the saloon on a dog sled. Ginger Rogers can be sitting in the sled and I'll be driving the team."

As unit manager it became my task to make the dog sled skit come to life. I located a soldier who found a dog team to use. We came back later that night to do the show. Bob leaned down to pet the dogs and almost lost his hand. These dogs were used to the snow and cold outdoors but we had them on a stage in a warm theater. They were growling a little bit and quite nervous. I told Mr. Hope, "Don't ever lean down to pet the dogs."

Bob Hope and me in the wings at one of our USO shows.

During the actual show, it was time for the scene. The batwing doors opened and Bob Hope glided into the saloon set on a sled pulled by dogs. As Ginger Rogers stood up and took off her fur coat, which was quite revealing, all fifteen thousand kids in the audience let out a howl. That noise scared the dogs who took off right for the orchestra pit where Les Brown and his band were sitting.

I ran out on stage to guide the dogs off set which I was able to do, however, they turned very close to me. When I looked down, I realized the sled had gone over my shoes cutting them, and I was looking at my socks. Back on stage, Bob let the crowd's howl calm down and said, "Well, there'll be a white Christmas in the barracks tonight."

Mickey Mantle was also a guest on this show. When we weren't performing we were in our military housing, which included a bar and a kitchen. We were having a few drinks one night when Mickey said, "Oh," and he started to cry. I asked, "What's the matter?" He said, "I just realized I'm not gonna be home for Christmas with my boys."

I said, "It's a little late to figure that out, but that's the way it is." He said okay and went upstairs to bed. A short while later, I turned around and there was Mickey Mantle in his BVD shorts outside in the snow in temperatures that were significantly below zero, building a snowman which he said he was going to take home to his boys. It took about three of us to get him back inside because Mickey Mantle was quite stout and had his own mind about what he wanted to do. There was no problem with him freezing because he had too much alcohol in him to let that happen.

The next day we went to Fairbanks where it was forty-five-below zero and we had to have Caterpillar tractors stretch out the cables because they were frozen in coils. It was quite an experience. We finished all the shows and planned our return home the day after Christmas. I got the whole crew together and we went down to the flight line to get on the plane. No plane. The one assigned to us had a mechanical problem, so we went back to the barracks and played poker for a while.

I kept going back to the flight line to get updates. Our film crew members were on an eight-hour day plus overtime afterward. After eight hours, we still hadn't taken off, so I went to the colonel who was my project officer and said, "We've got to cancel this. I can't pay these guys this kind of money. We're going to have to go tomorrow." The officer said, "There's no way you can go tomorrow because tomorrow you won't even have a plane. There aren't any available. You'll have to take this one tonight."

We took off about seven o'clock that night and flew back to Los Angeles. The guys kept telling me all the blood was going to run out of my boots because of all the overtime I owed them. As it happened, not one person put in for the full overtime. They took their eight hours and a little more but they didn't dig us for the whole amount. They said, "It wasn't your fault, and we were glad to do it." That was the end of the Christmas show.

The Bob Hope Chevy Show from Alaska aired on NBC on December 28, 1956.[39]

CHAPTER TEN

Bob Hope & the One-Star General Explore the Orient

After working with Mr. Hope on that one Christmas show in 1956, I was asked to be associate producer for Bob for all his shows, live and filmed. Hope's prior associate producer, George Habib, who had been with Bob for a number of years, decided to move on after he finished the 1956-57 year. He recommended me to replace him and that's how my work with Bob Hope started.[40]

As the associate producer, I now had a unit manager working with me. He did what I did before I moved up a notch, if you want to call it that. Associate producer was a better title, a better recognition.

Bob did one television show every four weeks. I went to Bob's house at ten in the morning and worked on the script with the writers. Afterward, Mr. Hope went to Lakeside Golf Course and played golf in the afternoon. I went to the studio and coordinated with a singing group or a dance group or any activity that didn't involve Mr. Hope. I broke for dinner and went back to the studio at seven thirty in the evening. Bob and a guest actor worked until one o'clock in the morning. That was our routine while we did shows in the studio.

Hope had a huge office on his property in Toluca Lake, plus his house had a three-hole golf course. One Tuesday, he invited guest star pro golfer Sam Snead to the house to work on the script with the writers. He persuaded Mr. Snead to give him a few golf tips. Snead jokingly said, "You paid me to be a guest on your show, not to give you golf lessons."

Bob called Snead later that night at the Knickerbocker Hotel and asked if he would do an interview with a lady from a local paper. She showed up at seven that evening at Snead's hotel room and asked if she could freshen up in the bathroom. She came out stark naked according to Sam. On Sunday, we were all in Bob's dressing room at NBC and Bob asked Snead, "How did the interview go with the lady reporter?" Snead replied, "She's been with me all week. We're finishing the interview tonight. I told her to send you the bill." Bob said, "If I knew that, I would have asked for more lessons."

Bob had a big, very impressive desk in the middle of his office and I had a work space there as well. One night I was working and Bob said, "It's time to eat. Come have dinner with us." I sat down to dinner with him and his kids. He was just like any other father, asking his kids what they did in school that day, what they did after school. He was as normal as any father would be. That gave me a new insight into him.

Another time, he invited me to go with him to visit a friend he used to work with in vaudeville. His name was Charlie Cooley. Bob and Charlie were such close friends because they went way back. Bob relied on Charlie. When Mr. Hope moved to California, he bought Charlie a house nearby. Then, Charlie got sick.

Often when we worked late in the office after the writers left, Bob would say, "Walk with me over to see Charlie. I want to see how he's doing." He didn't want to walk alone but he was worried for his friend. He was a very caring person.

After I went home, Bob sometimes called to read me his monologue. He'd ask, "Do you like that?" I'd say, "Yeah, I like it." He'd ask, "How about this gag?" I'd say, "No, I don't think that's funny." He'd tell me, "Just wait." His delivery, where he paused, which line he emphasized. When he performed it, he got a tremendous laugh. Then he'd look at me like, "Told you so." He wasn't mean about it, but he knew his craft. They all did.

When I did the Hope shows, a couple of them were big musicals which were shot in color. Some were taped and some were live. We went live a lot of times. That was scary. We did a show in the days of beatniks, the guys with the hair and goatees and the whole thing. I forget who the guest star was. Hope had a goatee and was dressed like a hippy in this skit in which he and his girlfriend were having a baby. We were supposed to cut to the nursery where there were four babies in bassinettes lined up against the wall. One of the babies was to have a goatee, which was the tag line.

We hired the babies but they could only be under the lights for a very short time. That was by labor law because they were afraid the lights would hurt the babies' eyes. It was a good rule. Out of the four babies, Hope picked the one he wanted to be his "child" in the skit. We had the four babies lined up in a row. I was backstage with the make-up man who was going to make up the baby. He couldn't put the goatee on too far ahead of time because he had to glue it on. He had to wait almost until the last minute.

Let's say the baby Hope picked was in bassinette number two. Just as we tried to glue the goatee on, that baby started to cry and moan. I told the make-up man, "Move down to four." We threw the goatee on number four and when the camera came in I said, "That way!" and pointed. Anyway, we got the shot.

As I said, some of Hope's shows were taped because videotape came into the studios at that time. This worked out great and it was a time-saver to an extent. However, if we had to make a cut, which we often had to do with Bob's monologue, it was a very tedious process. The tape was about two inches wide and had barely-visible little black lines about every quarter of an inch. If we cut one of the lines, we got video roll-up on the television screen. The editor sprinkled talcum powder on the tape to make the lines show up, and then used a razor blade to cut between the lines. It took about thirty minutes for each edit. There were many sleepless nights working with editors after the others had gone home as we readied the show to go on air.

That same year of 1957 when I became associate producer, Bob wanted to do a Christmas show in the Orient. This was quite a feat because Bob told us the scope of his plan before we left for the survey: a troupe of seventy-six people flying from base to base in two DC-6 airplanes. I flew out of California to survey the locations with Johnny Pawlek and Jack Bachom. Jack was part of Jacmar with Marvin Coil, the company that edited our film for *Matinee Theatre* and the Alaska Hope show in 1956.

Jack Bachom's function was to take the film shot each day, pack it up for Customs and send it to Hollywood. Partner Marvin Coil was to pick it up at the lab and break it down. All this had to be planned ahead of time.

Johnny Pawlek's survey task was to check sound. Johnny was a sound engineer and he did every radio show that Bob Hope ever did for years. Bob relied on Johnny because they were together for so long. Johnny had to make sure we had quality sound because without sound, a comic is nothing. Lots of the shows were going to be performed inside plane hangars, Quonset huts, wherever. We ended up with parachutes hanging from the ceiling to deaden the echo. Johnny laid out those plans. I also had to hire a sound engineer to work the machines because it was an I-A crew, but they got along fine with Johnny.

Our orders were cut out of Washington, D.C., and they authorized us to travel to all the bases the USO wanted us to film. We were basically going to do a two-hour stage show at each base for a total of twenty-one shows in fourteen days including travel with the entire troupe. It was a hectic schedule.

We could tell on the survey how well things were going to go by who met us at the front gate. If we were greeted at the base by a Lieutenant, we knew we were in trouble. A good sergeant, okay. A Colonel or up? Yes. We knew things were going to get done.

Me talking to Bob Hope over his left shoulder, along with Bob's brother and producer Jack Hope (right) and make-up artist Bill Morley (left with moustache).

Our visits were sanctioned by Washington and the bases knew we were coming, but the people in Washington couldn't specify who would be assigned to us on any given base. That's why they gave me the military rank of a one-star general. I had it written down on a piece of paper that I kept in my coat pocket. If a Captain gave me a little guff, I said, "Here are my orders. You're working for me. You don't want to work for me, I'll find somebody else." I had to do that a few times. Once they saw what my rank was they realized I wasn't some flunky trying to put something over on them.

Jack, Johnny and I left the day after Thanksgiving. We flew to San Francisco and were met by the military and driven out to

Travis Air Force Base. We were greeted there by a colonel who showed us around and fed us lunch. After lunch, he said, "You're going overseas, so you have to get your immunization shots."

We went to the dispensary. Jack and Johnny said, "Since you're our leader, you have to go first." There was a short sergeant standing there who had four needles in his hand. He shoved my sleeve up, gauzed it with a little alcohol and bingo! Four needles went into my arm all at once. I looked down and he was playing them like a pump organ. It was quite a shock. Never had four needles at once. Nor had Jack or Johnny who were behind me with long faces now that they knew what was gonna happen to them.

We left Travis Air Force Base late that afternoon in a DC-6 airplane carrying military dependents headed for Honolulu. We were an hour out when the plane lost a motor. As we turned around to go back to Travis, we lost another motor. We limped back into Travis barely skimming the water. That was our first flight with the military. When we landed, I called the colonel who saw us off and told him what happened. He got us a room at the Officer's Club. Of course, my brigadier general orders gave us a bit of clout, so we got the best billeting on the base.

We didn't have our rooms long, though. The colonel called us about two o'clock in the morning and said, "I have a flight out to Hawaii but you have to get down here in twenty minutes." I got the other two men up and we went down to the flight line. This time we had a big Boeing cargo plane. We walked up the back ramp where they put in two rows of seats for us on one side, and a row of seats on the other side. On the other side, there was a military policeman and a soldier. The soldier was handcuffed to the chair and handcuffed to the MP. The GI was going back on a murder rap, and it gave us a little chill to know we were sitting there with a potential murderer.

We flew into Honolulu and did some work there. Our plan was to stay the night and fly to Tokyo the next night. The military had a hard time finding us a hotel because it was a very busy time of year. We found a room at the Royal Hawaiian Hotel at a cost of seven dollars a night. This was one of the swankiest hotels in Hawaii at the time. The next day, we finished our work and got ready for the flight to Tokyo. The military folks picked up our bags around four o'clock which gave us time to have dinner. We started to look for a restaurant when all of a sudden it began to rain, and I mean it was a downpour. Water came up over the curb. We decided to eat at the hotel.

The three of us didn't look too bad, but we weren't in any fancy clothes. We went to the hotel and they wouldn't let us into the dining room because we didn't have a tie. We went to the bar to have a drink. Our luggage was already on the plane so all we had was what we were wearing. We got to the hotel bar and they wouldn't let us in because we didn't have a tie.

I found a busboy, gave him some money and said, "Find us three ties." Twenty minutes later he came back. He had three ties that looked like they'd been dragged through the mud, but we put them on. We went back to the hotel dining room, but now it was too late for dinner. So, we went back to the bar. When we got into the bar, there wasn't a soul in there. It was completely empty, yet they wouldn't let us in because we didn't have a tie.

That ticked me off and I complained to the bartender. Then I ordered a gin martini. The bartender showed me the martini he made. It was huge. It was like a bird bath, a big bowl with a hollow stem. He said, "Here's your martini." I asked, "What's that gonna cost me?" He said, "The little one is ninety-cents." I asked, "Well, how much for this one?" He said, "It's ninety-cents." I asked, "How can you do that?" He said, "I'm like you. I'm mad at the company, so have a nice drink." That's how we started our trip to Wake Island, the refueling point on the way to Japan.

I drank the fourteen ounces of gin, and then the colonel showed up to take us to the airport. When he found out we hadn't eaten, he stopped at a different restaurant. We couldn't get in there either, so we had another drink. A little one. We decided to go to the cafeteria at the airport. By this time we were crazed to get something to eat. As we were going through the food line, they called our names to board the plane. My civilian rank of a one-star general gave us priority boarding. A couple drinks, no dinner. I buckled the seat belt and didn't remember taking off. When I came to, we were landing at Wake Island.

Wake Island was hot and sticky. We were loaded onto an open-air bus and taken to a shack that served as the restaurant. I knew we were in trouble when they had us pay for our breakfast as we went in the door. There was nothing to order; we got what they cooked. I sat down to a dish of stewed prunes. Not what I really wanted with the hang-over I had. Then we got some powdered scrambled eggs. That was our lunch. It only cost us two bucks, so I guess that wasn't too bad a deal. Then we flew on to Tokyo.

In preparation for the very full USO schedule we were there to set up, I created a survey checklist of things that had to be done at each base for each leg of the trip. In Tokyo, I sat down with the brass and went through it. I was in my late-20s and had never done anything of this magnitude. It was my responsibility to make sure that our seventy-six people coming in had ground transportation that met the plane to get us to the base. I had to arrange for the best-available housing and food. We had to have stages erected, platforms for the cameras. Everything and anything needed to put these shows on was my responsibility. I had to lay everything out for every base where we were scheduled to perform.

On the survey, we went to each base, but not in the order of the performances. After the survey, I determined which shows would be first, second and so on. The twenty-one stage shows would be in Japan, Okinawa and South Korea. We surveyed the places for the shows in and around Tokyo, and then we flew to Okinawa.

On the island, I was settling in to one of the barracks when the colonel came in and said, "Your transportation to get to the other bases in Okinawa is here." I walked outside and saw a chopper. This helicopter had no doors. It was a two-seater for the pilot and me. There was a glass bubble over my head that went down underneath the seat. It was a Navy chopper that was used mainly for hovering and looking for submarines. It had a blade going one way, and another blade going the other. What a thrill it was riding around all day in that thing.

Then we went to Korea and did the survey there. The three of us were billeted in one room at the officers' quarters in town. We walked up three flights of stairs and entered the room. When we shut the door, we saw a big sign on it that said, "Please lock yourself in the room." With a padlock. They were afraid we would be hijacked while we were sleeping.

I went into the bathroom. It consisted of a sink, a shower and a hole in the floor which was the toilet. Johnny Pawlek said, "Gee, there's no soap or towels. I'll go down and get some." He came back upstairs with the soap and towels and said, "I got the stuff, but there's no water today and may not be any tomorrow." That was the officers' quarters in Seoul, South Korea. It was a hell hole.

We left there and flew back to Okinawa for the first show because, by that time, Bob had flown in with the production crew, the writers and the talent.[41] We did four shows in Okinawa.

For the first show, I was on stage setting everything up for the final check. I had to coordinate with the talent to get them on stage at the right time, get them off the stage and make sure they were in the correct wardrobe. We brought people with us to do that, but it was my responsibility to see it was done correctly. It was like being a stage manager in a theater.

I was out on stage with the crew when all of a sudden, I heard this deafening sound. I looked around. We were in the middle of nowhere. What could it be? I looked again and five thousand soldiers came in from this direction, and another five thousand from that direction and even another five thousand from a third direction. They marched in and I mean in step and in tempo. They sat down in front of the stage so they could watch the show. The marching feet of fifteen thousand soldiers! I started to cry. It was an experience I can't describe. These shows we put on were a lot of work, but it was worth it because it was important to the soldiers. I loved every minute of it. We got such a reaction from the service members. They just *loved* it.

From the production side, I call what we did film show productions. Each show was about two hours long. A singer came on stage and did three numbers, a dance group did their act, and then someone else. We didn't film the full show every time. If a singer did three songs, we filmed one song here, one song in another location and another song somewhere else. All of Bob's monologues were recorded at every base. We travelled with two of his best writers, Mort Lachman and Bill Larkin. As soon as we hit a base, those two found out the names of the brass in charge. They took certain jokes and put in the local names, and the troops loved it. The joke was the same, but the names were changed. Making fun of the brass was a great thing for the kids to hear.

We also did a lot of handheld camera work with shots of soldiers in the audience. Bob wanted us to show the audience. The letters Bob got after the shows came in a full mail truck, not just a sack. There were bags and bags and bags. They said, "I saw my son on television!"

The Orient show had Jayne Mansfield, Peter Leeds, columnist Hedda Hopper, a great, great group of people that Bob brought over. Sleeping quarters for the celebrities and crew were a little tight on these trips. I assigned Peter Leeds with Jayne Mansfield's boyfriend, Mickey Hargitay, and I had Jayne Mansfield with Hedda Hopper. I slept in a bungalow with six other people.

One night Peter Leeds knocked on my door at one o'clock in the morning and asked, "Where am I gonna sleep?" I said,

"You're in with Mickey Hargitay." He said, "Yeah, lucky me. Mickey Hargitay has Jayne Mansfield in there with him." I said, "Well, there's an open bed with Hedda Hopper." He said, "No way. I'm not going there." So, he came in and slept on a couch in our room for four nights.

As for Bob Hope, he never really slept at night. He took a lot of catnaps. During the shows he did his dialogue, skit, or whatever and when someone else performed, he went off stage, sat down on a box and went to sleep. He could sleep just like that. I shook him for his cue to go back on and he got up wide awake.

A couple of other stories while doing the Okinawa shows...I told everybody we were going to be out in a ball field away from everything. I said there were no bathroom facilities and suggested they use the bathroom before we left the base. Once we got there, Hedda Hopper came to me and said, "I have a problem. I know what you said, but I have to go to the bathroom real bad and I can't use a soup can so what are you going to do?" We had a tent for makeup and wardrobe. I said, "Everybody clear the tent," and I pointed to a corner for Hedda to use.

The Navy put two ships side-by-side. I took one of the cameramen with a handheld camera to photograph all the stars coming aboard. There were two sailors positioned at the gang plank to welcome everyone. All of a sudden, a car drove up on the dock flying flags to indicate it was a general's car. The two sailors said, "Holy sh*t, there's a General coming aboard. Get the Captain."

The General got out of his car and was about halfway up the gang plank as the Navy Captain came out of his quarters still putting on his tie and coat. I asked the General, "Where the hell have you been? We've been waiting for you." The Captain and the sailors looked at me as if to ask, "Are you crazy?" I said to them, "Don't worry. He's one of our actors dressed as a General." The Captain said, "You should have warned us earlier." I said, "Relax, we all need a good laugh."

While we were traveling from base to base, we used our flying time to help Barney McNulty. That's a name you may not recognize, but he was a great man. He did all of Bob Hope's cue cards, and when he got busy we *all* did cue cards. We stood in the plane's aisle writing them.

When we got close to landing, Jayne Mansfield and Mickey Hargitay went into the bathroom. The bathrooms on a military plane were smaller than they are on a commercial plane even today. There was no door, just a curtain. Mickey Hargitay helped Jayne change clothes so she looked glamorous when departing the plane. We heard all these noises, elbows hitting the walls, and everybody laughed. Finally, Jane stepped out looking great.

I got off the plane first with the director and camera crew and set up the cameras for everybody to exit the plane. I signaled Bob, and of course, he came down first to cheers. When Jayne got off she stopped at the top of the stairs, looked around, found all the cameras, and walked by everyone sideways to show off her figure.

The shows were great to do. Bob was a wonderful person. The military loved him and he loved the military. One of my responsibilities for every base we visited, even if we stopped for re-fueling, was to make sure we had ground transportation for Bob and any of the cast that wanted to join him to go to the base hospital. Bob entertained the troops who couldn't get to him. I went with him a couple of times, but, uh, it was uh, it was tough.

Bob went through the wards and brought life to these kids who were shot up and in bad shape. They had grins when he left and they all thanked him. It was a wonderful, wonderful thing that he did at every base. I respected him for that. These kids were in rehab. They were the wounded. Some of them lost legs, some in traction. This was 1957, so it wasn't too far after the war. They didn't bring a lot of those fellows home right away. They didn't have the facilities to bring them home. We stopped in Guam, Wake Island, Kwajalein. He hit the hospital on every base we went. If we did a few shows at the same base, in between he went to the base hospital. Bob was in a class all by himself.

On Christmas day, we were in South Korea to film at a place called the Bayonet Bowl up near the 38th parallel demilitarized zone. Everybody flew up in big helicopters because there were no roads into the place. I was in a helicopter with an empty seat across from me and an empty one beside me. Suddenly, the window across from me blew out. The glass flew over my right shoulder and landed in the empty seat. Had I been sitting there, I'd have had a face full of glass.

Many times flying around in planes on the Hope tours I thought, "Man, I'm going to go home in a box." The biggest exposure was during the surveys rather than during the actual shows. If we were at an Army base and had to get to an Air Force or Navy facility, we had to scramble. The Army didn't have planes to fly us to a different service's base. We had to find someone from the Navy or Air Force to pick us up unless we happened upon a cargo plane or transport that was going to our destination. We flew in any kind of plane and always wore a parachute. We sat in bucket seats with no insulation and scraped the frost off the inside of the plane. But it's what we had to do. One time we went aboard a plane and I asked, "What are you carrying?" The pilot said, "Ammo. All ammo." I said, "No, I'll wait for another plane." I wasn't having any part of a plane full of ammo.

As for the Bayonet Bowl on Christmas Day, I started to set things up on stage and the band was getting ready, wearing gloves because it was so cold. The kids marched in and sat on the hill leaving a big vacant area in the front. I asked the project officer, "Why aren't the kids sitting near the stage?" He said, "They're going to move some chairs in later and the brass are going to sit in front." I said, "Don't do it." He said, "I've got my orders." I said, "You've got my orders, too. Don't do it." He looked at me. I said, "I'm tellin' ya."

A little bit later, Mr. Hope flew in with a general. He asked, "Is everything going all right?" I said, "There's one problem we have to solve. Maybe the general can take care of this. There's a big vacant area in the front where they're going to move in chairs for the brass."

Me on stage far right talking to Bob Hope along with Les Brown (left) and his Band of Renown. The young soldiers are up front.

Hope looked at the general and said, "The hell they are. I didn't come over here to entertain the brass. You people who have seniority in the military, you get all kinds of perks. I'm over here to take care of the troops who have nothing. Either the troops are down front and you're off to the side or I won't go on." The general said, "That's the way it will be because I want you to perform." The general went out, picked up the microphone and told all the kids on the hill to stand up and gradually move forward. They moved up right to the edge of the stage. The show went on and it was a real success.

Later that same day, we went to another location whose name I forget. The general in charge there said to me, "This is the closest to the border we've ever had twenty thousand kids in one contained area. If the North Koreans wanted to do something, if they really wanted to start this war up all over again, this would be a good time. They keep flying over and buzzing us."

He asked me, "You see that path over there?" and he pointed to a hill. I said, "Yes, sir." He said, "Along that path there are people stationed all the way back to Seoul. If there are any problems here, you and your company get on that path and walk back to Seoul because that's your route of escape." That put a thrill in my throat. Thankfully, all went off without a hitch.

We went on to Seoul, South Korea, where we lost a big light we used on the stage. I was told by someone to go to some American guy for a replacement. The American said he'd get it for me but said, "You can't come with me. Go stand on such-and-such a corner and I'll come by."

I got the money and stood on the corner with my briefcase between my legs so it wouldn't get swiped. Sure enough, this truck came down the street with a big stage K-10 light in it. I transferred it into my truck and we got it back to the base. That Seoul, South Korea was a strange, strange place. Regardless, we ended up doing four shows in one day there.

At every base we went, the brass wanted Mr. Hope to come to their house for dinner. Bob had a rule about that. He said, "There's no one more important than anyone else in this troupe. Anybody who wants to give a party, it's a party for seventy-six people because that's the entire group. We're working hard and we're working together." I had to tell the generals, "He's not going to come to your house under any circumstance, but if you want to give the whole group a party, we'll be there."

Christmas Eve they gave us a party. It was about midnight. I was talking to a one-star and a two-star general and they wanted to know how things went. Jack Hope, Bob's brother, came up and asked me a question. As we were talking, the two-star general asked Jack, "Would you like a drink, Mr. Hope?" Jack said, "Yes, I'd like a Scotch and water." The two-star turned to the one-star and in a very gruff voice said, "Get Mr. Hope a drink." He barked it at him like an order. The one-star bounced it off somebody else and so on. By the time the last guy got to the bartender, he was probably shaking in his boots. Rank has its privileges. Two minutes later, Jack Hope had his drink.

Then long about one o'clock in the morning, Jayne Mansfield decided to sing "Silent Night." We set up a little platform for her. She got up with the small band that had been playing and she sang her song.

After we flew home to the states, we worked on assembling the show to air on the network. Marvin Coil had collected all the film Jack Bachom sent back and now we had ten days to put it together. We worked night and day. Marvin put up bunk beds in the studio for folks to sleep or to step away from it all for a bit. We worked our tails off getting that show edited.

One night, Bob Hope was working with one of the five editors. The guy was a little off-kilter with a toothache. Bob drove home at three in the morning and came back a bit later. He walked up to the guy and said, "I went home and got you this medicine. It worked for me and I thought it might work for you." How many people would do that?

The whole trip was quite an experience for me. It was the first time I'd ever done anything of that magnitude, to have all those people report to me and to do what it took to get everything done and done right.

The 1957 *Bob Hope Far East Christmas USO Show* aired January 18, 1958.[42]

CHAPTER ELEVEN

The Road to Europe

Back state-side in 1958, we were still doing Bob's TV shows in Los Angeles. Bob also had a commitment to do a movie for United Artists. He did a film in Paris previously,[43] but I was not involved in that one. It went way over budget. For this next picture, United Artists said, "Here's your budget. If you go over budget, it's going to come out of your salary. We're not paying any more than this amount."

Bob asked me to work on the film and said, "You've got to keep track of this budget because I don't want to spend any of my money." The movie was called *Alias Jesse James.* It was my first feature film. We shot at Paramount Studios on stage and we did a lot of second unit work out in the Valley near what today is Westlake Village.[44] It was released the following year.

At Christmastime this same year, Bob and the USO determined we would go to Europe for the military again.[45] Jack Bachom, Johnny Pawlek and I left to do the survey right after Thanksgiving. The same routine as before. We went to Washington and got our orders. They gave us the list of bases which took us all over Europe and the Mediterranean. Once again, we were scheduled to do twenty-one shows in fourteen days including travel. Our first stop was in the Azores, on to Morocco and then Spain, Italy, Germany and Scotland. The last show was in Keflavik, Iceland.[46]

A few things about this survey. I was in Frankfurt, Germany, in a room full of people and a colonel came in. I've seen colonels and I've seen colonels, but I never saw an officer with so much brass and so many decorations on his uniform in my life. He turned to me and asked, "Are you in charge of this troupe?" I said, "Yes, sir." He said, "You sit at my right at this table." I sat down. He asked, "Do you have a checklist?" I said, "Yes, sir." He said, "Go." I started reading off things that needed to be done and the Colonel was crisply assigning each task to his team. We were making great progress.

We got to one part of the list and all of a sudden, a voice way over in the corner, a lieutenant who was not even sitting at the table, said, "Sir, sir." You could hear a quiver in his voice. He said, "The local fire marshal in Frankfurt will only allow five-thousand people in the building you're talking about using for the performance." The colonel sat back and asked, "Now, Lieutenant, you mean I have to tell Mr. Hope we're going to have only five-thousand people in this performance instead of fifteen or twenty thousand?"

The lieutenant said, "Sir, it's not me. It's the fire marshal." There was a long pause. The colonel looked at the lieutenant and asked, "This is a tank base, isn't it?" The lieutenant said, "Yes, sir." He said, "I guess you'll have to get a couple of tanks and run 'em through the walls to get the required exits in this building because we're going to have fifteen to twenty-thousand people. And that's it!" We came back to do the show. There were holes in the wall, some of them covered with blankets, but we had almost twenty-thousand people in that building. It was a great show.

In Italy, Bob and I planned to do a show in the Bay of Naples aboard the aircraft carrier the *USS Forrestal*. Bob wanted as many ships as possible from the area to sail in so the Seventh Fleet could be in the background. I was in Naples setting things up and I had to talk to the Admiral on the *Forrestal*. The only way to get to the ship was to fly out, so they put me in a two-seater fighter plane and we landed on the carrier. It was the first time I'd ever done that and boy, that was quite a thrill. I met with the people on board and finished my tasks. They sent me back the same way—in a fighter plane. They shot us off a catapult. Wow!

When the troupe came over, we did our first show in the Azores, then Morocco, and southern Spain. When we were leaving the last location near Seville, one of the pilots doing the safety check discovered someone put jet fuel in our prop plane by accident. They had to drain it all out. It was quite a hold-up, but I'm glad the pilot realized it. Had we taken off with the jet fuel, we would have crashed.

Next was the show in Madrid which we performed late at night. Folks in Madrid eat dinner late in the evening, as is their custom. We did, too. After the show and dinner, I returned to the hotel about two o'clock in the morning. There was a note for me to call Mr. Hope. He beat me back to the hotel by five minutes. I went up to his suite and he asked, "Where the hell have you been? You should've been in your room." I said, "I just got back." He said, "I was looking for you." I said, "You just got back." Anyway, we bantered back and forth. He said, "I saw a dance group tonight and I want to film it tomorrow morning before we go to the next show." I said okay.

I went back to my room and contacted people at the base we just left to see if they could arrange a permit to put generators on the street. I had to file a whole new flight manifest because Bob told me to take the rest of the cast and the band to the base in northern Spain. He would join us later in the day after he and his film crew finished. He also told me to start without him if he ran late.

I had all that arranged and left early in the morning to fly up to northern Spain. It was a bad day. It was raining like a son-of-a-gun, lightning flashing around us. The plane was bouncing around. Everybody was getting sick including me. It was not a fun trip.

We got over the base and tried to land. We kept dropping and dropping. We hit a lot of air pockets and dropped like crazy. We made about four or five passes over the base to land and the pilot called me up to the cockpit. He said, "Mac, I can't land this plane. I'm afraid. We keep hitting these pockets, and we may hit one we're not going to pull out of. What do you want me to do?" I said, "It's not what I want you to do. If you tell me you can't land the plane, I suggest we go back to Madrid." The pilot said, "I think that's the best solution."

We turned around. I said, "Radio ahead and tell Mr. Hope and his plane to stay there because there's no sense in him getting into this mess either." We were back in Madrid by mid-afternoon. I got off the plane and went into the terminal. Hope was there, mad as hell at me. "Do you realize this is the first show in all the shows I've done for the troops I've had to cancel?" He was really upset. He kind of chewed my buns out. I said, "Bob, if the pilot tells me he can't land the plane?" He said, "You should have tried anyway." I said, "We did try, but I had all the cast members and the orchestra and I wasn't going to put those people's lives in jeopardy." He was still mad at me.

We continued talking and the subject of the movie *Alias Jesse James* came up. He said, "You know what? I think we should go to the Rose Parade. I should get a stagecoach and ride down Colorado Boulevard so we can advertise the movie." I said, "Bob, the Rose Bowl Association won't allow that kind of advertising." He said, "Oh, hell, we could get away with it." I said, "They won't do it." I had done the Rose Bowl coverage as I mentioned previously, so I knew what I was talking about.

He said, "Who do I talk to?" I gave him the phone number for the president of the Rose Bowl Association. We placed a call to the office in Pasadena. Bob talked to the president and came out of the conversation with the same answer I gave him, but now he was mad at *me* because he couldn't do it. Sometimes Bob was a little gruff. We had a few words, but for the most part, we got along great.

The day before Christmas, we were in Naples to do the show on the *USS Forrestal* which was berthed in the bay. We were all on the ship and had lunch. Mr. Hope was talking to the Admiral on the flight deck. Bob said, "Boy, look at that scenery. The Bay of Naples is just a beautiful sight. Maybe we should just shoot in that direction."

I said, "No, we talked about having all the ships in this area at sea so we could have the Seventh Fleet in the background." He said, "Yeah, but the Bay of Naples. No one's ever seen that at home. That's a bigger draw I think than anything." He turned to the Admiral and asked, "You *can* turn this thing around, can't you?" The Admiral said, "If you want it turned around, we'll turn it around."

At that point, Bob's work on board was done, so he left for the hotel. I was still on the ship working with the crew when I heard the boatswain mate's whistle over the loudspeaker. "All shore leave is canceled. All shore leave is canceled." Remember, it was Christmas Eve. In order to turn the ship around, the sailors had to take the *Forrestal* out seventy miles. All the crew that had shore leave Christmas Eve in Naples didn't get it. I never told Mr. Hope the end of that story because it would have upset him. Had he known, I don't think he would have asked the admiral to do it. I was upset like Bob would have been but I just let it be.

We did the show the following morning against the Bay of Naples. Ten minutes into the show, a cloudburst opened up and it rained the rest of the day. The Navy people came out with their heavy duty Caterpillar forklifts, picked up the stage in three pieces and moved it down to the hangar deck where we did the show. We hardly saw anything because it was so dark, like working in a hole, but that's how we did the show on the *Forrestal*. No views of Naples.

The rest of the shows in Europe for the most part were uneventful except for the last one. We landed at Prestwick, Scotland and did a small show there. While we were there they had mechanical problems with one of the planes, and we had a four hour wait while they flew in a part. We left Prestwick late, which put us late into Iceland. Per Hope, that was my fault. I should have anticipated.

Bob never admitted the truth that the shows he did during World War II were smaller. There were only four or five people in the troupe. It was all radio so the crew size was minimal. Now we had seventy-six people. I wanted to keep us together as a unit in case something happened so we didn't have people over there and people over here. That was my reason for keeping the show together in Scotland. I never pressed the radio versus television discussion with Bob, but ours was the more difficult of the two.

Still, Bob was upset about our wait in Scotland and the delay which put us into Iceland at three in the morning. The kids were waiting for us inside, and we put the show on at three o'clock in the morning. It was a hell of a show. Then, we finally came home to the States and did the same thing with the editing to get the show ready in ten days. We succeeded and the *USO Xmas European Bases Show* aired January 16, 1959.[47]

I look at my three years with Mr. Hope as being the experience that made me what I am. Working with NBC in a studio, I got things ready to go on the air, but it was a lot different to hire a crew, to be in charge of something, to be out there on your own. I wasn't in that position until I worked for Hope.

Working the Hope tours defined my ability to organize outside a controlled area. In a studio, I picked up a phone to get anything I needed. That was easy. If something happened, I got it corrected immediately. When I did the Hope shows, I got things done by the seat of my pants. It was the first time I had that much authority and responsibility. I set things up in the survey with people I didn't know. We never quite knew if what we requested was really going to happen until we came back to do the show. It did, but we didn't know for sure.

As for Mr. Hope, I got along with Bob quite well. I liked him. I respected him. I mean, you can't not respect a man like that. God, he had such timing and talent. He was bigger than life, really. In those days, if you said you worked for Bob Hope, it was important.

After the European tour, Fenton Coe contacted me. I had to decide which direction my career path would take. Although assigned to work with Bob Hope, I was still an NBC staff employee. Fenton approached me in 1959 and asked me to decide whether I wanted to stay with Mr. Hope or to return to NBC and Fenton's film division. The film division had become extremely active by this time and I felt drawn to that call.

I told Bob my decision to leave him and he said, "If that's what you want to do, that's okay." I recommended Sil Caranchini to take my place partly because Sil had worked with Bob before. Sil was originally an engineer in radio back in New York and had moved out to California. He got into television as a technical director then became a unit manager. He was my unit manager on the Hope shows. He didn't go overseas with me, but I worked with him directly. Hope wasn't upset with me and he felt comfortable with Sil.

A funny story about Sil, who was a very smart engineer. He had a back problem and went into the hospital to have an operation. He was on the operating table but they hadn't started anything yet. This was in the early days of doctors using monitors with a camera during procedures. The monitor went on the fritz. They brought in four people to fix it, but they couldn't. Sil, in his hospital garb, got off the operating table, got on his knees, stood up on the operating table, put his hands around the back of the unit, and fixed the monitor. Then he got back on the table and they did the operation.

Sil stayed with Bob for many, many years after. He stayed with him longer than I did, because I really focused on film and never went back to live or taped television.

CHAPTER TWELVE

Forging Friendships with *Outlaws*

One of my first assignments after Mr. Hope was a half-hour mystery called *Philip Marlowe*[48] starring Phil Carey. It was sponsored by Viceroy Cigarettes. In the course of the show, Phil Carey smoked Viceroy cigarettes. Back then, if the character was a good guy he smoked a filter cigarette, and if he was the heavy or a bad guy, he smoked cigarettes with no filter at all. That was one of the rules for Viceroy. Kind of strange, but true.

We shot at MGM Studios. I was associate producer. The producer/writer was Gene Wang. He produced *Perry Mason*[49] for many years. Gene Wang didn't like to write ahead of time. He wrote under the gun. For *Philip Marlowe*, the gun was me. I went to the production office at MGM and found out which stages were available on the days we were scheduled to shoot. I made a list of them and went to see them. I went back to Mr. Wang and took him down to the stage I chose and made him say, "Okay, we can work on this stage." Then I told him, "You have to write enough so we have a day's work." He wrote it overnight. That's the way Mr. Wang worked.

I went into the office about four-thirty or five o'clock the next morning and found the script on my desk. I made a few copies and sent it off to mimeo to get all the scripts ordered. Then I broke it down for shooting. Bobby Justman was my first Assistant Director. He came in a little later in the morning. By seven o'clock, we were shooting the show. We shot two shows back-to-back. NBC had a crew doing *The Lawless Years*[50] which was a detective series. That show used the crew for two days, and then I shot three days with the same crew. We filmed a half-hour show in three days. That went on for the year.

In January of 1960, we began a pilot called *Outlaws*.[51] Doug Heyes was the producer, director and writer. I was associate producer. The show starred Don Collier,[52] Barton MacLane, and Jock Gaynor. We filmed that at MGM, too. It was a good, good Western, kind of a thriller with a twist.

Set in the Oklahoma Territory of the 1880s, it was shot from the perspective of the outlaws as they were pursued by the law. This made it different and gave viewers an unusual angle of events as the episodes unraveled. It was during the filming of the *Outlaws* pilot that I met several colleagues who, over time, had recurring parts in productions I did. Those folks also became good friends in my personal life.

I reached a point in *Outlaws* where everything was set up and my job was basically done. I had no preparation for upcoming shows since I was only doing the pilot. I was present on the set, but in the background. Bobby Justman was the AD on this one as well.

Bobby Hoy[53] was doing some stunts for us. He came off the set after he did his stunt, went to Bobby Justman and asked, "Who do I talk to about money?" Bobby Justman said, "You'll have to talk to Kent McCray." Bobby Hoy asked, "Where is he?" and Justman said, "Over there in a card game." Bobby Hoy said, "A card game? I was in that card game and I thought that guy was a driver." He came over and talked to me. That was the first time I met Bobby Hoy.

We worked out the pay. Bobby was happy with the number I gave him. That first meeting turned into a lifelong friendship with a wonderful guy. He was one of the greatest stunt people I ever worked with. I respected him dearly.

Then there was the friendship I formed with one of the stars of *Outlaws,* Deputy Marshal Will Foreman. Don Collier[54] remembers:

I had an interview at Paramount Studios for a show called The Egyptian, *so I went over there for the interview with Doug Heyes. I walked into his office and he asked, "Why are you here?" I said, "I'm here to interview for* The Egyptian." *He said, "You're not remotely close to what I'm looking for." I said, "I'm sorry, Mr. Heyes. I was told to come over here." He said, "Go on, get out of here."*

I started to leave and Mr. Heyes said, "Wait a minute. Get back here. I wrote and I'm going to direct a pilot over at MGM called Outlaws. *That's a Western. You're more suited for something like that. I want you to have your agent get you an appointment and go over there and interview for the* Outlaws *series. Make it today because they've already interviewed about fifty guys and they're getting close to choosing."*

I called my agent and he made me an appointment at MGM. I read the copy for the folks. I read it and I read some more. I read for a couple of hours and we talked. They asked if I could come back the next day and I said, "Sure." They didn't say I had the part.

I came back and they had me read the part of the Marshal with a bunch of guys reading for the deputy. I read with about eight or ten of them, I guess, and we finally got done. Frank Telford, who eventually was the producer of Outlaws, *said, "Go on down to wardrobe. I want you to try some clothes on." I went down to wardrobe and the old man there fitted me up and put the hat on me, and I looked pretty good! He said, "Good luck. I hope it goes a long time." I said, "What?" He said, "You got the part." I said, "I did?" I didn't even realize I had the part! He said, "Yeah, you got it. They called down here and wanted me to tell you that you got the part."*

Kent and I first met in January 1960. We did the Outlaws *pilot and I started to get to know him very well. I think it took us four weeks to shoot that thing. Kent was just a great big guy and full of fun. We had a lot of laughs, but he knew exactly what he was doing. Kent had been with Bob Hope. Live TV. He went to that school of pretty hard knocks. You learn a lot there.*

NBC had two pilots they were going to shoot in '59 and '60. January and February they were going to shoot Outlaws *and* The Blue and the Gray.[55] *Kent worked on the* Outlaws *pilot and then he...finished out that entire second year with us.*

Retired stuntman Jack Lilley now owns Movin' On Livestock which provides animals and period-wagons for motion pictures. I met him on the set of *Outlaws*, too. Here's what Jack says:[56]

Kent smoked a pipe then. He had that pipe and he'd be laughing. He was always just a sharp, very intelligent man. A good guy. His personality radiated off him. You liked him as soon as you met him. The way he had a sense of humor that no one had. As a producer, he could be as tough as they come if they had problems, but he was always a fair man. He would take it right to them. There was no temperamental actor or actress. He would say, "Hey, let's knock it off. Let's get it done."

The pilot of *Outlaws* aired on September 29, 1960. Before I realized I'd be returning for the second season of the show, I found myself working halfway around the world with a daytime star who put my "Let's get it done" motto to the test.

CHAPTER THIRTEEN

Someone's in Denmark with Dinah...

In the spring of 1960, I finished editing *Outlaws* and planned to take a few weeks off. After one week, I came in to get my paycheck and to see what was going on. Dick Larson, Fenton Coe's assistant, asked, "Do you want to go to Europe on a survey?" I asked, "For what?" He said, "Dinah Shore wants to do three shows in Europe during the summer. Jack Donohue is the producer/director." Jack Donohue was originally a choreographer and director in the early days at MGM Studios. He had quite a nice background.

Dick Larson said, "You'd be gone like two weeks." I said, "What about my vacation?" He said, "We'll have to do that later." I decided to go to Europe. While I was in the office getting things set up, I ran into Lee Zuckerman, an auditor who had done some shows with us. He asked, "You're going to Europe? I'm going to take my vacation and go to San Francisco." I asked, "Why don't you come with me? I could use you. We could do budgets while we're over there. It will cost you airfare because they won't fly you over there, but I can take care of your room and meals." He got the money for the ticket.

On a given night, Jack, Lee and I boarded an SAS plane and took off for Denmark, our first stop. During the flight, the stewardess came by and said, "The plane is not too crowded, so I've changed your seating. All of you have three seats across so you can stretch out a little bit." Great! We started this trip quite comfortably.

We woke up the next morning and landed at a refueling stop in Greenland. Lots of people came on board. Greenland is a territory of Denmark, so a lot of Danes who worked there were going home on leave. They got in the back of the plane and sang songs. Some introduced the three of us to a little after-dinner drink called Aquavit, a very powerful one, but very tasty. We attempted to teach them English and they tried to teach us Danish songs. It was a nice flight into Copenhagen.

It turned out our survey lasted six weeks instead of two. In Denmark, I went to studios and tried to find out what they had to offer us. We went to Norway. We went to Sweden. We then went to Portugal. We went to Italy, France and a lot of places I went for Bob Hope, so I had a little knowledge of what we were doing. Then we went to Spain and checked everything there.

When we were in Portugal, I had a meeting with a production specialist at one of the studios. I don't speak Portuguese and he didn't speak English. We were supposed to have an interpreter. I took a cab to the studio. We sat and looked at each other for fifteen, twenty minutes when his secretary came in and said, "The interpreter can't make it." The two of us sat there kind of smiling at each other. I took a shot at trying to negotiate. I asked him about equipment and crews. Within the language of the film industry, and after a two-hour meeting with sweat coming off my head, I had all the equipment I needed from him plus the crews, although the crews, he said, may be a problem. I made that note.

Jack, Lee and I also went to London to meet with some people there. We needed continuity and I wanted to hire the film and sound crew from England because they could all speak English with our people. I talked to two production companies in London and made a commitment with one of them. While we prepared to return to the States, our auditor Lee Zuckerman was dispatched to

Rome to work for a while. They had trouble with a show there. This time, NBC actually reimbursed him for his airfare.

Jack and I came home and I did all the budgets to present to Dinah Shore and her entourage of auditors and agents. It was decided it was a "Go." I went to Dinah, who was not my favorite person to work with.

Going back a few years, when Dinah was doing her fifteen minute show for NBC, she wanted to do a show in Nashville and in Minneapolis-St. Paul for the Winter Carnival. I was dispatched to do the survey for what would have been a live show. Sil Caranchini from NBC engineering and I investigated if we could get the equipment we needed. We came home and went over everything with Dinah in her dressing room one day. We ended up scrapping the idea because of the time of year and the high cost.

While we were in her dressing room, Dinah's wardrobe gal, Carol, came in and began to get things ready for Dinah's show. Dinah said, "You know, Carol, that blouse I had yesterday, that would look great on you." I was told Dinah had agreements with the clothing designers in which she got to keep her clothes for an advertising plug.

She said, "Carol, I want you to try that blouse on." She turned to all the guys in the room and said, "We're through with our business, so get out of here." We all left and Carol tried on the blouse I was told. I saw Carol the next day in the hallway and asked, "How'd the blouse fit?" She said, "It fit great. It only cost me twenty dollars." That was my introduction to how Dinah worked.

Regarding the European tour, it was decided that we would film one show in Copenhagen, Denmark, and one show in Madrid, Spain with a side trip down to the Alhambra and Lisbon, Portugal. We would do the third show in Paris. All the film would be shipped to London for processing.

Before I left, I met with Dinah and her entourage. She had her choreographer, her piano player, her voice coach and many others.

I said, "It's up to you how you want to work this. I can put you on per diem and you pay your own bills for meals, or you can bring me the checks and I will pick up the tab." They wanted to be on per diem. I said, "That's fine." I set up everything and I went back to London to secure things. The crew met us for the first show in Denmark.

After I got there, I found out that during the winter, film crews in Denmark worked a six-day week but in the summertime when the weather was nice, they were on a five-day week. Because of the cost and time of being overseas, I wanted to work a six-day week. I had to go to the unions with the head of the studio and make a deal so we could work six days.

We traveled with a large troupe including two writers. I had an assistant director, Bud Brill, and Lee Zuckerman came in from Italy and met me in London. He stayed with us the whole time.

A couple of days into it our first show in Copenhagen, one of Dinah's people came to me and said, "Dinah told me to pick up the check last night at dinner and here's the bill." I said, "That's good for you." He said, "No, Dinah told me you'd pay for it." I said, "I told you in L.A. that wasn't how it was going to work. You go back to Dinah and remind her of that." He said, "But she said." I cut him off saying, "I don't care what she said. I'm not paying it. You're on per diem." It bothered me that she tried to pull something like that after we agreed to the terms. It put a damper on our work relationship.

We had a good show in Copenhagen. Most of the work was at night which was rough to do. We shot a lot of it at the Tivoli Garden. That's such a beautiful spot.

We left Copenhagen and went to Madrid, Spain. Before we left the States, I made sure the people in London had all the equipment we needed. For travel purposes, I had them write out an inventory. I had them number the equipment boxes and make a numbered content sheet for each one to make it easier to match things at Customs. We had the sheets translated depending on our next location. In this case, the sheets were translated from English to Danish, and then Danish to Spanish. That way, when we got to Madrid, we wouldn't have a language problem with Customs. Even with all that preparation, it took us three days to get the equipment out of Madrid Customs.

Alex Quiroga, who was an NBC consultant and a very good technician, also went with me on this trip. He and I went out to Customs every day. Finally, they said we could get our gear. The gentleman at Customs took out a pad with a form on it and started filling it in. I gave him the list of the equipment and he walked around and checked all the boxes and the numbers. He took a pen out, dipped it in an inkwell and started to write. Dipped in the inkwell and started to write. We were already three days behind, so I offered him a ball point pen. He shook his head. "Ball point pens are illegal" for official forms. He wrote the first form, picked up another form and copied the information from the first form to the second form, then copied it again so he had three. Everything was in triplicate. We were there all day while he wrote out things until the equipment was released to us. It was nerve-racking.

While waiting to shoot during those three days, I asked Dinah about doing some pre-recording in Madrid. I told her we were going to pre-record the Lisbon songs in Madrid because there were no decent facilities in Lisbon to record a full orchestra. We scheduled a night that worked for her and I ordered the orchestra. As the orchestra rehearsed, Dinah showed up with a very gravelly voice and said something like, "I can't sing tonight, I have laryngitis." I said, "Okay." I walked her back to her car with its chauffeur and she got in. The car window was open and I heard her say to the driver in a very clear voice, "Take me to such and such restaurant, please." It was all B.S. with her.

I went back and told Jack Donohue we had to record the orchestra on a separate track because there was no way we could record in Lisbon. That's what we did. These particular songs also involved a chorus that was supposed to sing with Dinah. I'll get to that in a moment.

After shooting in Madrid, we moved down to the Alhambra to shoot there. It was a very picturesque spot but offered very limited accommodations. We all had to stay at the same hotel and we ate there, too.

Dinah came to me and said, "We're all going to eat together," and she meant her group of people. She said, "I'd like to have you set up a dinner for us." It was about fifteen people. I made arrangements. As we were walking to the table, Dinah said to me, "I want you to sit right next to me." I said, "Okay," and sat down. We had a very nice dinner and at the tail end when the check came, Dinah leaned over to me and said, "I would like to have you pick up the check."

I knew that was coming and I was prepared. I said, "That's fine." I paid the bill for all seated there and then I got up and walked around the whole table. I looked at the bill and looked at what they had and said, "You owe me so much. You owe me so much." I went around the table and collected from all these people who were on per diem. I walked back to Dinah and said, "Dinah, out of my personal per diem, I would like to take you to dinner." I turned around and started to walk away. She said, "You know this is very embarrassing, don't you?" And I said, "I don't care."

We finished the show in Spain and moved on to Lisbon. I told Alex Quiroga, "Find a location where we can record the chorus and Dinah." He did that while I went to the university to see if they had a group we could use for back-up vocals. They did but the singers were going on tour. They were only able to give me two available dates before they left.

I told Dinah our limitations on dates with the chorus. Out of the two choices, she picked a night that was convenient for her. We set everything up and went out at night to record the chorus with Dinah singing to the playback of the orchestra. Dinah never showed up. Now we were stuck again, but I had the crew record the chorus.

I got Dinah to commit to another night to finish the songs. She had on earphones and in one ear the orchestra played while in the other ear she heard the chorus. In other words, she had to do her singing part with two sound mixes playing, one in each ear. She did and then we blended the three parts and put it all together. It came out okay. It wasn't great.

Within the next couple of days, I got a phone call from Fenton Coe at NBC. He started to chew my rear end out for making Dinah record a number like that. He said, "That's inexcusable. Why would you do that?" Oh, he kept chewing me out. It was my fault that she had to be subjected to recording with a playback in each ear. She couldn't sing properly and it was not very good. I asked, "Do you want to hear my side of the story?" He said, "No, it's your fault." I hung up and didn't call him back. I never heard another word about it.

We shot in Lisbon in a picturesque fishing village outside the city called Nazaré. Because of the crew problem in Lisbon, which the man I met with warned me about, I brought the crew from Madrid.

On the last day of shooting, we ran late. Lee and I got the bill from the head gaffer who was overseeing the whole Madrid crew for me. He said, "It's all itemized with who gets what. Just give me the total amount and I'll pay the guys when we get on the plane." That sounded fine with me. We went over the bill, checked it all out, and paid the man who then left to catch his plane.

About twenty minutes later, the gaffer came back and said, "You made a mistake." I said, "Oh, no. I hope you're not going to miss your plane." He said, "No, we'll make it all right, but you did make a mistake. You paid us too much." He gave me some money back. Inadvertently, we had given him too much money for what the bill was. It was our mistake, not his. Here's a guy who could have walked away with some extra money, but being a very honest gentleman, he gave us the money back.

We moved on to Paris and did the show there. We pre-recorded one of Dinah's songs for the show. We all liked what we recorded, but Dinah said she wanted to do another take. Then another one. We did thirty-five takes of this one song! The musicians got tired, the crew got tired and even Dinah got tired. She finally said, "I think Take 5 was the best. That's the one we should use," and she walked out of the studio.

Next, I had a problem with the sound crew who complained about things that had nothing to do with the show. They didn't like their accommodations and they didn't like the food. One day three of them started their tirades again. I took about as much of it as I could and said, "You won't have to worry about it any longer." I fired the sound crew. One of them said, "What do you mean? We're going to finish the show." I said, "You're finished as of now." I handed them each a ticket and money and said, "Take a cab to the airport. You're outta here." Alex Quiroga and I took over the sound department. Alex worked a recorder and mixer and I was the boom operator. The two of us handled all the sound for the Paris show.

That's my sojourn with Dinah Shore.

Her group left for home. I took all the film to London and I stayed there until Thanksgiving Eve. Jack Donohue and I did the editing and post-work there then shipped home the final cut print, which saved duty taxes on a lot of film we shot.[57] I was gone a long time and it was a very difficult work situation, so it wasn't the best of all trips.

We came home and turned in all the bills for the show. Before returning from overseas, I took Dinah's wardrobe, boxed it up and shipped it home so we didn't have to carry it all. Anything that she bought I packed, like dishes, jewelry, books, and I put it with the wardrobe. It was shipped to her house and saved her money on Customs. After we got home, her agent called me and said, "The people want their wardrobe." He meant the vendors we had consignment deals with. I said, "Dinah has it at her house." He said, "No, she says she doesn't." I said, "I shipped it all to her house."

I told the agent to look for different things like books, china, and the like. He went to her house and found everything I mentioned, but Dinah still insisted that she didn't have the wardrobe. I said, "It's there someplace, but that's your problem, not mine."

One last Dinah story. When we traveled, I had a list of all the crew. I collected their passports and gave them all to the Customs agent. Dinah never gave me her passport. The group walked through Customs very quickly, while Dinah stood in a separate line. I said to Dinah, "You know, if you give me your passport, you could get through all this a lot easier." She said, "No, I like going through Customs." She didn't like it. She didn't want to give me her passport because she didn't want me to see how old she was. As you can tell, I was not enchanted with Dinah, and neither were a lot of other people.

CHAPTER FOURTEEN

Riding with *Outlaws* Again

Once I got settled back in Los Angeles after returning from Europe, I went to my boss Fenton Coe about some unfinished business. It was December 1960 and I said, "I'd like to take my vacation now." He said, "I have a pilot I want you to do." I said, "Fenton, what about my vacation? I put it off once already." Eventually I agreed to do the pilot, but I ended with, "I'll just take my vacation in January when the pilot's done."

He said, "No, it's an NBC rule if you don't take your vacation in a given year, you lose it." I said, "Fenton, I haven't shown up for seven months. No one's going to know if I don't show up for another three weeks. If I work the pilot now, in January I won't come in for three weeks." He said, "I can't allow that." I said, "Then screw you. I'm going on vacation." And I did. I came back the first part of January and Fenton assigned me to another pilot. The pilot he wanted me to do earlier didn't get shot until February.

Fenton Coe was one of the first people I ever met at NBC. I respected him a great deal. He taught me and helped me a lot, there's no two ways about it. I wouldn't have gotten into the film business had it not been for Fenton. I'm truly grateful to him. Fenton and I got along very well for the most part. We played golf together and he and his wife socialized with my family. I really liked him. However, Fenton was a company man, by the book, and that mindset just irritated me at times.

Once, I was asked to do a survey that put me on the road for four weeks. I went to the comptroller of the company to ask for an advance of money. He said, "No, you spend your own money and we'll reimburse you." I said, "I'm not a friggin' bank," and I didn't say 'friggin', either. The comptroller said, "No, we can't do that." I walked out of that meeting and told Fenton, "I'm not going." It irritated me. It was ridiculous. Petty.

When I did the Dinah Shore show, I went to Dinah's people and the head of NBC programming and said, "I'm going to be working overseas for seven months. As associate producer, I'd like to get a fee in addition to my salary. My fee is the cost of airfare for my wife to vacation with me for a bit while I'm in Europe."

Shore's camp and some at NBC agreed but Fenton said, "You can't take money on the side." I said, "Send somebody else. I'm on staff. What do I care if I go there or stay home?" Fenton went to Tom Sarnoff who was his boss, and Tom Sarnoff said, "Send somebody else." Fenton said, "I don't have anybody else." Sarnoff said, "Then pay him."

When Jack Donohue and I did the post-production of Dinah's show, Jack had to return to the States to direct a Dean Martin special. Fenton called me and asked, "Will you go off per diem while Jack's gone?" I said, "The only way I'll go off per diem is if I come home." He said, "No, you stay there." I asked, "I'm supposed to stay here for three weeks on my own and keep working without being paid per diem? You finish it up." Well, they paid me.

It was just nitpicky stuff. They tried to save a few bucks in the silliest ways. As the years went on, I got better at working those issues out with them. I became a little bit more independent about interacting with the NBC corporate side. GE was even worse when I worked with them in the 1990s. Good God, they were stupid.

Anyhow, that dust settled and I was assigned to the second year of *Outlaws*. They changed the cast for the second season. Slim Pickens and Judy Lewis were added and Bruce Yarnell returned. Don Collier's character was back as the main star, promoted to Marshal. We filmed mostly in the Los Angeles area and at Paramount Sunset Studios. For one episode, we had Cliff Roberston as director. I thought very highly of him. It was one of the first shows he ever directed.

Cliff rehearsed a dance sequence all day long. Every day at eleven o'clock in the morning and at three o'clock in the afternoon, I had to report to the producers what we had shot so far. That day, they called and asked, "Where are you?" I said, "We haven't shot anything yet." We didn't shoot anything until four in the afternoon. Cliff shot one take of the big dance sequence with the camera moving all around. At five o'clock we wrapped and had our day's work.

Don Collier was in his second year of the show and his first full year of working with me. He remembers:

Kent and I became instant friends. We had a lot of the same likes and a lot of the same dislikes. Our interests were the same: girls and booze. No! (laughing) His general appearance appealed to me. He was a nice-looking specimen. He loved to play cards and we played a lot of casino. We played a lot of pitch. We played poker on Friday nights.

There was an old bowling alley at Sunset and Gower that Paramount bought and turned into a big soundstage. We shot a lot of our interiors for Outlaws *on that stage. In the old tradition of shows, we had a wrap party at the end of the production. In TV, you finish a show theoretically every Friday, so every Friday would be like a wrap party.*

Kent would break out the booze Friday after work and we would usually have a poker game. We would drink and play poker like at five or six o'clock until maybe nine. Slim Pickens was on the show then. Me and Slim were drinking and the boys and Kent, about six guys, were playing poker in the other room.

Slim and I got the idea of taking a big container of ice water, you know, like they have on the football fields that they pour on the coach? We carried this big ice bucket in there and snuck up on the guys and poured the whole damn bucket on the table right in the middle.

Kent—I think he had the winning hand—got thoroughly upset. I thought he was going to kill us! Me and Slim just took off and ran out of there. We got the hell out of there. They finally got settled down inside and got everything cleaned up. About an hour later, we went back in and everything was okay, but Kent was thoroughly pissed. That's the only time I think he got mad at me because other times, we would, of course, do anything he asked us to do. If it was in our power to do it, we'd do it. Basically, we got along fine and we formed a friendship that's lasted until this very day, and I hope it goes on another hundred years!

I don't remember the ice bucket incident, but I do know that on the second year of *Outlaws*, I really got to know Don Collier. I always loved him. He's great. A natural. There isn't a mean bone in his body. So agreeable: "Whatever you need, we'll get it done." And he did!

Unfortunately, *Outlaws* was canceled because of a policy called "pay or play." Don Collier explains:

NBC owed Ralph Edwards an hour of prime time and he wanted that hour in 1962.[58] *NBC only owned two hours of prime time. That was* Bonanza *and* Outlaws. Bonanza, *of course, was a color show, and NBC at the time was owned by RCA, and RCA wanted to sell color television sets. So, they kept the color show, which was* Bonanza, *and they canceled ours. They gave our hour to Ralph Edwards. He used that hour to produce a show called* Wide Country *with Earl Holliman and Andrew Prine. It lasted one year. It wasn't a very good show.*

Of course, *Bonanza* was just that—a huge production full of colorful weekly Western fare. I made even more lasting friendships there and went on to do more productions with people who became like family.

CHAPTER FIFTEEN

A *Bonanza* of Color

I was tickled to death to get the Production Supervisor position on *Bonanza*[59] because I liked the show.[60] NBC assigned me to it in 1962. That's the first time I ever met David Dortort.[61] My office during *Outlaws* was at Paramount and when I had time, I drifted from stage to stage, sat down and watched how other shows ran their productions. Observation. It was good to get a different idea or perspective. I sat in on *Bonanza* several times during shoots and I saw David Dortort, but I really hadn't talked to him. When I was assigned to the series, I got to know David very well.

He was a procrastinator, but a brilliant man. He knew his facts about historical things. He wrote books on the historical Southwest, some very fine books. He came out West as a writer and worked a lot of shows as a writer before he became a producer. He produced the series John Payne did, *The Restless Gun*.[62] That's where David met Michael Landon,[63] who was in the pilot.

David had his quirks. He came in at eleven o'clock because he liked to watch the stock market, which was driven by East Coast time. He showed up between eleven and twelve o'clock, worked a little bit in his office, then went to lunch. Dailies were shown at two o'clock. Then, he went back to the office again. The re-write man came in with the next day's dialogue, and David re-worked it. They often went into the evening with the re-writes. We needed the changes to be in everyone's hands the next morning by seven o'clock so the copy department folks worked all night.

David drove me nuts because he wouldn't do things on time. Always last minute. Pressure. Pressure. But that's the way he worked, so what are you going to do? Fortunately for us, Michael Landon and Dan Blocker[64] came in early in the morning. They went to the script supervisor to find out what scenes we were shooting. She handed them a three-ring binder. Maybe a five-page scene. They reviewed it about five times and knew it. Photographic memory. Both of them. They read it five times and they had it in their head no matter how much dialogue there was.

Michael was a little more on the nose than Blocker. Blocker ad-libbed a few lines if he got caught and didn't remember, but he gave the right cue lines for the next person to speak. He was great. Great, great actor. Made you cry, made you laugh. Some of the shows with Michael and him were hysterical, like the one about those two raising rabbits."[65]

I wasn't laughing at all the first time I met Michael Landon, though. We worked our first episode together on location at Vasquez Rocks, I think. Mike was in every scene. He was up in the rocks between takes and he called down to me and said, "I need a car at one o'clock. I have a big meeting at NBC." This was all news to me but I didn't say anything. I went down to the pay phone about a half a mile away. Remember, no cell phones back then. I called the Studio and asked if they knew anything about Mike having to go to a meeting at NBC. Mike was in every scene in this episode so it was impossible to let him go. We would have had to shut down.

I called back when they did some research. They knew nothing about anything. I called Fenton Coe and he said, "Call me back." I waited, called him back and he knew nothing about it.

About an hour and a half passed by the time I went back to the location. Mike came down after a take and asked, "You have my car ready for one o'clock?" I said, "No, and I don't think you really have a meeting at NBC." He said, "No, I really don't. I was just testing you."

That upset me and I told Michael, "Look, don't test me or we're going to have problems. You're honest with me, I'll be honest with you and we'll get along fine. Otherwise, you're going to be in big trouble. Had you walked off the set, I could have fired you. You could be suspended from the Guild and you wouldn't get paid, so think twice when you threaten to do something."

That was the start of my friendship with Michael Landon which lasted thirty years. It was a great friendship. The best! I loved him.

CHAPTER SIXTEEN

A Production Manager Keeps It All Going

Let me explain some of the duties of a Production Manager. My main concern was keeping the show's costs within the budget established by the network for a given show. The budget was based on the sales department. In order to do that, I came up with a process to get the most from our shooting days without running up costs.

When the first draft of a script came in, I read it and broke it down scene by scene. I then put it up on what we called a production board. I had one in my office and I had a smaller one I used outside the office.

The production board was like a table or a spreadsheet with each cast member listed on the columns across the top while the scenes were broken down and listed on the rows to the left. Each scene was placed on a colored strip based on its location. I used white for interior scenes, yellow for location scenes, green for street or special locations, and pink for exterior night shooting. After I did the breakdown this way, I took those strips and scheduled them for the number of days for the show. For *Bonanza* and *The High Chaparral*, we did the shows in six days.

Using the board, I noted where we had heavy location scenes. Since location shooting was always more expensive, I tried to figure out what scenes we might move to an interior set to reduce costs. Or vice versa. I would then go to the producer and re-write man to see if they agreed with what I wanted to do. Sometimes yes, sometimes no. If no, then I went back to the drawing board to figure out something else.

Subsequently, the script might have writer changes or director changes. Each time the script changed, I adjusted the board accordingly. When the final script came in, I sat down and did a detailed budget on what the cost of the show would be.

I also worked with the directors to pick locations for the show, whether they were local or in Tucson or Tahoe. Wherever. If the director wanted a story changed somehow, it went back to the writer, but if the director wanted something a little different to get the shots he wanted, something physical or mechanical, he and I sat down and talked about it.

A couple of times we needed a seventy-foot boom, which was quite expensive. The director and I would discuss it and I'd say, "Ok, I'll give you that if maybe you give a little on this." It was a matter of give and take to get all the shows done within budget. We had to be creative to be cost-conscious without destroying the integrity of the script.

I also worked many times in postproduction. It was interesting because it was a little different from production. In postproduction, I worked with the editors for sound and with composers for music.

The composer came in to score a show. After that was completed, we looked at an upcoming show for his next session to determine where music should start and stop. Certain scenes needed music. The music editor made notes as the scenes we chose for music were timed out to a third of a second. The composer wrote the music to those times. He had a week to do it. We weren't allowed to track anything—that means we couldn't use music already recorded. We had to record live music for every show. Union rule. Plus, we had a separate session for the title music, which was recorded once every year.

We did a lot more music for *Chaparral* than *Bonanza*. Harry Sukman[66] and David Rose[67] were wonderful. Probably twenty minutes of music was normal. I sat on the scoring stage when the music was recorded and really enjoyed the experience.

After all the music and editing was completed, I went to the dubbing stage and worked with three audio mixers to blend twenty audio tracks into one. That was an all-day process, but it was certainly a very enjoyable time for me.

Our *Bonanza* production schedule gave us quite a few shows on location. We filmed in Tahoe twice a year. We spent two to three weeks at a time there. We went to Big Bear and to Frazier Park to get the pine trees and other shots from that backdrop. We also did a lot of shows locally in the Thousand Oaks area in the Conejo Valley.

One time, we were shooting on location in Big Bear. It was a show with Ed Begley. He and his sons were transporting nitroglycerin over a mountain.[68] We started the show up at Big Bear in the Baldwin Lake area in a dry alkali bed, which was the look we wanted. Long about eleven o'clock, the clouds opened up and we had over two inches of rain in twenty minutes. Of course, the alky bed just became glue. All the trucks got stuck except the camera truck.

I called the hotel and told my auditor to book the restaurant because the caterers lost all the lunches. The salads and everything just washed off the table because it was raining so hard. I got the crew back to the hotel so we could serve them lunch, and I moved the company to Cedar Lake which had no rain at all. They got some shots but very few. I spent most of the day at the alky bed getting the trucks out, lying down in the mud and putting chains on tires and vehicles. I went back to the hotel and took off my pants which were so covered with dried mud that they literally stood up by themselves.

In the meantime, I told director Bill Claxton and assistant director Don Daves to go to my room for a drink and wait until I got there. When I arrived, I called the studio to tell Jimmy Lane, our associate producer, about our problem. He said, "I can't talk to you now." I said, "Jim, I have to talk to you. We've had rain all day and we barely got anything filmed." He said, "I can't talk to you." I said, "Jim, we're in big trouble and I have to talk to you so we can figure this out." He said something like, "Didn't you hear me? There's a sale on underwear at Sears and I have to go." And then he then hung up on me. That was the kind of cooperation I got from Mr. Lane.

Another time, we set up to film a special episode for Lorne Greene's[69] character. The story was about Ben coming West with one of his wives. I made special arrangements for Lorne during the shoot to make things easier for him. In those days, the actors and crews reported to the studio and we sent them by bus to the location. For this particular show, I went to Lorne and asked if we could put a make-up table in the den at his home because he lived in the Valley. It would be more convenient for him to do make-up at his home rather than go to the Studio, have make-up done there and then drive all the way back through the Valley. It probably saved him a good hour and forty-five minutes. He agreed and I set it up.

Because he portrayed a younger man in the episode, Lorne had to have a different toupee on his head, darker hair along with some other make-up. I pretty much knew what time to expect Lorne on set, but one day, he showed up forty-five minutes sooner than normal.

I said, "Oops, something must be wrong. They shouldn't be here this early." I went to the make-up man and asked if everything was all right. He said, "Yes, everything is fine. Lorne went through the script and he never has to take his hat off, so we just touched up the sideburns and around his head. The back of the hair is darkened, but there's no toupee on top."

We set up to shoot the opening scene of the day which took place around a grave in the camp. A child had passed away and they were having a service. I went behind a truck and hollered out, "All the men around the grave should have their hats off." Then I went around another truck and yelled out, "All the men around the grave should have their hats off." I repeated this three times.

Me in sunglasses with Lorne Greene on the *Bonanza* set.

Lorne kept looking around and looking around to see who made the comments. He couldn't take his hat off because he had no toup on. He finally said, "That's right. I shouldn't even be in this scene. This scene is for the immediate family only. I'll be in my wagon ready to roll." He walked out of the scene. We shot it with just the immediate family. I told him later it was me, but he was okay with it. We generally got along fine.

Let me explain one thing with Lorne Greene. Lorne Greene had three toupees, but no one was ever supposed to know that he wore a toup. Everybody on the set knew it, but we weren't *supposed* to know it. He had one toup that looked like he just had a haircut, and another one after it had grown out a couple of weeks, and then a third one when it was getting longer. He rotated them and the hair dresser maintained them. If he finished his work day early, he hung around until everyone left so he could get them to the hair dresser without anyone knowing. The hairdresser worked overtime to take care of them and keep them clean. That was the situation with Lorne Greene and his toupees.

Dan Blocker lost his hair a little bit. He didn't want to wear a toupee. He just sprayed his hair with a little shoe black or shoe brown polish to cover up his bald spot and blend it in with his hair.[70]

I saw Dan every day of the week and we became close on the set. I called him on weekends if something came up that he needed to know. Dan could go with the flow during production. I never had to worry about him.

Michael was Michael. He wanted to learn everything he could at that age. He spent time with writer John Hawkins during lunch breaks talking about scripts, formatting, and writing dialogue. John gave him assignments and Mike sat in the outer office with a yellow pad. When done, he took the work back to John to critique and correct it. That's how Michael learned to write a script, by working with one of the best re-write men in the business. Behind the camera, he learned what different lenses could do. He was inquisitive and very thorough about what he wanted to create.

There was a time when we ran out of scripts and we were going to have to shut down production. Mike went to John Hawkins' office and found a script John said David Dortort wasn't sure he wanted to do. Mike went to David's office with the script and told him he'd re-write it over the weekend. I went to Mike's house on Sunday and read what he wrote to get a head start on the production side. We kept shooting Monday morning instead of having to shut down. That was the first time Michael got a writing job.[71]

Funny story. We always had a Christmas party, and David Dortort always made a speech which was usually quite lengthy.

He always thanked everybody. When it came time to hand out Christmas presents, I stood next to him to remind him of everyone's name.

In his speech, he said, "Michael has learned to be a good writer, and some day, he's going to be a great director." Michael said, "Yeah, you have an opening two weeks from now. Can I take that spot?" David couldn't very well say no. Michael talked David into saying, "Yeah, I think that could work." Michael directed that show and the rest is history.[72]

Pernell Roberts, as has been reported in many articles, was a bit difficult at times although I never had any problem with him. After the third year, he wanted off the show. He didn't feel the scripts were good. He really wanted to do Shakespeare, work in theater and be on the stage. He did not like the format of working on television.

This was the same year that NBC made a deal with Chevrolet and moved the show to Sunday night.[73] Chevrolet bought thirty-four new shows a year and sixteen repeats. In other words, Chevrolet bought fifty out of fifty-two weeks of the year and pretty much owned one hour on Sunday night. That was a tremendous sale for the network and was unheard of in that market as well as today's market.

Pernell went to NBC and said he wanted to be released from his contract. They went to Chevrolet and asked, "How do you feel about not having Pernell in the show?" They said, "We like the show the way it is. That's why we bought it." NBC informed Pernell he would have to work out the remaining three years of his contract. He did so with frequent disagreements.

Pernell was unfortunately bitter about everything. He had a tendency to cause trouble. On a lunch break one day, he went to a radio station in Glendale, which is near Hollywood, for an interview. An interviewer asked, "How do you like working with your fellow cast members on *Bonanza*?" Pernell answered something like, "It's all right if you like working with a has-been radio personality from Canada, an oversized oaf and a juvenile."

By the time he got back to the set, the cast heard about it and was ready to kill him. We had to separate them and ask them to calm down. There was never a dull moment.

Pernell was frustrated as hell. The last day of his *Bonanza* contract we were on location.[74] The director said, "Pernell, the show is finished. You are finished with the series. We appreciate you." The crew applauded. Pernell went into his dressing room, came out bare-ass naked carrying his wardrobe, put it on a rock and set it on fire. He said, "No one's ever going to wear it again." Of course, we had doubles, but that's how he reacted. Some years later he came back to television as *Trapper John, M.D.*

David Canary came to work as the foreman at the Ponderosa after Pernell left. They felt they needed another character on the show. He was a great guy who was easy to get along with. David appeared in almost one-hundred episodes off and on until the show ended in 1973.

Along with David, NBC brought in the boy Mitch Vogel. He was a good kid and wonderful to work with. He had a very big part in a movie called *The Reivers* with Steve McQueen, which was very successful, and NBC wanted him to be on the show. He played the role of Jamie for about fifty episodes.

When we shot in the studio, I spent time on the set and in my office. When we were on location, I was there all day. I loved working the show for a lot of reasons. One was knowing we were making history.

Remember, the original concept of the show was that it had to be shot in color. RCA gave us extra money to get better lighting and to hire the people needed to work in the lab to ensure the color was correct. People like Alex Quiroga and Ed Ancona spent a lot of time and a lot of effort to make sure it was correct. RCA even ran an ad campaign that said they would send a technician to someone's home to adjust the color on their color television set on the night *Bonanza* aired because it had the most accurate color.

Another historic reason was that Paramount was one of the first studios to allow a television show to be shot on their premises. Paramount always did feature films; they hated television. All the studios hated television. Television threatened their industry because they feared that feature films would be cut back—and they were. All the crews in those days were on Paramount's payroll. They paid these people fifty-two weeks a year guaranteed whether they worked or not. Paramount said, "We can't afford to keep doing this." However, by law and union commitment, they *had* to keep them.

Paramount absorbed all those costs until the studio said, "We have to do television." *Bonanza* was one of the first shows allowed to shoot there. Paramount needed to use these people they paid for. If it weren't for that, we would have never had the incredible cinematographer Haskell "Buzzy" Boggs[75] on the crew. He was with us for thirty years.

At first, we really didn't have a say-so as to who got hired from the studio although we could finagle a little bit once we got to know people. Initially, every day I attended a production meeting at the studio. Any production manager who worked on the lot had to go to this meeting. We each had a call sheet of people we needed for the next day. Say I needed five grips and seventeen electricians. The studio department heads got a copy of my call sheet and assigned their crew according to seniority.

That all changed in the late '60s, or at least by the time we did *Little House on the Prairie,*[76] when the unions gave up the practice of assigning jobs by seniority. The studios decided they had to go "freelance." That meant the crew members weren't paid a guaranteed fifty-two weeks anymore. When that happened, I picked anybody in the industry to be on my crews. No one had to follow seniority. If we chose the right people, we had a great crew.

For instance, say I hired a cinematographer. He had his own people he worked with for years that came with him. When we hired a prop man, he had someone he hired as his assistant, so it kept the "families" together. It usually worked, and if it didn't work, we said so and changes were made. That allowed me to assemble my crew of regulars.

NBC also made a change that impacted a lot of us as well. Remember when I was assigned to *Bonanza*, I was still on NBC's payroll? I was on staff until 1966. NBC finally signed a contract with the Directors Guild of America[77] which covered directors, production managers, unit managers, and assistant directors. Prior to that agreement, I had to hire a union unit manager on *Bonanza* even though I was the production manager. Production manager and unit manager were almost the same job, but one was a union position and one wasn't. We couldn't do the show without a unit manager because that was in the union contract with the studios. The unit manager did what I asked because he worked for me, but he had the union job and I didn't.

In 1966 when NBC joined the Guild, we production managers now got full credit without the union position. The transition hit in the middle of *Bonanza*'s season. When I joined the Directors Guild, I went off NBC's staff and I became freelance, too. Anyone hired freelance was hired only for the length of the show. When the show was over, we were automatically let go. In the contract with the Guild, a percentage of our checks was withheld for what they called "vacation/holiday." We could take that check at the end of the show's run to financially cover the time we weren't working.

We had a gentleman doing postproduction on *Bonanza* who handled the music scoring and the dubbing, and he wanted to retire. David Dortort came to me and asked, "You went to a music college, didn't you?" I said, "Yes." He asked, "Think you could handle the music and work with the composers as well?" I said, "Of course! No problem at all." I'd done it before but he didn't know that. I started working six weeks ahead of actually shooting the show and then stayed on for as many weeks as necessary for postproduction. I basically worked it out so I still had a paid fifty-two week year.

CHAPTER SEVENTEEN

Tales from the Ponderosa

FROM KENT

A large part of my job as Production Supervisor on *Bonanza* was keeping the costs under control. Weekly, I had to send a budget to New York for each show. If we were over budget, we had to say why; if we were under budget, we had to say why. Twice a year we brought in fresh vegetation to augment the tree trunks around the Ponderosa set. We fireproofed it and tried to keep it green but with all the hot lights, it only lasted a few months. Each time we replenished the greenery it caused that episode to be over budget. When I sent the budget in I explained the reason for the overage as "nursery set."

One time I mailed a nursery set budget off to New York. About six weeks later when the show aired, I received a frantic call from the gentleman who we reported all this information to. He said, "Ah, you've been lying to me. I proved it last night." I asked, "What do you mean you proved it last night?" "That show with the big nursery set was on the air." I said, "Yes, it was." He said, "I watched that show and there wasn't a kid in it!" Of course, our nursery meant shrubs and his nursery meant kids....

Michael Landon told me that during the pilot of *Bonanza*, the four Cartwrights went to get fitted at the Paramount wardrobe department. David Dortort and the director of the first show were there. The cast was asked to get dressed so David and the director could check the wardrobe for color since this was all to be shot in color. They wanted to see how the different outfits blended. Mike told the story: "All of us started wearing lifts because each of us wanted to be the tallest." They all ended up with lifts so high they could hardly stand up. Dan Blocker was the largest of the group, by far the tallest. Mike was the shortest so he did what he could to look bigger.

Lorne Greene was great on and off the screen. He played his part very well. He was very precise and in control and that's what made his character work. Lorne was a very nice man.

Dan Blocker was a gem. A person you liked from the get-go. He had a powerful attitude, politically and otherwise, so you had to be careful what you talked about. I say that's part of someone's personal life and I never got into it. He and Michael used to get into it. Blocker was a staunch Democrat and Michael was a Republican.

Ted Voigtlander and Buzzy Boggs were our alternating cinematographers. We brought in special lenses and shot things either on location or in the studio to show Michael the effect we got with different ones. When Michael started to direct, he used a lot of these techniques that we tested. He knew what he was doing. He became a fine director, one of the best in the business, but was underrated.

We had actor George Montgomery as a guest star. There was a big shootout at the end of the show with George and Michael Landon. We were set up to shoot the scene, and George said, "Wait a minute. I think I should win this shootout." Director Bill Claxton said, "You can't win. Michael's going to win. He's the star of the show. Let's be sensible about this." "No," Montgomery said, "I'm not shooting this scene unless I win."

I got involved in it and I had to call David Dortort. We had a big meeting on the set, held up shooting for over an hour, and finally convinced Mr. Montgomery that he was not the lead actor. Michael was the lead actor, and he was gonna win. We shot the scene and that's the way it ended.[78]

Mike and I were leaving for Tucson on a *Bonanza* survey. I sent a car to pick Mike up. I was at the airport waiting, waiting, waiting. I thought, "Michael, where are you?" He and wife Lynn had recently moved into a new home in Beverly Hills. He didn't know how to open the gate of his new house to get out! They were doing construction work on the house, so Mike found a ladder and put it up at a low spot in the wall. He climbed the ladder, perched on the stone wall, pulled up the ladder, put it on the other side and climbed down. Then he ran up the hill to meet his car. But he made it on time.

We came home from Tucson and Mike finished the script we were going to shoot there. We then travelled back to Tucson to shoot the show, which was a story about a man chasing Mike. If the guy caught up to him, he was going to kill him.

Michael was supposed to be out in the desert, and he was supposed to be parched and blistered and all that. The first day, we shot out in a place called Sabino Canyon but it started to rain. I mean, it came down pretty good. Everyplace we looked, there were puddles. How can he be dying of thirst when there were puddles around? Michael had to re-write everything to make it look like he was only being chased.

On the last day of shooting out at Ryan Airfield, we used a dirt runway they had for gliders and very light planes. This particular time, we didn't have an insert car, so we used our boom truck, which was big. We called it a Chapman boom for the company that made it. For general work around the set, it was there for the exterior because it was adjustable to go from people sitting on horseback to people standing to people sitting on a chair without having to move a lot of stuff. It had a counter-weight arm. A great piece of equipment. Very expensive.

Anyhow, in this particular case, I used the Chapman boom to follow Michael running. We had to have water because it had to match some of the rain sequences from Sabino Canyon. I went to the airport and asked if I could rent their water truck which they used to wet down the runway for the gliders. They agreed. We waited, waited. I saw the water truck start and it got about halfway to us and stopped.

I got in my car and drove over. The driver had a breakdown and he couldn't go any further, which meant we had no water. I got in touch with the special effects guy. We had what we called the "honey wagon" which was a dressing room plus toilets. The front end of the vehicle housed the crew's toilet, and the trailer had dressing rooms. There was a big tank on the front end of the truck filled with clean water. I piped into that water to get the rainy look that we needed.

As I worked the pump on top of the truck, Michael ran alongside the boom truck until he suddenly yelled, "Cut. Cut." Mike looked at me and said, "McCray, if that water has lumps in it, you're outta here!" Hey, you improvise wherever you have to.

When Michael was directing one day, he wanted a dream sequence. We put Vaseline on the lens which gave it a smoky look. We played with the edges to make them more or less clear or distorted. We didn't have enough Vaseline so we used Preparation H. I said, "You better get the shot before it shrinks."

CHAPTER EIGHTEEN

The High Chaparral

I continued with *Bonanza* and in 1966, I was scheduled to go to Hawaii on a survey with Bill Claxton, Fenton Coe and Buzzy Boggs, our cinematographer. NBC thought about doing a *Bonanza* episode on the Parker Ranch on the Big Island, so we went to check things out.

The night before, I picked up a pilot script we were working on called *The High Chaparral.*[79] I brought the script home with me, having gotten it from writer Denne Petitclerc. The next morning we took a flight out of Los Angeles. After we got airborne, I opened my briefcase and started to read the script. As I read a portion, I passed it back to Bill Claxton who was going to direct it. He read it and passed it back to Fenton Coe, and then it went over to Buzzy Boggs.

By the time we got to Honolulu, we finished reading the script and thought it was great. We looked at each other and said, "This is much better than a *Bonanza* at the Parker Ranch. What are we doing here?" We continued on the survey, but it was determined at a later date it was too expensive to film in Hawaii. We came home and I immediately started working on the script of *Chaparral*.

The High Chaparral is the story of Big John Cannon who comes west to settle the Arizona Territory in the 1870s along with his wife Annalee, his son, Billy Blue, and his brother, Buck. During the two-hour pilot, Annalee is killed by an Indian arrow. John visits his neighbor to the south, Don Sebastian Montoya, in order to forge a bond to stop Indians and bandidos from raiding his herd. He seals the agreement by marrying the Don's lovely, aristocratic and outspoken daughter Victoria. She and her carefree, womanizing brother Manolito join Big John at the High Chaparral ranch.

Not only did the mix of family, culture and religion between Anglos and Latinos come into play, but also the setting introduced Native Americans in a more humanistic light, including them in the triangle of interaction on a fairly equal basis. *The High Chaparral* was ahead of its time in minority hiring, casting Latinos in starring roles, and accurately casting Latinos and Native Americans in many support roles. It was very popular among Latino viewers.[80]

I was quite eager to begin production on the show. On weekends, I went to Arizona because this was the location we wanted. It was the setting of the show: the Arizona Territory which was also Apache Indian Territory. I met with Bob Shelton[81] and he and I traveled the area looking for different locations for the show. We tried to figure the best place to set up the homestead. I was concerned about putting it on somebody's private property. Would they maintain it? Would kids get into it and wreck it? We couldn't have that. We couldn't keep re-building a main part of the set.

Bob Shelton[82] of Old Tucson Movie Studios remembers our scouting visits in 1966:

I was in my office round about 1966 and my secretary said somebody from NBC wanted to speak with me. She showed him in and this big guy came in, told me he was Kent McCray from NBC and that he was on a scouting trip to search for a location for a future film project. I said, "Well, here we are. What can I do for you?" That was the beginning of our acquaintance. As I did with all film companies that came there I said, "Let's take a walk around our property. We have 320 acres and we have a rather substantial size Western town with a kind of Southwestern flavor."

Some time passed before I got a call from Kent. "We want to come back and take another look at your place." So, that happened. He already had in his mind kind of where he wanted to put the set...It was a major decision so everybody back in L.A. and NBC had to decide if that's what they wanted to do...He called me and said, "We have decided that we are going to select you, Old Tucson, to establish the set...for The High Chaparral *television pilot."*

By mutual agreement, we decided the show should be based at Old Tucson Studios which Bob managed and partly owned. Building the Chaparral homestead there ensured it would be guarded. The location also had a Mexican street and a Western street we could use in the show, and we did many, many times. Plus, the territory outside the back of the High Chaparral ranch was wide-open country. We did a lot of sequences out there. There were a lot of different roads to use. There were also some other great locations within a mile or two of Old Tucson. It became the hub of where I felt we should do the show.

When I got back, I laid out pictures I had taken at Old Tucson for the other departments to see where we would be working. Then I went back to the site with cinematographer Buzzy Boggs, art director Earl Hedrick and Bill Claxton, who was going to produce and direct the pilot. We sat around in the area trying to determine the angle the house should be built in order to get the best sun all day, which was important for added light. Earl worked on some interior design sketches and envisioned what the set should look like. All the permanent interior and exterior sets were his designs.

We started building it in May 1966. Every weekend I went someplace to try to improve our locations or to check on the building. I tried to make sure we got it all together. We knew we were going to have a lot of horse work done in front of the main gate. That whole area was open. Every time you have a falling horse, you have to bring in a lot of sand or some such material so the horse and rider didn't get hurt. I had the whole area in front of the main gate raked and all the rocks taken out. Then we brought in some loose granite gravel and laid that down. It looked good, but it wasn't harmful to the animals or riders. We had a pretty open range where we could do our stunt work. It wasn't confined to a certain area, which looks phony. That worked well for us through the whole series and paid off by doing it at the start.

We started shooting in June 1966 for the pilot. The set still exists on the same spot today. The show itself was very production-oriented, consisting of a lot of horse work and stunt work, so we hired Henry Wills to be our stunt coordinator. He brought in a great bunch of stunt people.

Former stuntman Jack Lilley remembers:

Henry Wills was the finest man you ever met. He was in the league of Kent McCray. He was my mentor as a stuntman, and Henry taught me more than I ever knew...that's the kind of people Kent kept around him. He had a cadre of us. If you were right, you were right-on with Kent. He ran those companies like just a big family. I doubled Leif Erickson on High Chaparral *and anyone else. We did Indians, we did everything. It was the best TV show I ever worked on.*

Henry Darrow[83] also appreciated the stuntmen.

I had the man who doubled me. He was ten years to twelve years older than I was. His name was Carl Pitti. Carl taught me to quick-draw, how to use a rope, how to throw a knife, how to use a bow and arrow, how to use a whip, because it used to be part of his father's act doing rodeo shows...Because of (Carl), I bought a couple of Australian whips, two six-footers and one eight-to-ten footer. I used one once (in the series). It was a scene when one of the Indian kids had a knife in his hand, and I whipped out and got the knife. As I pulled back, the knife went over my head, and with that I said, "That's the end of that!"

Bobby Hoy, a Golden Boot award-winner for all his contributions to the Western genre, was added not only for his stunts, but also for his acting talent, playing the character Joe Butler.

Stuntman/actor Bobby Hoy, (center with hat), prepares for a hand-to-hand fight with an attacking Indian. *Chaparral* **had a lot of action.**

Fellow stuntman Jerry Summers was cast as Ira Bean. Joe and Ira became part of what has become affectionately known as The Bunkhouse Boys, which also consisted of Pedro, Reno, and Vaquero and, of course, Joe's brother and ranch foreman Sam Butler played by Don Collier.

Don remembers how he got chosen for the show:

When the casting came up for High Chaparral, *I know that Kent McCray suggested me for the part of Sam Butler, the foreman, which was accepted. Casting director Bill Maybery called me and asked, "Do you want the part?" I simply said, "Yeah!" I took the part because it was an NBC show and I knew all the guys that were going to be on it and you always like a steady job. As it turned out, it was something I really enjoyed. Kent has been very instrumental in my career.*

Don's so easy to get along with and accommodating. I think that's one reason John Wayne cast him in several films.

CHAPTER NINETEEN

Mr. Burris' Homestead

We shot the *Chaparral* pilot in June during the hot Tucson summer. When we first got there, we kept getting a reflection from a building off in the distance. We figured out by talking to Tucson residents that it was probably coming from the airport hangar down at Ryan Field, a local airport. I hired county sheriff's deputy John Gammons[84] to work for us. I paid the Sheriff's Department and also paid John so we had crowd control and set security at all times.

In those days, there were no cell phones, so John used the radio in his truck to help us pinpoint the reflection. He called the Sheriff's Department and they sent another Sheriff's car down to the airport. I sent a painter and a couple of laborers down there and they kept putting red tarps on buildings until we figured out which one was giving us the problem. The painter painted that roof green so it blended in with all the saguaro and the cactus in the area.

On a daily basis, our cast and crew left the hotel at six in the morning. I was out before everyone else and didn't get back until I wrapped the company at night. Don Daves, Bill Claxton and Henry Wills were usually in my room when I returned. We talked about what we were going to do the next day to make sure everything was reviewed. The schedule was set, but a lot of individual problems came up when we enhanced a scene, especially in the pilot.

**Deputy Sheriff John Gammons (right) making me and director
Bill Claxton (center) honorary Deputies.**

We filmed the pilot in four weeks. It had a lot of heavy stunt work, Indian attacks and the like. In the script, the Cannons were travelling from the East to their new home in Arizona. They stopped at another ranch along the way and left after a short visit. Afterward, the other family's home got attacked by Apaches.

Bob Shelton and I coordinated with a local rancher, a Mr. Burris, who owned an adobe house out in the middle of the location. He agreed to let us use it as the house the Cannons visit. During the Indian attack after John Cannon and his family leave, we were supposed to have fire coming out of the windows caused by flaming arrows. I had the special effects people put tin all around the adobe and the roof and the interior so the flames wouldn't hurt the set. The day we shot it, I was up on the hill with Henry Wills.

The Indians started to circle the house, and they shot flaming arrows into it. Just as the technicians started the controlled house fire, the wind shifted and rather than the flames going toward the exterior, they did a one-hundred-eighty degree turn and went the opposite way into the interior. Unfortunately, Mr. Burris' homestead burned to the ground.

When I talked to Mr. Burris, he was a little upset. He eventually laughed and said, "I saw what you did to protect the place. It wasn't your fault the wind shifted. Don't worry about it." I felt very bad about the homestead burning down. It was a really great house and I always regretted that.

Toward the end of the *Chaparral* pilot when we filmed the big action sequence between the Indians and the Cannons, I was sitting off camera on an apple box. One of the stunt guys, Chuck Hayward, was in a Cavalry outfit. Inadvertently, his horse reared during the scene and he went off the horse. It wasn't supposed to happen. When he landed, he was really stiff and he stayed like that. I was only about ten feet away from him and my instinct was to help him, but I saw his eyes moving so I knew he was okay. He stayed like that, and the horses were running by and stepping over him like you wouldn't believe. Even between his legs.

After the shot was over, I immediately went to him and asked, "Chuck, are you all right?" He said, "Yeah." I said, "You were just lying there." He said, "I had to. I stayed still so the horses could see me and avoid me. Had I started to move around, the horses could have gotten spooked because they wouldn't know what to do. I could have been hurt even though the horses wouldn't mean to do it. They just wouldn't have known which way to go." It takes a lot of guts to lie flat while horses are running around you like that.

I can't say enough about people who do stunts in films and on television. They're very caring. They worked together, watched out for each other, and protected the actors and the animals around them. What a special profession. They dressed to resemble the actors they did stunts for, and prided themselves on turning their head away from the camera so no one realized it wasn't the actor doing the stunt.

Bobby Hoy was one of the best. He grew up on a ranch so he knew horses. When Henry Darrow first started, he wasn't a great horseman, which is understandable. No one faulted him for it. Bobby stayed very close to him so if Henry's horse acted up, Bobby was right there to rein him back. He protected Henry many, many times from falling off. Bobby appointed himself to do that. He never got paid for it, but that's just the way he worked. He was one of the best. I respected Bobby a great deal.

We shot the *Chaparral* pilot for under half a million dollars. Many couldn't believe it because there was a lot of action and a lot of stunts, a lot of bows and arrows being shot. The two-hour pilot was very well-received. It was a lot of hard work.

Once we finished, we came back to L.A. and did the postproduction work. Then NBC had to look at it and critique it as they do with everything. We waited to see if they put it on the schedule. Sometimes, you didn't know until May of the following year. Once we got picked-up, they allowed us to hire writers.

We got some stories a little ahead which helped when we started to shoot in June 1967. You have to remember, in those days we took six days to shoot a show. With the air date the same day each week and us working six days a week, it got a little tight from time-to-time. I think our commitment was twenty-two or twenty-four episodes. After the first season, we sat back and hoped we got picked up for the next one. That's how all of it was. A crap shoot. It was a lot of fun.

After the pilot of *Chaparral* was edited, I went back on *Bonanza* and then the following season we started filming *Chaparral*. I left *Bonanza* for that season and stayed only on *Chaparral*.

CHAPTER TWENTY

"*Chaparral* Was My Baby"

I liked doing *Bonanza* but I felt *Chaparral* was my baby because I was the first one to read it. I did *everything* to get it ready. Many times on location shooting in Tucson, Bill Claxton was busy prepping and wasn't always on the set. If there was a problem, they all looked to me to solve it. That's what had to be done.

Henry Darrow remembers:

He was the best production manager ever... He was always on top of it. That was one of the things that I'm sure David Dortort must've really appreciated with Kent...It wasn't until time had passed when I realized, my gosh, I just forgot how much Kent ran basically the whole operation...(Kent) was always ahead of the game. He wasn't surprised too often at all.

Bob Shelton shares his memories at the Old Tucson location:

I was President of Old Tucson and the responsibility for that studio was mine. Once Kent had notified me they were going to come over and work for a week or two weeks, whatever it was, they moved all their trucks onto the property, they stored things there, they used whatever facilities they wanted. My association with him was daily because he needed things from us and we needed things from him...Kent McCray, as far as his Western credentials and his work ethic, is head and shoulders above anybody I ever worked with. He was honest. He was straight forward. He never played games. If he had something unpleasant to talk about, he went right to it, no fancy dancing around it...

Stuntman/extra Neil Summers was new to the industry back then. He shares:

It has been forty odd years since I was getting started with my stunt profession on the series The High Chaparral. *Kent McCray was in overall charge of the production and he was admired and respected by his cast and crew alike. In Kent's working world, there was no difference between anyone under his leadership. We were all treated with dignity, kindness and care. He was a hands-on boss and was with us in the heat of the Arizona summers, and not running the show from an air conditioned office back in town.*[85]

Fellow stuntman/extra Steve DeFrance got invited onto *Chaparral* by Henry Wills:

The phenomenon of Kent McCray is that I think he had a twin because he seemed to be everywhere. We'd be shooting second unit. He'd be at the main set. We'd go out to the second unit location and he'd be there waiting for us! "How'd he do that?" Even when he wasn't there, it seems as though his presence was there...[86]

Don Collier gave me the nickname "Big Daddy." The first time I heard it, I was kind of flattered, actually. Don remembers it this way:

Big Daddy! That's right. Ol' B.D. He was a big guy. Also, he was almost like a father to us guys. We were all about the same age, but he...just looked after his flock. Made sure all his children were in line, got up in the morning sober, ready to work, and got to bed on time if he could control them...Someone had to be a father for us.

Veteran stuntman Jack Lilley has this to share:

Kent kept a crew. You were like a family. You could go into his office any time and ask him anything...If you had any kind of a problem, he'd say, "What is it?" and it'd be solved.

Don Collier giving "Big Daddy" a hard time on the set of
***High Chaparral,* and "Big Daddy" giving it right back.**

And you really had to cross him bad for him to ever fire you, because if you had a problem, he was the first one to step up if you were right, and back you. That's Kent McCray. He <u>was</u> Big Daddy. They put (that name) on Burl Ives in a movie, but there's the original Big Daddy is Kent. You could go to him with any problem you had....

I have a picture of me sitting on a bale of hay and I have a bale of hay in front of me as a desk as I'm breaking down a script. Your office is where you find it. I did that for *Chaparral* and *Bonanza.*

Chaparral I thought was special. I liked the chemistry of the cast. I liked the fact it had a lot of action in it. True action. The flavor of *Bonanza,* which was part of the concept of the show, centered on the Cartwright family and the Ponderosa. The characters didn't have to venture out to other places to do stories. People came to the Ponderosa ninety percent of the time.

I was always on location shoots and improvised as necessary.

Chaparral was meant to be different. It was never meant to take the place of *Bonanza*. It was simply a different concept. David Dortort did a lot of research when *Chaparral* came up. He wanted to show the Southwest Arizona Territory, a conflict of a rancher against the Indians and the Mexicans. All three groups were fighting multiple battles. It gave the show color. It had action and a lot of location work.

As production manager, I hired and fired the crew. I was the glue. My main function was to keep things moving. If there was a problem, we had to figure it out quickly. We couldn't waste time. It was forced on me to assume some of those roles as problem solver, and I just did it. I think the cast came to me because I tried to help them. I can't remember any major problems. *Chaparral* had a very cohesive group of people who worked together.

I was one of the first people in the industry to give the crew single hotel rooms. The first year of *Chaparral*, everybody shared a room. It got to be a bit of a wrinkle. I mean, they were working in 105 degree heat all day, and then coming home hot and sweaty. Who wants to share a room or a bathroom with some other guy?

One night that first year while on location, I got a call at three or four o'clock in the morning. The cook usually got up early to get breakfast for the crew and cast. He and his helper shared a room. The helper got up and went to the bathroom. When he came back, he tried to wake up the cook. He didn't wake up. He was dead. They called me about it.

I had to inform the police. Afterward, I went to the restaurant and asked the manager, "Can I borrow your cook so he can come out to location and feed the crew?" He agreed, and their cook fed our people for two days while I had another cook flown in from L.A.

CHAPTER TWENTY-ONE

Tales from the Sonoran Desert

FROM KENT

When we shot *Chaparral* on location in Tucson, we always had a doctor on the set. He was a licensed surgeon with one good eye and one glass eye. He also had a heart problem. After surgery to correct the heart issue, he developed a tremor in his hands. He could never go back to being a surgeon, but he knew everything and was very well-read and medically up-to-date.

For treatment due to the heat, Doc handed out salt pills. Plus, we took a big bucket with a chunk of ice in it and filled it partially with water and witch hazel. We dipped a rag in it and put it around our necks to cool our bodies as it dried. It gave you a stiff neck after a few days, but that was better than taking the heat. Cameron Mitchell would jump in the watering trough after almost every scene.

As for Doc's eye problem, he would lie on a rock and go to sleep but his glass eye wouldn't close. A glass eye, if you've ever seen one, always looks like it's looking at you, like it's tracking you. People walked past him and screamed. We had people look at him and pass out. That's when we woke him up and told him to move.

Leif Erickson was a big man, about 6'3". Very nice man. We did a *Bonanza* with him.[87] We hired different actors on *Bonanza* and tried to envision them being on *Chaparral*. It didn't come as a shock to anyone when we hired Leif as John Cannon.

Cam Mitchell was a great actor who did a lot of major films. He was the only guy I knew who chewed wine or ate with his gloves on. Look at some of the episodes.

Linda Cristal, I thought, was extraordinary. She not only looked beautiful and was a good actress, but also she worked in 105 degrees wearing heavy wardrobe complete with high necklines. Never complained a word!

Henry Darrow gave the show so much color. His laugh, his personality and his Spanish dialect set the tone for me. His performance bubbles! He did an incredible job.

As Don Sebastian de Montoya, Frank Silvera brought dignity and class to the role. He was a great actor.

Mark Slade was pleasant to work with and he did a nice job as the character Blue.

Rudy Ramos joined the cast during the last year. I didn't get to know him well, but he was very effective and well-cast as the character Wind.

High Chaparral had a sense of humor as well as a sense of drama. For example, one storyline had the boys getting Victoria a turkey for Thanksgiving.[88] The only turkeys to be found were the prizes at a turkey shoot in Tucson. Buck, Blue and Manolito entered and one won.

The turkey was in a crate in the buckboard. The wagon started down the street, but the turkey got loose and they ran around trying to find the turkey.[89] They captured the turkey and took it into the saloon with them to have a drink. The turkey got loose again and played havoc in the saloon. Finally, the turkey went back in the crate and back on the buckboard.

The wagon got stolen and John and the Bunkhouse boys saw a stranger driving it through the desert. The men gave chase and the wagon hit a bump. The turkey crate was supposed to fall out of the buckboard again and when it hit the ground, the turkey was supposed to get loose again. We had an Animal Humane rep on site who said, "You can't let the turkey fall out of the crate onto a rock because it might get hurt. You're going to have to kill the turkey so a dead turkey falls out of the crate."

Stuntman Jacky Lilley, in a very loud voice said, "Speaking for the turkey, I'd like to take my chances." Well, that broke up the set and we looked at the Humane rep who said, "I think you're right." Jack saved the life of the turkey.

Many of the episodes we did for the series were produced like a feature film. One is my favorite, "The Buffalo Soldiers." We had one hundred horses on the set.[90]

FROM BOB SHELTON

I had a house on the edge of town with a swimming pool out back. My wife at the time was out of town visiting her father in New York. Very early on in the relationship with NBC and Kent...I had them all out to my house for a barbecue. We were really having a good time. Everybody was enjoying it.

We had a big patio out back and there was a swimming pool in the middle of it. We were trying to get some more seats together closer to the house and we had a metal couch over on the far side of the swimming pool. Kent said, "I'll go get that and bring it over." He took one of the stuntmen, I think, and went over and each got on the end of it. It was pretty heavy because it was wrought iron. They were walking around the pool to bring it over...and they walked too close to the side of the pool. Kent misstepped and fell in!

...It was really a ball. Everybody had a hell of a good time. and soon, we were as wet on the inside as we were on the outside, and it was a lot of fun. You couldn't be around that bunch without having fun. Kent ran a very good, high-spirited crew of people. He was fair and he expected you to conduct yourself in the highest degree of your trade, and if you didn't, you didn't work for him. He would send you home. Everybody respected him because he was fair about everything. He wouldn't ask anybody to do anything that he wouldn't do, and there wasn't anything he *couldn't* do, either. He was a big, strong guy and he loved the business and he had a great sense of showmanship and executive talents about him.

FROM DON COLLIER

I remember being on location in Big Bear. It was probably in the summer of 1968 or 69. Summer in the San Bernadino Mountains is vacation time, and there were a lot of people up there. Kent went up early and tried to secure rooms for the whole company but he had trouble. He told me and Bobby (Hoy), "I haven't got enough rooms. You guys are going to have to bunk together," which was fine because we'd bunked together before.

Kent would get up at 5:00 A.M. or 5:30 A.M. and make the rounds to see if all the guys were up...It was summer time and Bobby and I just had a sheet up to our waist. We were wearing a pair of shorts, lying there each in our own single bed. We were talking to each other and I looked out the window to see Kent walk by. I knew where he was going. He was going to circle around there and wake one or two guys up if they weren't awake already, then he was going to come into our room and make sure we were awake.

I got out of my bed and I jumped into bed with Bobby. There we are together shoulder-to-shoulder, just wearing a pair of shorts. We figured Kent was going to walk into the room and catch us in bed together and we were all going to have a big laugh. Bobby and I are waiting for Kent. We were silent, not saying anything. And we waited. And we waited a little more. Kent didn't show up! Now, it was getting a tiny bit awkward.

Finally, Bobby turned to me and said, "Okay, pal, it's your move." We both fell out of bed laughing and that was the end of that! It was just a funny, weird thing. We told Kent and we all got a kick out of it.

CHAPTER TWENTY-TWO

Consolidating Resources

The year I was doing *Chaparral* only, we went to Tucson and shot for maybe three to four weeks at a time. While we were gone, *Bonanza* would go to some of my non-descript sets at the studio and use them for *Bonanza*, which I didn't mind. When *Bonanza* went on location, I was not allowed to use any of their non-descript sets, which I thought was stupid since it was all NBC's money.

At the end of the season, I complained about this heavily to NBC and said, "Right is right; fair is fair. It's all your money and you should be able to save it when possible." They asked, "What do you think we should do about it?" I said, "Since both shows are produced by David Dortort and both shows are owned by NBC, put one person in charge of production. We can consolidate things and control them."

NBC said, "Lay out a plan of what you want to do." I laid out a whole schedule showing how we could save money by eliminating one casting director and using the remaining casting director to do both shows. We could have one secretary and one receptionist. Same thing with the editorial crew. Same thing with the draftsmen. A lot of areas we could double-up and save money while still doing both productions.

They said, "Do you think you could do it?" I said, "Of course." They said, "Jimmy Lane's got seniority since he started *Bonanza*. It's only fair that we ask him if he wants to do it." I said, "Fine."

I already mentioned Jimmy Lane who was actually my boss, but he frustrated me. One day we were shooting *Bonanza* in Tahoe, and we had bad weather. We discussed working Sunday because of the weather, but Sunday was an expensive day to work. At least it would have put us back on schedule. It was sometimes better to work a Sunday and pay the overtime than it was to stay in hotels for two more days down the road. I had to weigh one against the other.

I said to Jimmy Lane, "Let's wait and see." Jimmy said, "No, I think we should." I said, "Look, if you want to work Sunday, I've got to know by Saturday at one o'clock. I've got to make sure people have lunches, make sure we have security, all kinds of different things. If we're going to work Sunday, I have to order that ahead of time." He said, "I'll come out to the set before one o'clock." I said, "If you're not there by one o'clock, I'm not going to order anything."

He showed up at 3:30 P.M. Remember, we were working in Tahoe. He asked, "Do you have everything set for tomorrow?" I said, "No!" I chewed his ass out in front of everybody which ticked him off. He said something like, "I had to go to Reno to get my wife a pillow." He had no concept.

Another time we were working in Kernville which is outside of Bakersfield. We were staying at a motel that had a nice restaurant. It was one of the only good restaurants in town, so everybody congregated there for dinner. Jimmy called me over and introduced me to the owner, who was at his table. Jimmy said, "Mr. So-and-so is going to be open for breakfast so the cast and crew can eat here." I said, "That's great!" Jimmy said, "Yes, they'll open at nine o'clock in the morning." I said, "Nine o'clock? We leave at six! What the hell is nine o'clock going to do for us?" I mean, he was my boss and he had been a production manager. He just had no concept of what was right and what was wrong.

Anyhow, NBC asked Jimmy Lane if wanted to be the production person in charge of consolidating *Bonanza* and *The High Chaparral*. He more or less replied, "Under no circumstances can this be done." He turned it down and lost his job. They fired him and I took over both shows. This would have been the second season of *Chaparral*.

When he left, there wasn't one piece of paper in the file cabinet relating to anything that had taken place on *Bonanza*. It seemed the material had been removed or destroyed so I wouldn't have any references to go back to. Stupid. The material belonged to NBC. No one had any right to take it or destroy it.

By 1970, we were shooting both *Chaparral* and *Bonanza* at Paramount Studios. However, due to some contractual disputes between NBC and Paramount, we were no longer offered an extension of our lease, which meant we had to find a new agreement. Warner Brothers came to us and said they would like to talk. We went to Warner Brothers and made a deal with them to shoot both shows at their studio. Charlie Greenlaw was head of production. A really great guy. We worked with him very closely.

In our original deal with Paramount, when we constructed a set, we paid a percentage of the cost that went into a strike fund. When we were finished with the set, Paramount had to strike it, that is tear it down, but there would be no cost to us because we had paid up front. We tried to buy the sets for both shows from Paramount and take them to Warner Brothers. Paramount refused to sell them.[91] They were very mad that we were leaving and they wouldn't negotiate at all.

We had to re-create all new sets at Warner Brothers, and get new furniture to match. At that same time, MGM Studios was selling all items in their prop and set dressing departments. We scoured around and were able to reproduce all the furniture that we had on the sets. If we didn't have it, we made it, which was a lot of extra work. We opened up the following season at Warner Brothers Studio and continued on there for two years with *Chaparral* and *Bonanza* until they both ended.

CHAPTER TWENTY-THREE

Introducing Susan Sukman

Susan Sukman grew up in a house filled with music. Her mother, Francesca (Paley), was an accomplished organist, pianist and composer who worked in radio. Her father, Harry Sukman, was an Oscar-winning composer and respected concert pianist. Harry, who was a child prodigy, began his career at age eleven and spent more than sixty years composing and performing. His early work as a musical conductor in New York took the family on the road until they settled on the West Coast.

Susan remembers:[92]

I was born in Chicago. I grew up in California. My dad was doing the music for a production called, "Pardon Our French." Two men named Olson and Johnson had a big hit on Broadway called "Hellzapoppin." Then they came out a few years later with "Pardon Our French." It started in New York. We went there. And then it went on the road to San Francisco and Boston and all over.

We were travelling on the train, so I never settled in a school. I was in and out of them. When you're a kid like that and you can't get settled or established in one place, or really be able to have permanent friends like normal kids, it's very disconcerting. I would get to the point that in the morning when I would have to go to school, I'd feel sick to my stomach because I was scared. My best friends were my parents or some of the cast members in the show. Actually, that was a great experience for me because it helped me in my casting career later. Being close friends with actors in the show made me understand what they went through with interviews and rehearsals.

Then we settled in California and I was registered at Fairburn Avenue School in West Los Angeles. I loved it, my grammar school. Then, dad got a call, and he thought, "Maybe I'll go back to Chicago." I said, "If you go, I'm not going. If you're going, I'm staying right here." Dad started to laugh. He said, "You are?" I said, "Yes, I am. I'm not going."

That's when my mother's sister called from Chicago and said, "You know, Harry, I think you should stay in California because there's not much for you to do here anymore." Thank God he did, because, obviously, his career was here. He started a successful career first as an on-staff pianist at Paramount and continued on to compose for multiple television series.

I didn't know about the call. I thought I was responsible for us staying here. I was so happy. From Fairburn Avenue School, I went to Emerson Junior High, and was in school with people like Liza Minelli and Jim Lancaster, Burt Lancaster's son. We became friends[93]. I used to go over to Burt Lancaster's house. They had a private screening room there. We used to make chocolate chip cookies for Burt. He was really sweet. He'd say, "Oh, these are the best chocolate chip cookies." Out in his back yard, he had a big trapeze set-up that he would work out on. He was a tremendous athlete.

We moved to Dalehurst Avenue. It was a Spanish house which my dad later called High Chaparral, absolutely beautiful. My parents had two Steinways in the living room. There was music in the house all the time. It was a great house. I loved it dearly because all the people who came to the house were well-known composers, musicians, and I must say, when I was five years old, I always sang. I was a singer. That was my instrument.

My father would accompany me at the piano. My uncle Victor Young would visit. I call him my uncle because he was like my father's brother. They grew up together in Chicago. Victor Young was a well-known composer of songs like "Stella by Starlight," "When I Fall in Love," all the wonderful songs that are well-known today. "Love Letters."

I was the first person to sing the song, "When I Fall in Love," and I was accompanied by my father. He was a great accompanist. He knew what key I should sing in. I never did but he would say, "Let's start with this," and he was always right. Every time we would go to a house to visit or have dinner, they would say, "Susan, get up and sing 'When I Fall in Love.'" Apparently, at that time when I was so young, I sang like an old experienced woman. I don't know. It just happened. I just felt the lyrics, the words, and everybody would cry and everybody would say, "How wonderful." You know, here I was a little girl in pigtails singing "When I Fall in Love." But I was known for that.

My dad won an Oscar for composing in 1961[94] *for the movie,* Song Without End: The Story of Franz Liszt. *I remember attending the awards ceremony that special night.*

First of all, I heard that when actresses get ready to go to the Oscars, they take all day. They get their hair done, their make-up, and they take forever. I tried to take forever to put on make-up and all this stuff. I was ready in ten minutes. It was 1961 and I was a teenager. My dad said, "You know, Susan, we're having a limo pick us up." I thought, "Oh, my gosh, I've never been in a limo before."

Up drove this big, long stretch limousine. Oh, my God. I got in the back seat. This was just amazing. I couldn't believe it. My dad got in and my mom got in. My mom looked so gorgeous. She had on a black satin dress that she had bought in Westwood with little jet beading up on top with spaghetti straps. She made her own wrap. She made this green satin cape, and at the edges, she sewed a little fringe. She looked stunning, as if she'd purchased the most expensive thing.

We got to the Santa Monica Civic Auditorium which is where the ceremony was. The lights were flashing and the cameras were going and people were all crowded in. There was the red carpet and the big Oscar they set outside the entrance. We got out of the car, and it was like, flash, flash, flash. It was the most exciting thing in the whole world. It made you feel like you were a star, even though you weren't. They were looking at me like, "Who's that?" My dad looked so handsome, very debonair.

We got in and sat down. He was seated on the end seat of the aisle in case he won. I was sitting between my parents holding hands. Bob Hope came on. He was the host. Dad knew him. He was very funny that night. Then, he introduced Bobby Darin and Sandra Dee, who had just gotten married a few months before. They were announcing his category.

My dad was nervous, not because he was up for the Oscar, but because he was afraid they were going to mispronounce his name, because it had happened so many times before. Bobby Darin announced his name absolutely perfectly, so he loved Bobby ever since then. He announced it, "And the winner is Harry Sukman!
Song Without End: The Story of Franz Liszt.*"*

My father went running up there, you couldn't even see him he was going so fast. Bob Hope grabbed his hand and said, "Harry, I'm so proud of you." It was just incredible. The woman sitting next to my mother was the wife of the owner of Sara Lee cakes, who was the big sponsor that year. She said, "I'm going to make sure to send you a cake every month. This is so wonderful." Every month for a year after that, we got a different Sara Lee cake. Their chocolate fudge cake, their banana nut cake with the white frosting. I mean, they were delicious.

After the Awards were over, we went to the Beverly Hilton. My aunt was with us. I went ahead with my aunt. My dad walked into the ballroom with my mother and the Oscar in his hand. My aunt was just beside herself. The first thing she said was, "I wish ma and pa were alive to see this." We went to the ladies room, and in the ladies room, there was Greer Garson, the actress, who took a hold of my aunt's hand and said, "This is wonderful. I'm so happy for you!" They became close friends for years. They kept in touch with each other, my Aunt Rose and Greer Garson.

It was an incredible, incredible night. I screamed when he won. Then the next year, when he was nominated for Fanny, *we went again. Unfortunately, he didn't win but when we went to the ball, Henry Mancini, who did win,[95] came over to my father and said, "Harry, you should have won this. Your score was far better than mine." I mean, can you imagine? That's something.*

Henry Mancini was a man who remembered everyone. He remembered your name. Years after that, we were at a concert at UCLA and I saw him. He walked over to me, years later mind you, and said, "Susan, how are you?" I said, "I'm fine, thank you." He said, "What a wonderful night that was, right?" Amazing!

As I got older in my late teens, I think I used to feel embarrassed about getting up in front of people to sing. I really thought to myself, "I don't want to get up and do this." As time passed, I never really knew what I wanted to do as careers go. I was very interested in English, I was very interested in Psychology, which I took at UCLA. I was very interested in Art History. This was after I left University High School. When I left Uni High, I went to Santa Monica City College first and then after a year, I went on to UCLA, which was right up the street from where we lived on Dalehurst.

After being in college a while, I was floundering. At the time, my father was under contract to a record company and he mentioned to the president of the company that I was a singer. The gentleman came to the house and said, "Let me hear her sing." Apparently he was very impressed with me because he said, "You know, I would like you to record a few things." I was thrilled. I couldn't believe it! And where did I go to record? Nashville. And whose songs did I record? I recorded some pretty well-known people that wrote for me, the same people who wrote for Roy Orbison, whom I appeared with on stage. I also appeared with Ray Stevens and I appeared with Boots Randolph, a great sax player.

When I appeared with them, I was singing my song, which was "Say a Prayer for Michael," (under the name Susan Sands) which became pretty well-known in the Midwest. Then I was asked to go on tour with them. After I appeared with them at the Playboy Club on Sunset in L.A., I decided I didn't want to start traveling. I said to my dad, "If they make this a hit then I'll go traveling, but I really don't feel like pushing it and traveling around." My dad said, "You're going to have to do something." I said, "Yeah, I am and I don't know what to do."

My dad and David Dortort were very close. At the time, dad was writing music for Bonanza *and* High Chaparral.[96] *They had met at a party given by the attorney for ASCAP. They were all very good friends. My dad was at this party and David asked my dad, "Harry, do you think you could write Mexican music?" This was before* The High Chaparral *series started but after the pilot. My dad said, "David, nobody could possibly write better Mexican music than I." And they laughed and then came* High Chaparral, *and NOBODY wrote Mexican music better! "Montoya's Theme" was David's most favorite thing. Every time David and Rose, his wife, would come to the house, my father would play that theme as he walked in the door. David would say, "Oh, Harry, that's so beautiful."*

Dad talked to David Dortort and said, "You know, my daughter is back from Nashville and if you ever have anything open, she's a great secretary." I had worked at a place in Beverly Hills that owned and operated Cinerama theaters across the country and I had done a lot of the secretarial work. Kept the books for them, what they took in during the weeks and weekends. He said, "She can type like crazy," and the like.

David said, "It's a funny thing. We are adding on a big reception area in front of the casting offices and we're going to need somebody out there. Why don't I send her over to Dick Larson who is our liaison for NBC and the show?" Before I went to Dick Larson, I was to meet Kent McCray who was the production manager of both shows and he was really in charge of all the people and the offices and the whole staff. I got a little nervous, but we went.

I even remember to this day what I wore. I wore a beige long-sleeved dress, very short, and a very wide belt. I always loved wide belts. Off I went. Of course, I had little heels to match the dress in the same kind of cream color. I walked in with my dad. Mr. McCray was in a meeting upstairs so I looked around his office and sat down. I saw some pictures on the back of his desk. My dad said, "That's Kent McCray in that picture." I said, "Oh, he's very good-looking." My dad said, "He is one of the nicest people I've ever met. Boy, if you could ever find a guy like that to marry, that's the one. He's a good guy. There are a few stories about him, but he's a good man." I said, "Oh, that's very interesting."

Kent walked in and he was just as tall and handsome as in his picture, very tan because he had just returned from Tucson where they were filming High Chaparral. *I thought, "Gosh, what a handsome man. Deep voice. Very personable. Very sweet." I talked to him for a while and then he said, "Let me take you upstairs to Dick Larson who's with NBC." I met Dick Larson and then I went home with dad. We found out the next day that I was hired as the receptionist.*

My duties were to type music cue sheets for my father and take them home to him. It was really a lot of music when he did The High Chaparral *and* Bonanza. *My dad would come home and say, "It's an Indian show. Wall-to-wall music." He would be in the back room with his piano, and I could hear him working for hours and doing a chase scene or whatever was called for.*

Some of my other duties were to take care of Mr. Dortort's scrapbooks for both his shows. I thought, "What kind of a job is this? I mean, a scrapbook? With glue and all that stuff?" I thought, "This isn't really my cup of tea, but hey, it's a job." As the receptionist, it was also my duty to greet visitors in the office. Under my desk was a button I pushed to let people in to see the casting secretary. I met all the agents and I met all the people coming in for interviews. They all had to sit in my office. This would be very helpful to me as my career started to take shape.

I also remember the day I met Susan for the first time. She became our receptionist. My first impression of her? There was a spark there.

CHAPTER TWENTY-FOUR

Ending an Era: Cancellation of *Chaparral* and *Bonanza*

The Seventies became the decade when what few Westerns were left rode off into the sunset. *The High Chaparral* ended in 1971[97] and *Bonanza* in 1973[98]. *Gunsmoke*, the last of the classic Western shows, hung on until 1975.[99]

I think Bobby Kennedy's assassination[100] changed the tone of violence on all the networks in the country as a whole. Violence was looked at it in a different perspective. We were shooting a *Bonanza* at that particular time. It was the story about a kind of chain gang run by a man who guarded his prisoners with a number of dogs on leashes. This was a Little Joe story. Joe broke free and there was a big chase between Mike and the dogs. There was a lot of barking, a lot of growling, a lot of snarling. We had to change it all. I had to take a lot of the barking out and re-score it so we covered a lot with music, which sounded good and scary but wasn't violent. We had to change how we did things.

I think it hurt *Chaparral* more than anything. Our show was location driven with a lot of action. We had the conflict of the outdoors, conflict over cattle and different groups of people. However, the nation's mood was re-examining that. Now, if we shot someone in a scene, we had to show that person get up and run away so the audience knew the character didn't die.

By the time all this hit, we were doing year four. Frank Silvera had died. He was putting in his own garbage disposal and electrocuted himself accidentally.[101] We had to replace his character, and we did so with Gilbert Roland. We did a two-hour show with him which I thought was good. He eventually would have been, not replacing Frank's character, but stepping in as family member Don Domingo. He gave a lot of character to the role. We did that two-hour show and that was going to be his introduction to become a regular on the series the rest of the year and the following season.

At that point, NBC said, "We're not going to continue." Now why they did that, I can't remember. Our ratings were not great. *Bonanza* was flying off the charts because it had a better time slot, which was great for them. *Chaparral* never had a great time slot I felt.[102] That's the luck of the draw. You can't always have your wishes.

I think it was the violence issue and the network's decision to back off. We tried to do shows with less action and the audience started to fade. Once that happened, we were dead ducks.

Bob Shelton recounts the impact the show and its cancellation had on Old Tucson.

*I know I'm prejudiced, but I thought it (*Chaparral*) was really a great piece of drama and a great piece of entertainment and had a great deal of truism and a great deal of effort in it. It was a shame it went off the air. It affected a lot of people.*

After *Chaparral*, I continued to focus on *Bonanza* when tragedy struck. It was on a Saturday. That was a sad, sad day. I was at home and got the phone call. Dan Blocker had passed away.[103] I put down the phone and sat there. We had just started pre-production. I had hired the crew to come back to start work on the series. The opening show was going to be a love story that Michael had written for Dan.

Dan had gone into the hospital for a gall bladder operation. He came home but he got a blood clot and evidently he called the doctors. I think they rushed him back to the hospital. They couldn't stop the clot from moving and it shut off his breathing. Losing Dan Blocker was not only a tremendous loss for the show, it was a personal loss for those of us who loved him, most-especially Michael. In fact, Mike thought about it all the time and I think about it to this day. Dan was a great man. He had a great charisma. What he did, he did well.

Pernell left. Hoss was gone. Only Little Joe and Pa left. Mike had to re-write the love story he wrote for Dan and made Little Joe the main character.[104] We shut down for a few weeks, and then started up again for what would be our final season.

I loved Michael's and Dan's interaction on set because they worked incredibly well together. They could make you cry one minute and laugh the next. The camaraderie was irreplaceable and we could never get it back again. Without Dan, we lost a great flair.

To fill the void, we brought in another character, one the audience was familiar with: David Canary who played "Candy." David was good, very good, but he didn't replace Blocker. How can you say someone is similar to Dan Blocker? I mean his size. His acting style.

David was someone the audience knew and someone Michael and Lorne could work with. They couldn't do the comedy scenes but they could do dramatic ones together. It gave Michael someone else to play off other than Pa.

In the last year, we hired Tim Matheson, a younger, handsome new character. Tim, who went on to become well-known outside of *Bonanza,* had his own story line on the show. However, *Bonanza* was canceled when Chevrolet stopped sponsoring it. That was after a long time. The show was moved to Tuesday nights against CBS' smash-hit *Maude* with Bea Arthur. That did us in.

Westerns were playing out by then. All of them. Warner Brothers' Westerns were gone. *Bonanza* was one of the last.

Chaparral had gone two years before that. It was a change of an era and it's never gone back. It never will. The true Western for television became too expensive because a lot of the studios had destroyed their Western streets to make room for offices and parking lots. That's what happened at Paramount. The Victorian-style architecture is tough to build with all the balustrades and railings. That's expensive to reproduce.

In the early days, each studio had its own prop and set-dressing departments. They had furniture of all periods, three-story buildings of nothing but furniture. They sold it off.

MGM sold theirs off when (Kirk) Kerkorian[105] took over and built a hotel in Vegas. *Cleopatra* broke Century Fox. Went way, way over budget. They sold off their back lot which became Century City. They, like MGM, had two Western streets, rail tracks which went down both streets, and a train which is now at Old Tucson. Cobblestone streets that looked like Europe. Modern streets. English or Irish-looking streets. Andy Hardy's school house building. Esther Williams' swimming pool. Those were all shot on the studio lot. It was a different era.

Here in town, there's one Western street left. It's been re-built since. There used to be a place Gene Autry owned called Melody Ranch. That burned down in a fire and two guys bought the property and re-built the street from photographs. They laid it all out and asked me to look at it. They did a good job of it, too.

NBC canceled us after fourteen years on the air. I got the call at 10:30 in the morning. They said, "Finish the show at lunch and lay everybody off." The cast knew it by then and everybody was very upset. Mike and Lorne went to NBC to plead their case: "At least let us finish the show. Don't cut us off in the middle. What are you going to do with half a show anyway? It has no residual factor." NBC reluctantly said we could finish it.

The last shot of the show, Michael, being the prankster that he was, had himself rigged by the special effects guys. He stood by this large fake window on the stage and when the director called,

"Cut," on the last scene of the last show, a gunshot went off. Michael, who was on a shock cord, flew backwards through the fake glass window and then stood up and said, "Tha, tha, tha, that's all, folks!"

And that was the end of the series *Bonanza*.

Fenton Coe, who was still head of production, called me and said, "You know the Cartwrights (he always called the cast the Cartwrights) are going to want to take some souvenirs home with them and you have to watch it because a lot of the props are on rental." I said, "I have enough stuff to do, but I'll try my best." I told Lorne and Mike not to "steal" too much.

We had a big wrap party at the end of everything. Fenton Coe came in and Mike said, "Hey, Fenton, help me move this table." Fenton, being an ex-prop man, said, "Sure." He picked up one end of the table and Mike took him down one side of the stage and across the stage and headed toward one of the back doors. Fenton said, "Where are we taking this?" Michael said, "Fenton, I'm stealing the table. I'm putting it in my car." Fenton said, "Oh, okay," and he helped Mike out the door with the table.

CHAPTER TWENTY-FIVE

Little House on the Prairie

After the wrap of *Bonanza*, I worked for Quinn Martin on the series *Barnaby Jones*,[106] a show starring Buddy Ebsen and Lee Meriwether. It was a good show to work on and I enjoyed it very much.

When that ended, Paramount Studios called me to work on a show called *Love Story*.[107] *Love Story* was an anthology series. The only thing they kept from the motion picture was the title. We did different love stories each week.

In the fall of 1973 while doing *Love Story*, Dick Larson called and asked me to talk to Michael Landon over the weekend. Michael was directing a *Love Story* episode[108] and we made arrangements to meet. He told me he wanted to do a show called *Little House on the Prairie*, based on the books by Laura Ingalls Wilder.[109] He was very excited about the project and he wanted me to work on it with him.

I met with him over many weekends, and on other weekends, I went to Texas, New Mexico and Arizona to scout locations and take pictures which I brought back to Michael. One day, Dick Larson called me and said, "We're getting very close to the start of production on *Little House*. You're going to have to quit your job at Paramount."

In this business, that's something you don't like to do. I struggled with it, but thought working with Mike again would be a great pleasure. I said, "Okay, I'll go down and tell the production office I'm quitting." That was the Paramount Production Department run by Jack Sonntag.

I called Jack's office to make an appointment with him, but he was busy going back and forth on other projects. His staff said they would call me when he was available. Dick Larson then called me and said, "Don't quit your job. We're going to inform Paramount we're cancelling the *Love Story* series and they'll wrap it after finishing two more shows. You may still have to get off early, though. I don't know yet."

Now I was in a pickle. I didn't want to talk to Mr. Sonntag. When his staff called to set the meeting, I said I couldn't go because of a problem on the set with the show, which was not true. I stalled for a day and shortly after, I heard Jack coming down the hall to talk to somebody else on my floor. I was afraid he was going to talk to me, too. Fortunately, my office on the third floor of the production building had a fire escape door in it, so I went down the fire escape and hid out for an hour so I didn't run into him.

Eventually, Jack called me into his office and said, "I just got news they're going to cancel *Love Story*. If you have another project in mind, go ahead and take it." I said, "As a matter of fact I do." I told him about Michael's show. He said, "Go ahead. You can get off the show anytime, just finish out this week. I'll have to find someone to take your place as production manager." I said, "Miles Middough just finished his show. He was assistant director and he's certainly qualified. He can take over and do the last two shows as production manager." Which he did.

I was back on NBC's payroll on the pilot for *Little House*. This was in December of 1973. I found a great location outside Tucson in a town called Patagonia. It had a meadow and a stream, trees all around it and I thought it would work very well. There was also some good grass country that would work for Kansas.

I took Michael and cinematographer Teddy Voigtlander, executive producer Ed Friendly, Miles Middough, who was now our assistant director, and a few other people down to Tucson to show them the location. Some time had passed since I was there and I was unaware there had been a killing frost. Much to my chagrin, as we walked onto the meadow and looked around, all the trees had lost their leaves. Through the bare trees we saw nothing but cactus. That wouldn't work for Kansas very well.

I sat there with egg on my face, embarrassed. We all went back to the hotel and re-grouped. We decided that Mike, Teddy, Miles and art director Trevor Williams and I would scout in Northern California.

We flew to Sacramento and rented a car. I called some production location people in Northern California to help us find what we were looking for. We went to Marysville, but they weren't too helpful. We also went up to Oroville, but that didn't look like anything we wanted. We drove to Stockton.

It rained every day on the survey. We met a gentleman who took us out to where they shot the movie *Oklahoma Crude*. We rode in the back of a pick-up in the rain and got wet. Nothing came out of that location, either.

We went back to the hotel and the gentleman from Stockton called us again with another location he wanted us to see. It was on Route 4, the Orvis Ranch. The people who owned it bred Herefords. We went out there and it really looked good. We were enthused about it.

Next, we tried to find a place to shoot some winter scenes that also included a stream. I suggested we go back to Sonora, Calif., where we had shot some *Bonanzas*. Mike knew those locations pretty well. We spent a few days looking around Sonora, and then went back to the studio to start really laying out the pilot for *Little House on the Prairie*.

During all of this, NBC's casting department told us to test a few children for the show. We set up a stage at Paramount and brought them in. I forget how many children we had, but it was a bunch. At one point, Michael and I were on a break and we walked down to the men's room. Mike asked who I liked. I mentioned one girl I thought would be good as Laura. He said, "The other girl that tested for Laura, I think she'd be good for Mary." Mike and I agreed, and NBC, too, that Melissa Gilbert would play Laura, and Melissa Sue Anderson would play Mary.

Leslie Landon Matthews,[110] Michael's daughter who appeared in the series, has a funny story about our choice of Melissa Gilbert:

One of the times I almost got myself in deep water was my dad telling mom before he announced the casting for Little House *that he had found his "Half-Pint." He talked about Melissa Gilbert. Then he looked at me and said, "Leslie, I think she actually goes to the same school with you and Mike." I said, "Oh, really?" I didn't know her.*

So, the next day I asked a teacher where Melissa Gilbert was and she pointed her out to me. I walked over to her and I introduced myself and then I said, "Oh, by the way, my dad said you're going to be the next Laura Ingalls." She just jumped up from the table and ran off. I thought, "Oh, okay."

I got home that night and my dad came to the door. Oh my goodness, I was in so much trouble. Melissa knew before her agent, before anyone from my dad's office called him. That was very funny, and I learned from that moment on that I had to be very careful with what I heard at the dinner table.

We also talked about casting the other characters. The Greenbush twins were cast portraying the youngest Ingalls child, Carrie. NBC and Michael chose Karen Grassle as Caroline Ingalls, Michael's wife. She had a natural pioneer look in a pretty way and was suited well for the role. I reminded Mike about Victor French. Victor was a great actor who could do comedy, he could do serious stuff. He did a lot of *Bonanzas* and Mike remembered him well. I said he might be good for Mr. Edwards. Everybody liked that idea, so I felt good about that.

We decided to start shooting in January 1974, right after the first of the year. I laid out the schedule to work in Sonora for a few days, and then move the company down to Stockton to work at the Orvis Ranch. Everything was planned and we were ready to go.

I went to the location with Teddy Voigtlander the weekend before we started. Mike came up, too. The first day of shooting was scheduled outside Columbia, Calif., at a place called Yankee Hill. There was a little shack, a little old house, and it was to be part of the opening sequence when the Ingalls family left their homestead in the Big Woods near Pepin, Wisconsin, on their way to Kansas.

The night before we began the shoot, Teddy Voigtlander and I went to town to play poker at a local place. We got back to our rooms about midnight. I invited Teddy to have a nightcap, and as we talked and had a drink, I happened to look out the window. It was snowing. Really, really hard. And it wasn't what we planned on.

I called my friend Jim Opie who was a teamster. I said, "I need your four-wheel drive truck to check out the location." It was now about two o'clock in the morning. He came by and we drove up to Yankee Hill. It had been snowing on the mountain pretty heavily.

Through Jim's connections, we got a couple of plows to start plowing the roads because the company was flying in later in the day and we had to get them to the location. They did get there about noon, very late. It was a mess. We got in some work and went back to the hotel.

The next couple of days we shot in Sonora with different sequences of Mike hunting turkeys and things. We shot the snow while we were there to use for later shows. Then there was a scene where Mr. Edwards was supposed to cross the river on his way to the Little House for Christmas. He was supposed to cross in his underwear with his clothes above his head.

I found a place to shoot the scene. I made arrangements to plow out an area in the parking lot of a forest service headquarters so we had a big area to park the trucks. However, the river was about a hundred yards from where we parked, and there was still about three feet of snow all around. We had to get all the equipment down to the water. We laid plywood down and kept leap-frogging the plywood to move all the equipment, which was quite a chore. The only thing we planned to shoot that day was Mr. Edwards crossing the river, so we didn't have to worry about time.

Just as we got down to the water, we broke for lunch and still hadn't gotten the shot. After lunch, I took Victor upstream about fifty feet so his tracks in the snow would be out of view. That was where he was supposed to wade across the river in his BVDs. He had a wet suit on under his underwear and he had to sit down in the snow and wait for us to give him the cue to come forward.

Once again we were ready, but Mike changed to a special camera lens which needed sunlight in addition to the lights we had. The sun had gone behind a cloud, and we waited for it to come back out. Victor sat there shivering from the cold, so I had the prop man get me a bottle of brandy and I threw it over to Victor. He drank some to keep warm. The sun came out and Mr. Edwards crossed the river in his underwear holding his clothes over his head. And that was the only shot we got for the day.

We took all the equipment from the river back to the trucks, leap-frogging the plywood the same way we brought the equipment in. Our driver, Clyde, was in the last truck to leave, and I always rode with him. We tried to back up, but the snow thawed a little when the sun was out and the water froze as the sun went down. Clyde backed up but the tires of the truck kept spinning. This truck was about the size of a Greyhound bus.

I leaned on the truck and as it was bouncing, it started to slide. I kept pushing on the truck, pushing on the truck, and we did a whole forty-five degree turn until I lined up the truck so we could get out. I walked around and got in and said, "Let's go," and that's the way we ended the day.

After a few more days in Sonora, we moved the company down to the exterior set, a log cabin that we built for the show's scenes in Kansas. This was at the Orvis Ranch. We left early in the morning and I led the pack of trucks. We went into the ranch, opened up the gates and started to drive down to the cabin along the little river.

All of a sudden, the trucks got stuck in the mud almost up to their axles. While it had been snowing in Sonora, Farmington had gotten a ton of rain. I mean the trucks were really stuck. By the time Mike showed up, every truck except the camera and wardrobe trucks were stuck. I told Mike and the rest of the crew to go to the back-up set at the fairgrounds in Stockton where we had built the interiors of the log cabin. At least they could rehearse and get something done, which is what they did.

We worked all day to get the trucks out. We put hydraulic jacks under the axles and they just sunk in the mud along with everything else. At ten o'clock that night, we still weren't out. Earlier, I called my friend Jim Opie again and asked him to get me some heavy equipment, a D9 Cat, and bring it over. He showed up about three in the morning, and I told the driver of the Cat not to go in certain areas. He said, "Ah, these Cats will go anywhere." I said, "Be careful."

He didn't believe me and *he* got stuck in the mud and *he* couldn't get out. We decided to get some sleep in the honey wagon while Jim Opie went back to find another D9 Cat. That one showed up at seven in the morning. The first thing we did was pull out the other D9 that was stuck. Once that happened, we had two Cats to pull all the equipment out of the mud. We sent everything down to the fairgrounds location and started shooting in the interior of the log cabin.

The weather was still bad so we stayed inside shooting scenes in the cabin set for at least a week or more. In the meantime, some of the drivers and I went out to find a new road to the cabin exterior set. We searched and tested the ground. We worked out a place that was okay except in one area. This was after days of dragging hay, rocks and everything we could think of over the mud to keep our trucks from sinking again.

Then I remembered a gentleman in Hollywood named Al Mann. He had a lot of old Army surplus stuff. We reached him and sure enough he had the landing mats the military used during the war to land planes when they had deep sand and other soft ground obstacles. These mats were made of heavy steel mesh, very heavy, and they came in pieces that interlocked together. Al sent a truck up with as many landing mats as he had. We laid them down in the trouble spot and that solved our problem. We were able to get the equipment into the area so we could shoot the exterior of the log cabin for the pilot sequences.

We eventually wrapped the show in Stockton and came home to edit the pilot. After the pilot was edited and post production was complete, we took it to a testing house to run it in front of an audience. NBC tested the pilot with an audience and it tested higher than any show that NBC ever had. That was a good sign. We also had a special screening for the press. NBC immediately picked up the show and we prepared for the first season *of Little House on the Prairie*.

We felt we had done something special, but we didn't know the true impact until later on. *Little House* has a bigger audience today than when it first aired.

CHAPTER TWENTY-SIX

Walnut Grove Comes to Life

We established our offices at Paramount Studios and set up our organizational structure. Michael hired John Hawkins as producer and story editor. We worked with him on *Bonanza*. Mike and Ed Friendly were the executive producers, and Bill Claxton, who also worked on many *Bonanzas* and *High Chaparrals*, was a producer/director. He would produce the shows he directed. I was named associate producer and production manager.

Once that was done, we prepared full-scale for actual production. We needed to find a location for Walnut Grove. Miles Middough mentioned a place he knew that *Gunsmoke* used in Simi Valley. Michael, Teddy Voigtlander, art director Trevor Williams and I visited the site and laid out the town in a way we thought would benefit the show. Next, we started the construction of Walnut Grove and its members.

The townspeople had to be cast. This ensemble included Kevin Hagen as Doc Baker; Dabbs Greer as Reverend Alden; Katherine MacGregor as Harriet Oleson; Richard Bull as Nels Oleson; Alison Arngrim as Nellie Oleson; Jonathan Gilbert as Willie Oleson; and Karl Swenson as Lars Hanson. Karl, incidentally, was from Connecticut and happened to be friends of my parents.

While the casting fell into place, we built the town. We needed water for a stream that ran the water wheel that in turn made the saw mill work. It all had to be arranged with Trevor Williams. His crew worked hard to get everything ready. We also had to build Little House and the barn and a stream by the house for those locations to be ready to shoot. It was a big job.

We needed water for the streams and Michael was firm about having green grass around some of the sets. I heard about a company in Bakersfield called Rain for Rent which had an auxiliary office near us at Santa Paula. I asked them about putting in an irrigation system. They were known for supplying irrigation systems for farmers during the agricultural boom that was going on in the Valley at that time. They agreed to look at the job.

In the meantime, I made arrangements with the City of Simi Valley to allow us to tie in to a water main. Of course, it would be metered but at a commercial rate which was better than a residential rate. We tapped into a water main off Tapo Canyon and laid pipe and auxiliary pumps to get the water into the location, which was about a mile away.

We used four-inch water pipes for irrigation. I hired a man to install all the pipes and green grass and to fill the streams and all of the work associated with that. We had a lot to do to complete the projects. We actually started shooting in June 1974. Our NBC commitment for the first year was twenty-two shows, and that was expanded to twenty-four because the show started off doing very well.

During this time, there was somewhat of a rift between Ed Friendly and Michael Landon. They didn't see eye-to-eye. I was caught in the middle trying to keep peace, letting each person know what was going on, and trying to solve problems between the two of them. It became quite hectic. They were at odds with one another and argued half the time. It was not a happy work atmosphere. Michael finally went to NBC and said, "This isn't going to work. One of us has to go because we can't work with all this friction."

NBC knew Michael. They needed Michael because he was the star of the show, so they sided with him. Fortunately, NBC's contracts included a clause that said, "NBC has creative control," which meant they could make the final decision. I was told it was decided that Mr. Friendly would receive all his payments for every show that was produced and get an office at Goldwyn Studios with a secretary. He would get a copy of all the information regarding production, but he would not be allowed on the set while we were shooting. It was an unfortunate situation, but it had to be done.

The show did very well in the ratings, a complete success. In fact, it was such a success that we knew they would pick up the show for another year. It was never in doubt. In the early years, they gave us an early pick-up, which meant we started getting scripts ahead of time and kept production rolling.

By the start of the second year, I had eighteen scripts laid out on a production board before we started the shooting year. We saved a lot of money because we had time to really prepare. That gave us flexibility in shooting locations.

We went back to Sonora many times because we liked the high country. It gave us a different look for the Walnut Grove area and it had streams. Sonora became our second home. I can't remember how many shows we did there but there were quite a few.

Mike was a gem to work with because he had vision. He knew what he wanted and he was sharp. When Mike wrote a script, he knew what it was going to look like on the air. He envisioned his ideas. His imagination was incredible and he was clever. Very clever. In what seemed like little effort, he sat down and wrote a 54-page script in a day-and-a-half. He wrote left-handed in long-hand and his poor secretary had to decipher it, but she did. Mike knew how to get things filmed with the least effort. He knew the camera well enough to know, "If I put it here and we shoot this way, I can get my close-ups without having to move everything over there."

That's why he loved Buzzy Boggs. Buzzy was so clever in what he knew and how he thought. He worked effortlessly because if we lit a scene, he asked what Mike's next set up was going to be. If he lit a full shot and he knew the next shot was a close up of two people, Buzzy lit that scene at the same time. He just had to tweak the light this way or that way, but he didn't have to start all over. Buzzy always thought ahead. He told Mike, "If you come over here you get this, and if you go over there, you get that." He had an eye for what was going to be on the screen. Mike loved him for it and for keeping production going.

Working film shows was different than working live television because in live television, actors arrived, went to their dressing rooms, did their routine and left. There wasn't really time to spend with them. On a film set, however, actors sat for twenty minutes to an hour between scenes doing nothing, so we had time to talk and to get to know each other.

With Michael, over time a bond grew. He realized I knew my job. I told him what was going on and I never gave him stories or told him things that weren't true. If we were financially heavy on a show, I let him know. If I asked someone to grow a beard, it was for a purpose. I didn't make requests without a purpose; I didn't shoot off my mouth just to shoot off my mouth. Once we got on *Little House* Mike and I became closer. We never had a stand-off ending with him saying, "I'm the star." It was never that.

When we shot in Sonora, we were subject to bad weather. If it rained, I went to the office at three o'clock in the morning and laid out three different schedules for Mike to review. I tried to keep the trucks on paved roads because the dirt ones turned to mud quickly. By five o'clock in the morning, I called Mike to review the options I set up for him. He picked the one he thought was best.

I always thought of Mike and the show. Mike respected me for that. He looked at the production board with me. By the end of the day, he'd say, "We got more done today than what we had scheduled." It was true because he loved the challenge.

CHAPTER TWENTY-SEVEN

Casting the Casting Director

While lots of changes in shows and projects happened in my world, Susan took off in a very successful field of her own. She tells it like this:

As secretary/receptionist for Bonanza *and* Chaparral, *I met all the agents and got to know casting and casting secretarial duties very well. I was fascinated and thought, "This is a very interesting job, meeting all these people and creating in my mind who would be best for the roles." I would read all the scripts. When our casting secretary left for another job, Kent came to me and said, "You know so much about this job, it's just obvious that you take it and work on both shows for Milt Hamerman," who was the casting director. I said, "If you feel that I can do it." He said, "Yes, I think you can do it."*

He was right. All the agents knew me. I had no problem. It was very easy. I knew how to type up all the cast lists. I knew how to get people to wardrobe. I knew how to do make-up and hair calls. I knew how to call the actors or the agents and how to get the scripts to them. I knew how to bring the actors in and how to mark a script so they knew the right scene. It became second nature to me.

When Chaparral *was canceled, I continued on* Bonanza. *They brought in a new casting director and that person had his own secretary. I had to find something else. I was asked to start at*

Samuel Goldwyn Studios as Assistant to the Assistant General Manager of the studio, where I helped rent office and stage space for new shows. I wanted to get back in production again, so I left that position and worked for Quinn Martin whose production company had its own building on the Goldwyn lot. At Quinn Martin, I worked on Streets of San Francisco.[111] *Then, I went to Fox for the pilot of* Movin' On[112] *with Frank Converse and Claude Akins.*

I got a job working at Paramount as an assistant to two casting directors. We were doing Laverne & Shirley,[113] Happy Days,[114] The Odd Couple,[115] Mannix,[116] *all of those shows plus some other pilots and movies-of-the-week. My bosses, Pat Harris and Marsha Kleinman, were overwhelmed with the volume of work and they gave me shows to cast on my own.*

While I was working there, I met Sylvia Gold with the ICM Agency. Later, she became the head of Warner Brothers casting. She asked me if I would be interested in working on Kung Fu[117] *and a new series called* The New Land[118] *at Warner Brothers. It was with Bonnie Bedelia. I said, "Absolutely!" So I went over there. I was called back to Paramount by Harris and Kleinman to work with them again.*

When NBC agreed to do the pilot for *Little House*, they had approval of all the cast choices. We had no casting director per se other than the casting department that NBC had. That's how the pilot was set. When we started the show, a man at NBC called one of his friends to become the casting director for us, but there were problems. Michael didn't like him and I didn't like him. He was wishy-washy. Couldn't make up his mind. At the start of the second year, Michael said, "We have to make a change."

In the meantime, Susan worked for an independent casting agency run by two ladies. They were very good casting people. NBC contacted them to see if they were interested in doing *Little House*. The two women said to Susan, "If we get this show, we'll let you cover it." Susan told me that and I went to Michael, who hadn't made up his mind yet. I told him, "Listen, these women are going to have Susan cover the show if they get chosen." He said, "That'll be good." I said, "Wait a minute. If we're going to pay them to have Susan do it, why don't we just hire Susan?" He said, "I think that's a great idea."

By then, it was well known that Susan and I were seeing each other. I said, "I don't want to be the one who suggests this." I told Michael, "You're going to have to call NBC and suggest it." He called NBC and said we were going to let Susan do the show. That's how we hired her to do *Little House* from season two on.

Susan continues the story:

I was at home in my apartment and I got a phone call one morning from Kent who said, "Pack up your paper clips, you're coming over here." I said, "You must be joking!" He said, "No, Mike and I have been talking and he went over to NBC and told them he wanted you. They all decided we're going to hire you on a trial basis to see if you can do this without any assistance." I said, "My God!" Then he said, "You can't tell the women you work for until NBC has a chance to tell them that they're choosing you and not them. Don't let on until we do that."

Talk about an Academy award-winning performance. I walked in to work and the two women were odd with me, distant. "Oh, God, maybe they know," I thought. I had to play "Mickey the Dunce." Marsha looked at Pat; Pat looked at Marsha and said, "My God, she really doesn't know." I said, "Know what?" "They want you, not us." I said, "That's ridiculous! You must be joking. Why would they want me? I've never done anything on my own." Marsha said, "That's what I thought, too, but they want you." I said, "What can I say? Nobody's called me."

Do you know that when I packed up my things to go over to the new office at Little House, *they insisted that I be the one to hire someone to take my place? Until I found that person, I had to do all the work for them as well as* Little House. *I agreed and told Kent, who said, "They're full of it." I said, "Well, that's what's happening." I found someone who actually became a very successful casting director.*

I began making a list of suggestions for the first show I was to cast for Little House. *That weekend, I was to go to Las Vegas. Before I left on Friday, I left my list of suggestions with Michael. Before I walked out the door, I heard Mike say something under his breath while looking over my suggestions. "God we went from the frying pan into the fire. He's looking at the list."*

I had the worst weekend of my life in Las Vegas because I thought, "I'm dead. I'm going to be gone." I came back and everything was fine. There was no problem. I went ahead and cast, and the great thing was that I knew all these agents for a long time since being a secretary and receptionist. They were very helpful to me and wanted to be there for me. They were, and I appreciated it very much. I tried to make the fairest deals I could. They knew I was very honest. I was not trying to cheat them.

Who's good for this part? Who's good for that part? Susan said there was on-the-nose casting and offbeat casting. On-the-nose was exactly what it said in the script. Offbeat casting was choosing somebody who was going to give the role a different flair. She always brought in both.

In those days the actors' agent brought in photos and she had big stacks to go through. She sorted them by look and called in the ones she thought fit the role. She not only worked with Michael, but she also worked with other episode directors like Bill Claxton, Victor French, Leo Penn, Joe Pevney, a lot of good directors. They all had their opinion and she had hers and it was a matter of reading who was right for the part. Susan couldn't have been better. She did a hell of a job all through the years. In fact, such a tremendous job that many of the actors became regular cast members, like Stan Ivar, Pam Roylance, Moses Gunn, Matthew Laborteaux, Jason Bateman, Steve Tracy, Alison Balson, Missy Francis, Ketty Lester, Linwood Boomer, Robert Casper, Merlin

Olsen, Hersha Parady, Shannon Doherty, Dean Butler, Lucy Lee Flippin, Sherri Stoner and the Turnbaugh twins.

CHAPTER TWENTY-EIGHT

Prairie Companions

I already described how Michael got into writing and directing on *Bonanza,* and those skills just exploded on *Little House.* Mike was a genius. No two ways about it. He had the knack to do good work and to touch people. He loved doing stories that made an impact on people. We all cried when we read the scripts. We cried at watching the dailies. We cried at the rough cut. We couldn't help it. We all said we should have bought stock in Kleenex.

Michael's daughter Leslie Landon Matthews says this about her father's stories:

He definitely knew how to move the human heart. It's kind of nice because my dad had no problems showing his emotions. Tears could be for happiness. Tears could be because...he was proud of you...Tears could be for sadness. It's funny when I would hear people say, "Gosh, I've never seen my dad cry." I'm thinking to myself, "Wow, I see my dad cry all the time." It didn't mean it was for something sad. It could be tears of joy. He felt things one-hundred percent.

A lot of his stories came from his own life. For example, he had to put his adopted daughter in a rehabilitation center for six months without seeing her. They said, "She's here, but you can have no contact with her for six months." He did the same thing to Mary Ingalls when she went blind. As Charles Ingalls, he took her to the school for the blind and left without saying good-bye.[119]

That was in his heart. He was able to transform it into a good story that made sense. It touched a lot of people.

"The Lord is My Shepherd"[120] was a great episode. It starred Ernest Borgnine as a kind of mystical mountain man who helped Laura when she ran away. She was jealous of her newborn brother, who died shortly thereafter. Laura journeyed up a mountain to get closer to God and to ask Him to take her and return her brother. Michael and Victor French took off to look for her. The innocence of a young child and her attempt to make something right that she felt was her fault. It was a great show, one of my favorites.

Mike touched a lot of people in real life, too. He wanted to help everybody. If one of the guys got sick he asked, "Do you want a doctor? I'll bring a doctor in here for you." He would, too.

He hosted the Michael Landon Celebrity Tennis Tournament in Tucson for more than a decade. It was a weekend in which several actors came over to play with local folks. They had a big private tent for the celebrities to rest, get a drink or lie down to get out of the heat. Not Mike. He sat in the photo booth and had his picture taken with anybody who walked in. They paid for it, but he sat there for hours. People said, "Come on, Mike, let's get out of here." Mike answered, "They paid to get in here and I'm staying for them."

He also did a great many things for the Make a Wish program. He saw a young girl on the set one day and gave her a ride on a golf cart and showed her around. He took her up to the office and got pictures for her. He learned she was terminal with cancer.

Mike flew back East over a weekend to visit her. She wouldn't eat, but he got her to take a few bites. He put her in his lap and gave her a ride in a wheelchair up and down the corridors. He made her laugh. Then he asked her, "What's something you really want to do?" She said, "I'd really like to taste a beer."

She was about thirteen years old, maybe younger. Mike said, "You want a beer?" He turned to the nurse. "Get her a beer." The nurse said, "I can't do that." He said, "Honey, what's the difference?" The nurse got her a beer. The girl took two sips and that was it. But she had her beer.

Michael was in Honolulu on vacation when our office secretary received word that the young girl passed away. Susan and I sent flowers to the service with his name on them. Michael had more love in him for people than anyone I've ever known.

Leslie Landon Matthews agrees:

It's funny, my dad's been gone a long time and every so often, I'll either talk to somebody or run into somebody...who was either on the set or they knew someone that had been on the set of my dad's. It's always the same story: "People wanted to be on your dad's crew or on your dad's set" and how well he treated them and, "You just don't find that anymore," and "It's very rare to find an environment like what your dad created on the set."

Prop master Dean Wilson[121] explains the set's atmosphere.

It was really a fun place to work. Kent was full of gags...When we were not working, when we were sitting around waiting for the set to be lit, Michael always had jokes to tell and stories to tell about the Bonanza *days. It was fun to go to work. Kent ran a good ship. He had people who knew what they were doing and I felt honored just because he thought that I knew what I was doing.*

We never had production meetings, and most shows had production meetings. They were up to their ear lobes in meetings. We never had 'em. Everybody was supposed to know what they were doing and I didn't have to worry about taking my props and showing them to Michael because he trusted me to have the right stuff, and it seemed like I always did...It was a good relationship between all of us. We sailed along and everything clicked, everything worked well. I mean there weren't any unhappy people on the set. There wasn't any torment or anybody being jealous.

Dolly grip Clarence Tindell[122] worked closely with Mike and me:

We didn't work a lot of long hours. After a time, everybody on the crew got a forty hour base pay and then we got twenty hours guaranteed overtime. It's called a 40/20. It was very, very generous...Michael wrote the scripts and we didn't have to shoot anything we didn't need...

Brad Yacobian,[123] the current unit production manager for the television series *Scandal,* came on the set as a pretty new guy to the business:

... They were so open, especially Kent. "Do you want to learn this? Let me show you this, let me show you that." I soaked it all up but not all companies are like that and not all people are like that as far as bringing somebody young in and wanting to show them everything and help them out....Kent taught communication, being up front, facing a situation head-on, getting involved with the crew so you're there for them in whatever you can do to make things easier for them, but also keeping things moving and firm...

John Musselman[124] worked in Crafts Services.

We were doing the pilot of Little House, *and Michael took a second unit, which was just a few people, to get the shots he wanted to do. Then he came back and we didn't have Little House finished. So everybody pitched in. Everybody got a hammer in his hand, the make-up man, the wardrobe guys, everybody, and that was just the beginning of the things I can remember. Everybody. And Kent would be the first one.*

Mike would change the script now and again so you wouldn't know what to expect. If the special effects guy had a lot of work, we would all get together and help him. We did that house. We put the roof on that house in about three hours. I thought that was pretty amazing because I'd never seen that done before with all the others helping....

I never run a mile in my life, but I would run twenty miles to work on Little House. *No one will ever know how much I enjoyed working there. Nobody in the sixteen years that we did* Little House on the Prairie *and* Highway to Heaven *ever left. Does that tell you something? Sixteen years is a long time in the television business. It was all Kent because he took care of the crew.*

Vern Leyk[125] was in transportation:

We'd have the last big party after the series was over at the end of the year. Michael would always say, "Okay, my family, we'll see you next year when we start up again." We were considered his family. Kent was in that. He was involved in that. He was part of it.

Clarence Tindell continues:

They would get two or three buses and fill them up with all the crew and their families and take us out to the Santa Anita Race Track. We had a special Little House *section up there and we had a race named for us. Then when we got on the bus and came back to MGM, we'd pull in to Stage 15 and they would have Les Brown and his band playing. They'd have a giant bar set up, food everywhere. A full day of real partying. I never heard of anybody else doing something like that for the crew.*

Many times, NBC asked Mike to co-host the Rose Bowl Parade. In lieu of taking a salary, Mike had RCA donate TV sets, tape recorders and the like and then he would give them to the crew for Christmas.

The crew was generous to Michael and me, too. One Christmas during *Little House*, they gave me money to go to Mexico on vacation. They said, "You need to get out of here." I had no desire to go to Mexico. Michael liked to go to the Kahala Hilton in Hawaii. I decided to use the money the crew gave me to go there instead. I stayed at the Kahala Hilton, which is right on the ocean.

Every morning I got up and walked the golf course because I liked the exercise. One day I walked about a mile-and-a-half down to the store and bought a bottle of vodka. I walked back and ran into Mike in the lobby with three of the kids and his wife, Lynn. The family and some friends decided to fly over at the last minute. It was such a surprise because I didn't know they were coming.

From that time on, Mike said, "Come on. We're going to dinner." Sometimes I'd say, "Come on, it's my turn to buy." We shared all the dinner costs. I didn't sponge off Mike ever. I never wanted to do that or be thought of that way. During the day, he and I sat out by the pool and played cards.

Anyhow, at the end of my morning golf course walks, I had to pass Mike's cabanas. He always invited me in. "Come on and have some coffee and some breakfast." It was a very good relationship. It's hard to put into words how you can feel that close to somebody, but I did. I not only respected Mike, but I loved him dearly.

I also grew very close to Susan during *Little House*. She describes our early relationship.

When I began casting all those shows, my best friend Kent McCray and I would talk. I would call Kent at the end of a date to tell him how awful it was. That's the kind of friend he was. I'd say, "You won't believe this guy. He came over at 6:30 and wouldn't you think he'd want to take me out to dinner? Oh, no. I opened the door and he said, 'I've already eaten. Let's watch television.'"

Those kinds of dates. I'd call Kent and we'd laugh. You know, Kent and I had a very unusual relationship. It was certainly not romantic at the beginning at all. It was just girlfriend/boyfriend funny stories. If anybody tells a funny story better, I can't imagine because he just made me laugh.

I remember Kent saying to me once, "Maybe we should have some dinner and talk about this." I thought, "Yeah, we could do that." We went out.

We had a great deal in common. We had everybody in common. I grew up in the business. I lived it and I knew exactly what it was. He would work late; I'd work late. He'd get there early; I'd get there early—and understand why. And understand that when you got out late, you'd get a salad or a cup of soup or whatever. You couldn't have a big dinner. My office was just across the hall from his. If I had a problem, I'd go there to find an answer; if he had a problem, he'd come to me and say, "Is that actor available? How much is he going to cost?" Or whatever.

I'll never forget the first real date I had with Kent. He took me to dinner at a restaurant called Diamond Jim's. Diamond Jim's was in a building across from my apartment. It was a complex of three apartment buildings and one of the buildings had the restaurant on the first floor. Diamond Jim's was a very nice place.

He parked in the restaurant parking and we went inside. The restaurant was dark and it had leather booths with black and red décor. Very nice. Wonderful steaks. We started talking, and he held my hand. He leaned over and gave me a kiss. I thought, "Gosh, he's so sweet." Then, he said, "I'll walk you home," because it was just in the next building. I said, "Okay."

He took me home, walked me to the door, kissed me good-night and left to get his car. They had locked the parking lot. He thought to himself, as he told me later, "I'm not going to go back up there. I can't go back up there. She said, 'Good-night.'" He knocked at the door of the restaurant and somebody was there who apparently had the keys from the parking lot attendant. He tells the story better because I didn't live this part, but he said there was a woman who needed a ride home because she was locked out, too. So, he took her home. He did not come back upstairs. The next day at work, I asked, "Why didn't you come up?" "Oh, no, I couldn't do that. Harry wouldn't have liked that," he said.

We had a few dates after. We would go to dinner after work to a pizza place right down the block from where I lived. I'll never forget the first time I went in there with him. We sat in a booth and the guy came over to take the order and said, "And what will your dad have?" You have to understand, I felt really bad, but I started to laugh. To this day he remembers that with a smile.

We developed a close relationship for a long time. When it did become romantic, he had left his home and I said, "If you leave your home, don't come to mine because I don't want to be perceived as the reason you left." He found himself a little apartment. He never came over. We kept getting closer but it went on and on for a long time. He didn't want his children hurt; he didn't want to do the wrong thing.

CHAPTER TWENTY-NINE

Changes, New Productions & MGM

During the course of *Little House*, my dad passed away. A year later my mother passed away.[126] I was close to my parents, very close. It was a great, great loss. They both wanted to be cremated and their ashes spread in a rose garden at one of the mortuaries in town. They wanted a quiet burial. No big hoopla. I did what they wanted. I followed their wishes. As you can imagine by this time, actually way before this time, my dad was quite happy with my work. His original concern that people might think I got my job at NBC because of him had disappeared ages ago. My parents were always very proud of me. I miss them still.

Dad and Mother visiting with me on location

By 1976, Michael wrote a beautiful story that we produced, a movie-of-the-week called *The Loneliest Runner*.[127] This was a sort of life story of Michael's bed-wetting problem as a child. In real life, his mother hung the yellow-stained sheets out the window daily. As a teen, Michael ran home after school to remove them so people wouldn't see them and add to his shame.

Michael's character pursued running for his high school track team and eventually earned a spot on the U.S.A. Olympics track team. To get the flavor of an Olympic competition, Michael wanted to shoot at the Los Angeles Coliseum during half-time of a football game. Michael called the owner of the team, Carroll Rosenbloom, to see if that could be worked out. Rosenbloom was extremely receptive and supportive of the storyline and the shoot.

The Los Angeles Rams gave us permission to delay half-time for five minutes because that was all the time they could give us. Mr. Rosenbloom went to CBS for us because they were broadcasting the game and they had to agree to a five-minute delay, as well. We also got approval from the National Football League.

After all this was worked out, we filmed at the Coliseum all morning, doing shots that did not show the audience. Then during half-time, Michael ran out of the tunnel in his Olympic uniform. I bought a certain number of seats and filled them with our cast and crew members and their families. They waved American flags during Michael's run out of the tunnel to the finish line. It was quite an exciting show and it was well-received by the public.

Susan has a fun behind-the-scenes story about *Runner:*

I did the casting for Loneliest Runner. *There was one part left, a one-liner for a security guard at a department store where this boy slept through the night in the bedding department because he didn't want to go home. This was kind of a biographical story about Michael and it was just heart-wrenching. Anyhow, the boy was at this store and fell asleep. The guard's line was something like, "He slept in the store all night and he's all right. Come and get him."*

Michael was the kind of guy who would say to me, "If an actor needs insurance, we don't have to have him come in and read a one-liner for us. If he really needs it, just give it to him." I always did that. In this case, there was an actor who really needed it and I brought him in and talked to him. He said, "That's great. I really appreciate it." So, I hired him.

I went down to the stage, and in the rehearsal he delivered the line and milked it like crazy. "He...fell asleep in the store..." With the breathing and the delivery, it was like a John Wayne part for God's sake. He had one line! And I went, "Oh, my God."

I heard Mike say, "Can you just pick it up a little bit?" I cringed. Then they were rolling. One take, and there were two takes, three takes. Same thing. We went to dailies. I sat there and this man came on, "Sigh, breathing...." I started coughing through the whole thing. After dailies, we saw a rough cut. And it came to this guy. I saw him walk in and I started coughing again until he was done.

After the rough cut, we went to an answer print. An answer print is just before it's finished and the final answer print goes on the air. Again, the man came on and I started coughing until he was done. We went to a screening. The press were there. We were all sitting in the theater and this guy came on. I started coughing again through his whole dialogue.

Remember, this was like 1977 while we were doing Little House *off season.*

About ten years later, we were doing Highway to Heaven. *There was a small part needed. It was only one line. Mike said give it to whoever needs it. He started to walk out but stopped and said, "And do me a favor. Hire somebody you don't have to cough over."*

Ten years later! He never said a word before that. Never said anything. He hit me with it ten years later. I said, "You creep! You gotta be kidding me?" Then he started with that great laugh of his, that giggle. And he walked out. I couldn't believe it. "Try to hire somebody you don't have to cough over."

As production of *Little House* continued, Victor French became quite popular and was offered a show of his own called *Carter Country*.[128] He left and did that show for two years. This created a void because Michael always wanted a male counterpart to play off. NBC had a contract with former-football-player-turned-actor Merlin Olsen, and it was suggested that he might be suitable for a role on *Little House*.

Merlin met with Michael. They had a good rapport and Michael had a good feeling about Merlin's ability and size. Merlin Olsen was one wonderful person. He had a hand that would dwarf anybody's. Merlin was hired and Mike wrote a character for him named Jonathan Garvey. Jonathan had a family, including a wife played by Hersha Parady, and a son who was portrayed by Patrick Laborteaux. The Garvey family moved into a house outside Walnut Grove.

One particular show of note we shot in Sonora. There was a house that location manager Ernie Durham called me about. He said the owner wanted to tear it down. Ernie suggested we shoot it as it was getting destroyed. Mike wrote a show about Jonathan Garvey and Charles Ingalls who took a job putting up telephone poles.[129] All the men who were part of this crew lived in the house that was going to be destroyed. The cook was played by Ted Gehring. Unbeknownst to everybody, Ted's character skimmed the supplies and took the potatoes down to the basement where he had a still to make moonshine. While the men were out, the house blew up due to the still, and that's how Michael wrote the house into the story. It worked out to be quite an exciting show for us all.

After two years of *Carter Country*, Victor was available and Mike thought we should bring him back because Mr. Edwards was quite popular. I asked him, "What are you going to do with Jonathan Garvey? Now, there are three of you." Mike said,

"There's no problem. I'll write a show for Merlin Olsen. He'll have his own series."

Before that happened, we had more changes.

In October 1978, our producer John Hawkins passed away. Susan describes what happened next:

Kent thought to be a producer you had to be a good writer. I always said to him, "I'm sorry. I don't agree with you. That's why you hire writers. That's why you hire supervising writers. That's why you have a writing staff." I told him so many times he would be, that he is, a great producer and just because he doesn't have the title, he's already doing everything.

When that job became available and we were on location up in Sonora, I would have breakfast every morning with Lynn, Mike's wife. I said to her, "I don't understand why Michael doesn't ask Kent if he wants to be producer." She said, "I think it's because Mike doesn't think he wants to be." I said, "Well, let me tell you, he would never ask Mike. Never. It would never occur to Kent to ask him anything. If Mike felt he wanted him, that's another story. But Kent would never ask him. He's not that kind of person." Lynn said, "That's ridiculous."

The next day, Mike took Kent away from the set and asked, "How would you like to be producer on the show?" It just floored him. He came back to the room and said, "You'll never believe what happened today. I'm so happy." I said, "What happened?" "Mike asked me if I wanted to be producer of Little House.*" I said, "Well, thank God! You should be!" Kent said, "I can't believe it. I don't know how that happened." I always had Kent's back.*

I give credit to Susan. If Susan hadn't talked to Lynn, I might never have become a producer. I was always an associate producer, but a full producer credit I never had until that moment. I was actually happy doing what I was doing, and when I got the producer's credit, my work didn't change. I was still doing the same job but I had a little more clout working with the crew.

More changes.

Around the middle of *Little House's* run, we lost our lease with Paramount, a flashback to when we had to move away from that studio while doing *Bonanza* and *High Chaparral.* NBC put *Little House* out for syndication bids and Paramount gave them a bid. NBC went back to the studio and said, "Your bid is one of the lowest. Do you want to change it before we make a decision?" They said, "No, you take our bid the way it is or you don't have a place to shoot." They were kind of blackmailing NBC into a deal and NBC didn't like it. They said, "If you don't want us to do the show at your site, then we'll move someplace else."

Fenton Coe, Dick Larson and I went to MGM Studios, looked around and made a deal. We started shooting at MGM the following season, the beginning of Season 6. I hired a grip crew to take down the sets, load them on a truck and move them out to MGM. Within a few weeks, we had all new sets on Stage 15.

Stage 15 at MGM is the largest stage in Hollywood. It's about three-hundred-ten feet long, I believe, and over a hundred feet wide.[130] It was a huge stage and we placed all our sets there, which made it a lot easier. We had dressing rooms and I even had a department that made our own wardrobe. It was a great place to work.

Stage 15 is also historic. MGM shot a great deal of *The Wizard of Oz* on that stage, and there were still yellow bricks on the walls where they painted the yellow brick road in perspective. During the War, this stage was used to film the movie *Thirty Seconds Over Tokyo*[131] with Spencer Tracy. It had a lot of shots on top of an aircraft carrier. They built the aircraft carrier on stage and actually had planes taxiing down the runway on stage. Then, they cut to stock films for the take-off. But it was all done on this stage. It was so interesting. Quite a lot of history. We all enjoyed working there.

CHAPTER THIRTY

Killing Stone & Father Murphy

Another movie-of-the-week that we did during the *Little House* off-season was called *Killing Stone*[132] with Gil Gerard. In this story, Gerard's character was falsely accused and convicted of a crime. He spent more than a decade in prison before being released. Once out, he was offered a job to write about how the world had changed, having missed all those years during his jail time.

We shot a lot of that show in Arizona at Florence Sharp's ranch. Mrs. Sharp's ranch was near Patagonia. If you've ever seen John Wayne's movie *McClintock,* you've seen the house. It was used in a lot of other shows, too. What a great, great homestead from the late 1800s. A three-story house with a basement and a porch on three sides. All the beams in the house were brought down the Colorado River to Yuma, and then by mule train to Patagonia where the house was built. They made all the bricks right there on site.

Mrs. Sharp, who lived there for many years, took me on a tour. In the basement, the beams were worn at the gun ports by rifles fired at Indians and Mexicans and other intruders who tried to raid the homestead. Mrs. Sharp was a character and she had many stories to tell about the history there. The Mexican border was actually visible from her house.

We also shot scenes of *Killing Stone* at Folsom Prison. Mike, cinematographer Teddy Voigtlander, location manager John Warren and I went there to check out the facility.

The assistant warden showed us around. Mike wanted to go inside one of the towers to look over the prison's big exercise yard. We were on the exterior of the wall and the assistant warden called up to the tower to say Mike was coming up. Only one person was allowed to go. They dropped the key down on a rope and the assistant warden opened the door. Michael went up the stairs to the last part of the climb, which was a ladder going into the tower. As Mike recalled, he went up the ladder and entered the tower to find a guard with a shotgun pointed right at him. Mike said he stood back, and the guard told him, "They said you were coming up, but we have to be careful that something bad hasn't happened." We shot scenes from that tower later.

I was in a different tower when we shot other scenes in which I had to cue vehicles coming down the road. The guard who was with me said he and the other guards sat up there for eight hour shifts. I asked, "What do you do at night? You're up here in the dark. You have no radio, no books. You have a small toilet over in the corner. How do you keep yourself awake?"

They had a high chair that was built so the guards had a clear view of things through the windows even while sitting down. The guard said, "I hang a tin cup off my little finger, and if that tin cup hits the cement floor, it makes enough noise to wake me if I doze."

Each day on site, we had to undergo a search on our way into the facility. We went through the first gate and the guards used mirrors and other equipment underneath our vehicles to ensure there were no weapons, people or contraband brought in. Every vehicle that entered the prison was searched this way. They stopped us at another gate and finally we were allowed in.

If a vendor truck entered, the guards searched it and one of the guards went with the driver while the driver took care of his business. When the driver finished, the truck came back to the inner gate and the guard got out. Using hand signals, the guard verified to the tower guards that everything was okay. If it wasn't okay, the guard had other hand signals to alert the tower guard that something was wrong.

Our crew wasn't allowed to wear dungarees because that was the basic prisoner uniform. I forget what we wore, but the wardrobe people got us all new clothes so we weren't mistaken for prisoners. We also signed in everyday and the guards checked our drivers' licenses to make sure we were who we were supposed to be.

It was such a different work environment and such an unusual mindset that I found it interesting. We shot there for two days. I enjoyed working with the people who ran Folsom, but it was surely not a place I wanted to be long term.

When *Little House* production started up again in 1981, Victor French returned as Mr. Edwards and Michael followed through with his promise to create a series for Merlin Olsen. In *Father Murphy*,[133] Merlin played the part of a priest who ran an orphanage school for boys and girls out West. His co-stars were Moses Gunn and Katherine Cannon. Father Murphy also ran a freight line business, a wagon pulled by a team of six mules. The pilot was shot in Tucson.

When we did the pilot for *Father Murphy*, we had an actor by the name of Burr DeBenning who played the saloon owner. We knew Burr for years. He did *Bonanzas* and *Little House* and Mike liked him. However, he was killed off in the pilot.

Mike was sitting in the office with Susan and me one day. Susan said, "Boy, I think Burr DeBenning is real sorry he can't be with you on the series." Mike said, "I love Burr DeBenning. We're going to use him." Susan said, "How are you going to use him? He was killed off in the pilot." Mike said, "We didn't kill his twin brother!"

Susan called Burr and said, "Burr, guess what? You have a part in *Father Murphy*." He said, "I can't. I was killed off." Susan repeated the line, "You were, but your twin brother wasn't." He did the show for two years. That's what happened if Mike loved you. He loved Dub Taylor. How can you not love Dub Taylor? He loved Jack Elam. He also loved Strother Martin. Great characters!

We also had seventeen regular kids on *Father Murphy*. Susan cast all of them. My job was to deal with them after that. On the weekends I got calls from the mothers. "So-and-so is picking on my child." "Yeah, what do you want me to do about it? If these kids went to public school, who would you call? Would you call a principal to make them stop? I'm not a principal."

Every now and then I got all the kids in a room and said, "You, you and you are troublemakers. Either stop making trouble or your contract won't get picked up. Either work with us the way we want or you'll be gone." That would straighten them out for a while. They were old enough to understand and they relayed the message back to their mothers. Then the mothers called and said, "What do you mean my son will be gone?" I said, "Because he's making trouble. We can't put up with this nonsense."

We had two stages for *Father Murphy*. Different sets were on different stages. I made the mothers stay on the stage where we *weren't* shooting. In fact, mothers weren't allowed to be on the stage with the kids. I did it because the mothers were bigger pains in the ass than the kids. Always complaining: "My son this." "My daughter that." "She has a bigger part than my daughter." After I heard, "He has an intricate part in the show. He's been established," I usually came up with something. "Really? I'm sorry but I just read he had an incurable disease." There's always a way and you had to do what you had to do.

The show went on for two years and was cancelled. Later on, Brandon Tartikoff told me *Father Murphy* was a good show and it deserved a better time slot. We were on against *60 Minutes*. It *was* a good show.

CHAPTER THIRTY-ONE

Little House with a New Perspective

After eight years on *Little House*, Mike felt the story line should shift. He wanted it to center on Laura's marriage. He planned to make appearances on camera, like a recurring character, but the final year of *Little House* was basically focused on the story of Laura and her life with Almanzo as they raised their family.

Almanzo was played by Dean Butler,[134] who came on the show in season six. Dean is now producer of *Feherty*[135] for NBC's Golf Channel and for Legacy Documentaries,[136] where he has produced two original documentaries about *Little House on the Prairie* (the books) as well as several hours of extra content for the television series DVD collection. He shares the show's impact on his life:

Little House on the Prairie *has touched every professional experience I've had in my life since I did it and that's an amazing thing. I feel very fortunate for what* Little House *was and what it meant to people and what it meant to all of us who did it. I feel really lucky that I have a connection in my life to this amazingly beautiful and beloved piece of television that just goes on and on and on and on. So, I'm really lucky I was cast back in 1979. I feel very fortunate that it has continued to bless me for all those years since.*

It was obvious to me going into the situation that Michael was an iconic figure in television. At that time, he was one of the biggest television stars in the world and he had been for over twenty years...His executive officer, that's maybe the best way to describe Kent...was just masterfully able to execute Michael's vision seamlessly and logistically put it together so that everything worked exactly the way they wanted it to.

I never, over the five years I worked in the company, I never for a moment had a thought that everything wasn't going exactly the way they thought it was going to go. I never saw a moment's hesitation, doubt, anxiety, stress in anybody's face. Never, never once. It just all worked perfectly all the time. They really were like two great jazz musicians working together in so many ways because schedules didn't always work out perfectly, but their improvisations on schedules and scenes and so forth made it feel seamless and perfect. "Okay, we're not doing this, but here's Plan B." And, oh my God, Plan B was as good or better than Plan A was!

We also brought in Stan Ivar[137] to play a character named John Carter, and Pamela Roylance who played his wife.

Stan shares memories of his time on *Little House*:

I was working with Michael because he was directing. The first show I was just nervous as anything. I remember the first scene. It was out there at Simi Valley in front of the Little House, and we were all four—Michael Landon, myself, Pam Roylance and Melissa Gilbert—standing there. This is when the Carters were coming to take over the house...I just kept flubbing one of my lines and Michael said, "Cut."

He led me behind the Little House and said, "What's wrong?" I said, "I'm just nervous. It's Little Joe. It's Half-Pint. It's all this stuff." He said, "Don't worry about it. I'll never let you look bad, believe me. Let's just go out and have some fun and do it." That was it. He took the pressure off and after that there really wasn't that kind of pressure, the nervous pressure. Just the regular "Do your job" pressure like anybody has when you're doing an acting job....

The show played out and we completed two[138] of the three *Little House* movies-of-the week that NBC wanted. I was in my office working with my construction foreman because we had to take down all the sets for *Little House*. That was an agreement I had with Newhall Land and Investment Company, the people who owned the property. They used the area for cattle and they were afraid that if the cattle got into the buildings, they would get hurt. Also we had to take out the streams and all the piping to fulfill our promise to put the land back to its original state.

While I was going over all these details, Michael walked in and asked, "What are you doing?" I told him. We finished the conversation and I went on to something else. About twenty minutes later, Mike came back in and said, "I have an idea. We're going to blow up the town." I said, "What?" He said, "Yeah, the story will be about a land baron who's taking over the land of Walnut Grove. However, he doesn't own the buildings that are in the town. The people won't let him have them because Walnut Grove would never be the same." That's the gist of the story Michael wrote.[139]

We blew up the town bit by bit.

Prior to shooting these scenes, we had to do a few tests. First, we had to know how strong the explosive charges were so we knew how close our crew and cameras could set up to capture the action and still be safe. In fact, we had to build camera barricades for protection. They had a solid front with a hole for the camera lens to see out. They also had a roof and sides to protect the people and the cameras.

We used the Garvey house as a test. Our special effects man Luke Tillman set the explosives and detonated the charge. We came to find out our barricades were too close when they fell apart. We also came to find out the wagon we set up with a water supply had a hose so full of holes, it was useless.

We made the necessary adjustments and moved forward with our plan to blow up the town. I had to coordinate all this with the local emergency agencies so they didn't think the explosions were some sort of attack or accident. Plus, we had the fire department on site, which was a good thing as well. We agreed upon a specific date so everyone was ready and on site.

When the date arrived, we had five cameras running to catch all the action. I can't remember what order we blew up the buildings, but I do know that when it was the saw mill's turn, it broke my heart. Watching the water wheel fall from its perch made me sad. It had been the central part of the town's set, the thing that brought everyone together in Walnut Grove. Eventually, they all were blown up: the feed mill, Doc Baker's office, Nellie's restaurant and Olesen's store, the blacksmith's and the post office.

We never blew up the church and we never blew up Little House. It was a very sad day for all of us. Michael and I started to cry. It was a very emotional day. You have to realize we spent ten years of our lives almost every day out there. The set had a great meaning to us all, but it's something that had to be done.

Stan Ivar continues the story:

I asked Michael, "What are you going to do with the Little House?" He said, "Why, do you want it?" I said, "Sure," Michael said, "You can have the Little House. Just take it apart, but you gotta promise me you're not going to use it for any advertising-type thing or anything like that or any business-type of thing." I said, "No, I'm not going to use it for anything." I was thinking about just putting it on my place.

I got some cowboy friends of mine and we took it down. It was built like a set and we took it down wall by wall. I had it on a flatbed trailer for a long time and brought it to my property. At one time, we got to talking, Kent and Susan and myself along with Melissa Gilbert as well, and we wound up talking to Jesse Ventura, who was then Governor of Minnesota. What we wanted to do, we wanted to donate the Little House to Walnut Grove in Minnesota. They were considering putting up a little park, a little place representing Little House.

...I still have the Little House here and it's rotting away and nothing's probably going to become of it. It's been outside so long now and I'm not saying it couldn't be refurbished...but that's where that sits....

During the following year of 1984, we did a feature called *Sam's Son*,[140] based again on Michael's life. It's a story about Michael's belief growing up that he drew his strength to throw the javelin in track and field from his long hair, like Samson in the Bible. Eli Wallach played his father and Anne Jackson, Eli's real-life wife, played the mother. It was a lot of fun working with both of them. We shot most of it in South Pasadena and in and around Los Angeles.

CHAPTER THIRTY-TWO

Tales from the Prairie

FROM KENT McCRAY

Michael was a jokester most of the time. He kept the set alive. Many times when he did a dialogue scene with the kids, he opened his mouth to reveal a big bug or a frog or something in there. Or he'd see a tarantula and let it walk up his arm. He teased Melissa Gilbert all the time. It was one of his favorite things.

In a scene which required her to run, Mike told her, "Okay, start running." We rolled the camera, and she started running and running and running. He told her, "Keep going. Keep going." He cut the camera but kept her running. She went for a long way, turned around and said, "You *can't* be shooting this all on film." Everybody laughed--there was always a gag going on.

Hal Burton was Mike's double on the show. He also did stunt work including driving the wagons when it wasn't necessary for Mike to do it. Mike went to Hal one day and said, "You know, I've noticed you're eating a lot of breakfast in the mornings. You're going to get fat and then you're not going to look like me." Hal laughed and said, "Ah, no, that's not going to happen." Unbeknownst to Hal, Mike went to our wardrobe man, Andy Matyasi, and said, "Start taking in Hal's pants about a quarter of an inch a week." Andy had the wardrobe people make the alterations as requested. After about six weeks, Mike said Hal came to him and said, "You know, maybe you're right. I have to back off 'cause my pants are getting awful tight."

One Halloween we were on location in Sonora. Behind the hotels where we stayed was this old, old cemetery. I heard that the kids wanted to go up there on Halloween night. I ripped the sheet off my bed, went there ahead of them and hid behind a huge tombstone. As they came up the hill, I popped out and made loud moaning voices. Scared the shit out of them! They turned and ran down that hill so fast.

Prior to that, the kids went around knocking on everybody's hotel door to get candy. When they went to Michael's door he said, "Just a minute. Just a minute." He took a pair of his underpants and smeared them with peanut butter and he threw them in the candy bag. When they got back in their room, they were sorting the candy out. They pulled out the pants and said, "Oh, God. Ick!"

A lot of actors insisted on a special dressing room. A big plush motor home. Not Michael. He didn't want it. He said, "That's all B.S. Give me the last room in the 'honey wagon.'" That used to be a running gag with Susan when she was casting. An agent would ask, "What about my client's dressing room?" She replied, "I don't know really what they're doing. I don't get into that, but I'll guarantee you it'll be just like Michael Landon's!" "Really?" they asked. "Yes," Susan replied.

That put the actor next door to the last room in the "honey wagon." Mike's attitude was, "I'll change my clothes in the truck." He'd go into the prop truck and change his clothes rather than walk over to the dressing rooms which were sometimes further away because of the generator noise. He was not a pretentious man at all.

FROM SUSAN SUKMAN McCRAY

One day, I went to CBS to meet Jack Lord, who came in from Hawaii to meet me when I was chosen to cast the L.A. guests for *Hawaii Five-O*. I was casting *Little House* at the same time. I'll never forget when he walked in the door, he was in full make-up with that little curl he had on his forehead. I asked a co-worker near me, "Why is he in full make-up? We're not shooting anything." I was told, "That's the way Jack is." I said, "Oh, that's very interesting."

Jack was a very, I don't want to say difficult, a very unusual man. He was always in full make-up no matter what. You could go to his home and he would answer the door in full make-up. I think he did it himself. The interesting thing is that when he walked in he said, "Say hi to Michael for me." They had done *God's Little Acre*. I said, "I sure will." I went back to the *Little House* office. Mike asked, "How's Jack?" and I said, "Interesting." And I told him about the make-up and he laughed that great laugh. He said, "He's an odd-ball." I said, "No kidding."

FROM LESLIE LANDON MATTHEWS

(Talking about Season 9) I loved working on the set with my dad. I had done episodes of *Little House* prior to being a regular. As I said, the crew had been together for so long it was really like a home away from home. I've known Melissa since she was so young and it was always so comfortable being on the set. That was my dad's time to start branching off and thinking of new projects.

So, of course, when he got to actually act on the show or direct, that was so special. I'll always hold that dear to my heart.

FROM DEAN BUTLER

There's not a day that we're shooting when I don't think about Michael and Kent and our group and how we did what we did in those years. They have a huge influence on how I lead. They are the examples. They are the mentors that guide me in my thinking. "What would Michael do? What would Kent do?" are the rhetorical questions that come up again and again.

FROM STAN IVAR

Later (after *Little House* finished), Kent was a Regent with the Hartford University back in Connecticut, and so was Susan. They didn't like to fly and ended up driving back about three times a year. They asked me, "Do you want to go with us and share the driving?" Kent and I would drive two hours apiece. But that's when we really got to know one another was when we spent all those hours in their Suburban driving cross country....

I have to admit, as far as I'm concerned, they are my closest friends of anybody that I've got. I talk to them on the phone at least once a day or once every couple of days. I wish I had gotten to know him better when we did *Little House*....

FROM BRAD YACOBIAN (on production techniques)

(Michael and Kent) were doing things thirty years ago that we do now. Always having two cameras on an episodic TV show. Having one of the cameras be a steady-cam which is the more mobile unit that can move around. Kent and Michael had all that. They had that in the late 70's/early 80's and that's what we do now. Back then they had alternating directors of photography, so while one director of photography was shooting, the other one was up in the office prepping the next episode because you do one episode after another after another. They were doing that back then and we're doing that now.

FROM CLARENCE TINDELL

The late Ron Housiaux was the key grip and I was the dolly grip…We bought grip equipment and Kent and Mike rented it from us. The income helped put my kids through college. Thank you, again, Kent! He doesn't realize everything he did for my family.

My wife was diagnosed with MS. I came home right away from location. She was in a hyperbaric chamber every day for an hour and in the hospital for two or three weeks. I had to be home with the kids. A paycheck came every week. Every week I got my 40/20. Every week. Think about *that*. Tell me what other company would do that.

That's Kent, though. It went through Michael, too, but I kind of felt it was Kent because he signed all the paychecks…I told him how much I appreciated it. I let him know because I love the guy. I can't help it. He's like a big brother to me.

CHAPTER THIRTY-THREE

Introducing Susan Sukman McCray

Over a long time, Susan and I became friends. I can't give a
date, but I knew and she knew that we would be together. We
went out to dinner a lot. It was just a relief to have someone to
talk to, someone who knew what I was talking about. Susan and
I were in the same business. We discussed people we knew and
events that developed.

If I had a problem, I talked it through with her to see if I was
on the right track. Or she advised me in a different way, gave me
her opinion on things, which I liked. Not saying I always
followed it, but I never resented her input. I loved it. I needed it.
We all need someone to bounce things off. From my standpoint,
it is the greatest relationship I could ever have.

Susan's continues:

*My relationship with Kent went on and on and on for a long
time. Everybody thought I was a fool because they didn't think
he would marry again. I said, "There's hope for me. I know it."
And there was hope. But he never asked me to marry him. Ever.*

*We had a jeweler around the studios who would come by and
say, "This is from the Schultz estate and this is collected from
this estate." His name was Al and he was a very lovely man.
One day, he came by and said to me, "I found this ring. Isn't it
beautiful?" I looked at it. It was a wedding band. I thought,*

"God, this is gorgeous." It had all these different kinds of stones. I said, "Al, sit right there."

I went across the hall and I had the ring on my finger. I said, "Kent." He looked at me and said, "Yes?" "Look at this ring. Isn't it beautiful?" He said, "Yeah, it kind of looks like a wedding band." I said, "Isn't it beautiful." "Yeah. Are you trying to tell me something?" I said, "Oh, no. It's really beautiful and I'm thinking maybe I should get it." He said, "I'll get it for you." I said, "You will?" And he said, "Yeah." I said, "Does this mean we're engaged? He said, "Yeah." I said, "Oh, great!"

I went back and said, "Al, go see Kent. He's across the hall and he wants to buy the ring." Al said, "Oh, God, that's great." I said, "Yeah, it is great." About ten minutes later, Michael came up the stairs. He knew Kent and I were together for quite some time. I said, "Michael, you'll never believe this." He said, "What?" I stuck out my finger with the ring and he said, "Holy shit. Are you kidding me?" I said, "No." He said, "Oh, God, I'm so happy!" I said, "So am I!"

I thought to myself I better ask how long this engagement is going to be. Some time went by and I said, "I think it's time we decided what we're going to do here." He said, "I think what you need to do since this is a wedding band, is to have Al come in and see if he can make an engagement ring for you so you'll have both." I said, "That's a very good idea." So I did, and Al made an engagement ring.

Then I said, "How does January sound to you?" He said, "It's okay but there's Super Bowl weekend. I'm not going to miss the Super Bowl and all the people we're going to invite won't want to miss the Super Bowl." I said, "Heaven forbid! Let's pick a different weekend. We can go the weekend before or the weekend after."[141] "Okay," he said.

My kids came to the wedding. Susan asked Michael to walk her mother down the aisle. Her mom was thrilled. Her eyes beamed because everyone was looking at her. She was with Michael Landon! We had done *Little House* and we had just started *Highway*. Michael was still very popular. He was a handsome charmer. Oh, God, great hair.

Our wedding day

Susan talks about our wedding day so much better:

It was a beautiful wedding. We got married at the Bel-Air Hotel. Absolutely breathtaking. I planned it. I made it as lovely as I could. I dreamed of it as a young girl at twelve years old. I always said, "If I ever get married, Mom, I want to get married at the Bel-Air Hotel." It stuck in my head. So I did. And it was beautiful. All the guys who Kent was close to over the years at the studio became groomsmen. I had four gals as my bridesmaids, one of whom had been a friend since junior high. My dad walked me down the aisle and I thank God for that because the December after my wedding, he passed away. I'm always grateful he was there to give me away.

As Kent said, my mother walked down the aisle with Michael. Mike loved her. My mother Francesca was a pianist, organist and composer. If there was a script that had a church organist in a scene, they would always ask for my mother. Anyone playing an instrument on screen had to be a member of the musicians union. My mother was, so Mike and Kent would always ask for her. She appeared in Bonanza *and in* Little House *on the* Prairie *as a church organist. After her first appearance, they gave her a nickname—The Pump—since she was to play the pump organ. Mike would say, "Let's get The Pump!"*

When my mother became ill with ALS, Michael came to the house to visit her with big hugs and told her he loved her. It was incredibly special for all of us. Mike and I had a close friendship. We had things in common and would laugh about everything. He was truly a great best man at our wedding. After the first dance with Kent, then my father, Michael danced with me.

Through the years Susan and I have never had an argument. I think that speaks for itself. We've been married more than thirty years. Many said it wouldn't last. We grew out of a friendship, not a lust. I think more highly of her today than I did then maybe. Still very strong. I think she's a very creative person, she's a very loving person and she'll do anything for you. I've always felt that. I think she knows I would do the same for her. I think we've had a very good life together.

People asked, "How can you get up in the morning, get in the car and both drive in together, work all day in the same office, and drive home at night, even after you're married?" I answered, "What's wrong with that?" They asked, "Don't you want a break?" "No!" I loved it.

Susan always has my back. Completely. She's always there when I need her. Always. Still is. I wouldn't be here today if she wasn't like she is. I wouldn't want it to be any other way, and I love her just as much today as the day I met her. When you marry your best friend, you can't go wrong.

She loves what she does and she does it extremely well. An author of a children's book about her father, developing her own perfume, producing a CD of her father's music, and the work she's doing now for two radio stations is amazing. She never thought she'd be hosting radio. A new adventure and she loves it. She has a natural talent. She's great at interviewing and ad-libbing live on air with her co-hosts.

From Susan's point of view:

I don't remember ever having an argument with Kent. We may disagree about things, but never, ever a bad argument. If we disagree, I was taught, no matter how you feel, you give that person a kiss goodnight before you go to sleep. That's just the way it is. I've never found anyone to stray. I've never been with anybody else. I can't imagine being without my best friend, not being able to talk with him, not being able to be with him.

I'll tell you what Kent's like. Most people don't realize that Michael Landon was a very shy man. He would never, ever admit that but he was. I saw it. Kent is a shy man in his own way and I think because of that, and because he would never put himself above anybody else, he won't say he's good at this or good at that or great at this. There were things he did for shows that he would never say he did. He would never want to take the credit, but he should.

Kent is not only talented at what he does, he's very smart at what he does. He's a very caring, compassionate human being for everyone. There is one thing about him I think everyone who worked for him knows and that is if you make a mistake and you tell him the truth, he'll deal with it; if you make a mistake and you lie about it, he doesn't like that at all and won't put up with it.

Kent has always been honest with everyone, so they reciprocate in kind. He is an emotional man. He has deep feelings for his friends and for his family and he will do anything he can for anyone close to him. Whoever he has helped is very grateful.

Harry Sukman and I got along very well after Susan and I were married. He passed away that same year. He was performing at a fundraiser for the hospital at Palm Springs. Every year, he gave a Gershwin concert for that cause. It was his birthday, December 2nd. He performed and got up to take a bow. Frank Sinatra was off-stage ready to wheel a birthday cake on stage for him. Harry collapsed and died on stage from a heart attack while the audience gave him a standing ovation.

Susan was devastated. I was on location in Sonora and she was here in town. She called me and I couldn't believe it. I flew home the next morning. It was really a shock for everybody. Then her mother Francesca got sick with ALS, a very devastating disease.[142] You become a prisoner in your own body. Your mind works but your body doesn't. Her mom was an artist, an organist, a pianist and a composer.

Susan with a new friend given to an ALS patient at the Fashion Show luncheon in honor of Susan's mother Francesca Paley Sukman.

After Francesca's passing,[143] Susan started fundraisers for the ALS Foundation. She did a luncheon five or six years in a row and all the monies they raised from the luncheon were designated for communication devices so patients could type into a computer and a voice would speak for them.

CHAPTER THIRTY-FOUR

Highway to Heaven

After *Little House* ended, Michael came up with another show called *Highway to Heaven*[144] where he played an angel. Victor French was his sidekick. This show was special for several reasons.

First, when they tested the pilot as we did *Little House*, *Highway to Heaven* got a higher score than *Little House* did, and it has held on for the highest audience test rating of a two-hour pilot. We shot the opener in Tucson and also at the Santa Anita Race Track as well as other local sites. Helen Hayes was the guest star. She was a wonderful lady to work with. We enjoyed her very much.

Second, Michael made a different deal with NBC this time, one in which *he* owned the negative, the rights. That meant NBC gave him X number of dollars to do each show, but any time it was over that amount, it came out of Mike's pocket.

Third, Mike sat down with me and said, "I never want to be over budget because I'm not going to spend any of my own money." I said, "That's fine. We'll work it out." And we did. For the five years *Highway* ran we were never over budget. At the end of each season, Mike gave a bonus to all the cast and crew.[145] He said, "You're the ones who brought the show in under budget. I'm sharing it with you." And so he did.

If that wasn't generous enough, Mike said to me one day that I was the brother he never had, which made me start to cry. Then he said, "You will be a partner in my company and you will receive money from any residual checks the show makes, foreign or domestic." He made me a ten-percent partner. He said, "You helped me make the money. Let's share the wealth." I would never have asked for such a thing. Michael said, "That's it!" To this day I get residuals from *Highway to Heaven*.

Michael said I was the brother he never had.

As to why Michael was drawn to me like a brother, I don't know. I was flabbergasted when he said that. I think he felt close to me; I was close to him. He never had a brother. He had his kids, but they were at a different age level. He could talk to me about a lot of things.

Susan shares her insight:

Kent McCray is very much like Michael Landon and I think that is why Michael always called him the brother he never had. Mike was a workaholic and he loved it; Kent was a workaholic and he loved it. You couldn't keep them away from the studio. Kent would walk in the door and someone would say, "Where's Mike?" One could start a joke, and the other one would finish it. One would start a thought, and the other one would finish it. That's the closeness. If you asked Michael why he loved Kent so much, it's because he's the most endearing, loving, caring, helping human being I've ever known. That's what Mike would say, because he said it to me about Kent.

I loved Michael. He was a tremendous part of our lives and so it is very hard to talk about him. It is like losing a right arm with him, because he really loved us, not only because we worked with him, but he worried about us, he cared about us. Kent worried about him, cared about him, loved him. It was mutual.

Leslie Landon Matthews comments:

...My whole memory of going to my dad's office was that I could hear Kent and my dad laughing down the hallway before I even reached the office. Those two always had so much fun together. Really, I think Kent brought such joy to my dad outside of his regular family...I always did think of Kent as a brother that my dad never had, never got to grow up with. Because my dad grew up in such a dysfunctional home, I think it was really important to him to establish such a wonderful, close friendship with a man like Kent.

I cannot say enough about Michael that will do him justice. He was a pleasure. He knew everything. Michael learned his craft well. Everyone said he had an ego. We all have an ego to some degree. Every now and again he pushed something. When he did, I commented, "Hey, you're showing your actor's ego again, aren't you?" "Oh, I don't want to do that," he answered. We were very honest with each other.

It was a very warm relationship because we relied on each other. He respected what I could do, how I handled the crew. He respected how I laid things out and how I got things done. It was a load off his mind that he didn't have to worry about. I respected what he could do. He had the final say, yes, but I wasn't ever afraid to say, "Let's do it this way." If something he wanted didn't work, we sat down and talked about it, but it was never a matter of him saying, "I want it this way. I want it that way."

When we shot the *Highway* shows, Susan and I picked up Mike each day at five in the morning and drove him to location. "Mommy" and "Poppy" sat in the front seat and "Sonny" sat in the back. That's how Michael referred to us. He seemed to think in terms of family. His childhood wasn't the best but we all created a production family.

Often we worked in the car because on *Highway*, it was impossible to get him alone. He and Sue did a lot of casting on those trips. Sometimes he read the newspaper. He loved to read the newspaper from cover to cover and tell stories about a lot of the little articles. If he said, "Geez, that would make a hell of a story," he'd sit down and write a script around it. He had an uncanny talent to do everything.

We also told jokes back and forth while driving. I had a great sense of humor; Michael had the greatest sense of humor. He told stories in all types of dialects. On set, if he was in a scene and came off after a shot, he'd start a story while waiting for his next scene. When he heard, "Michael, we're ready," he went back for his scene, maybe cry or whatever it called for, then walked off the set and continued on with the story. It truly made for a lot of fun each day.

I think back to all the good times and boy, we had a lot of them. Mike made it fun. If we got into a problem schedule-wise, if it was raining or something, it was a challenge for him to work it out. He *loved* that challenge. Lots of times while doing *Highway to Heaven*, I picked the locations with the location manager. We showed Mike the still pictures. This was before we had a tape machine.

He'd say, "Yeah, that'll work. That'll work. That'll work." However, still pictures don't show the size of a room or an area. Many times when we got there he said, "Oh, boy. Pictures lie, don't they?" Or, "You got me in a pickle on this one." That kind of thing. But at the end of the day, he'd say, "See. I made it work for you." He didn't want to pick the location, even if he had time, because that took the spontaneity away from him. He loved walking in and making it happen. I think that's what kept him going.

A good story kept Mike going, too. Author/actor Tom Sullivan,[146] who is also a singer and motivational speaker, brought us several on *Highway*.[147] If you don't know Tom's body of work, you should check into it.[148] He's an incredible man.

Tom talks about how we all ended up working together:

I had written a script for Highway to Heaven *and it was a spec script because everything I was writing back then was spec. The deal was nobody wanted to hire a blind guy. The only way I could get things to do as an actor was to write the stuff. So, with a wonderful woman named Jodie Lewis, we wrote a* Highway to Heaven *script not knowing whether we'd get it made or not.*

It went first to Kent, and I got a call one afternoon from the big fella. He said, "You know, this is a remarkable script. Landon has to see this." I said, "Is he open to that kind of thing?" He said, "He's open to anything that's good." With Kent's drama background that most people didn't even know about, the script went over to Michael, and the next morning, the phone rang. It was Landon. He said, "Tom, I've loved you on all the shows you've done. I think we could really do something with this."

What ended up being over the course of probably a year or year-and-a-half, I got to understand the dynamic of Mike and Kent. When you would be in a story meeting with them, Michael would let his imagination run. He'd take a story anywhere he wanted it to go in his head, and I always remember the big guy sitting there very quietly. Afterwards, I would be fortunate enough to be in the room when Kent would say, "Okay, what's the practical shooting schedule? How are we going to do this? Where are we going to do it?"

In fact, in one of my scripts Michael decided, because I was the principal actor in it, he wanted it shot in sequence. Well, you never shoot in sequence. Kent said to him, "Michael, how are you going to do that?" I'll never forget Michael saying to him, "Well, Kent, you're going to have to go out and figure that out." And they did! They shot the entire hour episode, scene-by-scene, in sequence, and from an acting standpoint. Boy was it wonderful because you could stay in character and you knew where you were as the piece went along.

We did a ninety-minute *Highway* one time. It was scheduled to be an hour, but it stretched into ninety minutes. Mike went to the network rather than chop it up, which he didn't want to do. He asked, "Is it possible one night to get another half-hour?" The network re-worked a few things and said, "Okay, you can have such-and-such."

Michael put the show on as an hour-and-a-half. However, in syndication, no one wants an hour-and-a-half show. That screws things up completely. Michael's business manager came to him and said, "They insist you take a half-hour out of the show." Michael asked, "What are they paying us per show?" I can't remember the amount of money. He said, "Okay. I'll write a non-descript half hour and we'll add, so we'll have two one-hour shows rather than an hour-and-a-half show. We'll get paid for two shows instead of one." That's what he did.

Syndication, as you can imagine, is a large part of the revenue from a show so that was always important. It was during trips to sell *Highway* that I met and became close friends with Michael's business manager, Dennis Korn. Dennis is now the co-trustee of Michael Landon's estate and the distributor for all Michael's shows. He comments on *Highway*:

Kent and Michael were busting their butts to produce the show and (representing my firm) I was going around to find a domestic distribution deal for when Highway *to Heaven* went into *syndication...You know you need over four seasons to be able to syndicate something, okay? So,* Highway to Heaven, *the ratings at the end of year four weren't great and NBC was thinking of canceling it. Michael and Kent went over to NBC and I believe it was Brandon Tartikoff at that time. They said, "Hey, we need your help. My business manager Dennis tells me that we need at least one-hundred-ten episodes so we can go into syndication." Brandon says, "Then you only need thirteen more episodes. Fine. We'll pick you up for thirteen next year...."*

See the way things worked differently? It would never happen nowadays.

Brandon Tartikoff, president of programming, was a wonderful man who loved Michael. He and his team came out every year where we were shooting to talk about the show. I arranged a motel room for them and Michael and I met with them. They gave us feedback for the show. Brandon would start out, "I think we should tailor the stories this way, this way and that way." Mike would sit and listen.

When they were through, Mike gave them a whole line of stories he wanted to do off the top of his head, which were ten-times better than what they wanted him to do. They all acquiesced and said, "Yeah, that's great, that's great!" End of meeting.

CHAPTER THIRTY-FIVE

Tales from the Highway

FROM KENT

Susan and I never did go on a trip for our honeymoon because we were shooting *Highway*. At the end of that season, we decided to go back East. At first, we went on a cruise through the Panama Canal and some of the islands, and then flew into Boston. Susan had never been to New England, and since I grew up there, I wanted to show her around.

During part of our trip, we went to Cape Cod and spent a night at a hotel. Across the street was a nice restaurant, so we went over and sat at the bar to have a drink. The bartender fixed our drinks. A few minutes later, he called out to everybody at the bar, "Is everybody taken care of because I'm going to be busy for a few minutes?" Everybody was fine.

He went to the end of the bar, turned on the television, and there was the start of *Highway to Heaven*. He said, "This is my favorite show and I can't miss it." We said nothing.

At the end of Act I, he came back to see if we wanted another drink. I turned to Susan and asked, "You know what I think is going to happen in this next Act?" I kind of related what the Act would be about. He just looked at us, filled everybody's drinks and went back to see Act II. At the end of Act II, I did the same thing about what was going to happen in Act III. At the end of that, he came back and I said what was going to happen in Act IV.

At the end of the show, he came over and said, "Boy, you picked everything right on the nose. How did you know what was going to happen? Are you a writer?" I said, "No, I don't write." I took out a business card and showed him that I was the producer. Needless to say, we got the best service of anybody in the restaurant that night.

There are things in the business that are done right; there are things in the business I think that are done wrong. You don't have the right to destroy anybody's property. When we did *Highway* and we used a lot of practical locations on city streets and residential streets, the one thing everyone hated was all the trucks coming into a residential area, blocking driveways. They were 18-wheelers and they'd spill out over the front of someone's house.

We used to give those residents a gift basket of some kind before we started shooting. The location manager had to get permits from them and pay them, but he always gave them a gift basket of wine or food or something to ease the burden a little bit. It made them happy and they were more cooperative.

We were shooting a *Highway to Heaven* episode and we were in a restaurant at a marina in Southern California. It was kind of a Polynesian restaurant. The singer was up on the stage and all the extras were sitting at a table. We started to shoot the master. "Stop. Wait. Wait. You, this couple right here," Mike said. "Stop chewing gum." "Oh, sorry, sorry," they said.

We did another take and another. Four times Mike had to tell these people to stop chewing gum. This is their profession. You don't chew gum on the set. You just don't do it. Certain things you know about your profession, the do's and don'ts. This is a don't. Each time Mike had to stop, he got a little more agitated. He said, "Once was enough."

We broke for lunch. These two actors who were chewing gum came over to Mike and asked, "Mr. Landon, are you mad at us?" He said, "No, why should I be mad at someone I'm never going to see again?" Isn't that a great line? Then he turned to me and said, "They'll never work on this set again." I said, "Of course not." They never did. "Why should I be mad at someone I'm never going to see again?" I wish I'd have thought of that.

Mike used to wear his wardrobe home, whatever he was in at the end of the day. One day, he was wearing a priest's outfit. He got in the car and told the driver, "Stop here at the liquor store. I want to get a bottle of wine for dinner."

He went into the liquor store, picked out a bottle of wine, took it up to the front desk, and the clerk said, "Father, you're spending too much money. I can't let you buy that wine." Mike said, "Don't worry about it because I'm not really a priest. I'm Michael Landon." The man said, "I don't care. You're spending too much money, and I won't let you buy it." Mike had to call his driver in from the car to explain to the clerk that he was not a priest, that he was really Michael Landon.

My love of trains actually started when we were doing *Little House*. I was often up in the engine. I learned how to run it. They taught me how to be the brakeman and how to stoke the fire. I had my radio and I was liaison between the train and the camera assistant and the director. The train had to enter the shots at certain speeds or back up or whatever. I was on a walkie talkie with them and I spent my whole day in the cab. Believe me it was hot.

Later on, Susan bought me a large gauge train set and I had shelving built and track installed so it travelled from room to room at our house above our heads. Then, Susan arranged for us to throw a party on a train to San Diego.

Me on the train in *Little House*

This was an old-fashioned dome diner, and we had forty-four people on board. We took the car out of Los Angeles. We had balloons on the ceiling, we had a band, we had a group of people we knew, and we served hors d'oeuvres and drinks. Upon arriving in San Diego, we got off the train and took the trolley to a restaurant, had a fine dinner and came back. The diner car was now attached to a train going back to Los Angeles.

We did this a few times, and then, the agent who made all the arrangements for us told Susan, "You know, you can rent a rail car. They will attach it to the end of an Amtrak train and you can go anywhere you'd like."

The rental train cars are eighty feet long. You have the back platform. You have a living room inside. You have three or four bedrooms depending on the different cars that you take. You have your own bathroom, and then you have a dining room and crew's quarters and a kitchen. You travel with your own chef and steward. A totally decadent trip, but one that I will never forget. We took many trips to Chicago, trips to Denver, and one year we went all the way to Boston and back. It was a lot of fun. You just relax and enjoy the scenery.

FROM LAUREN LEVIAN (ACTRESS AND WIFE OF HENRY DARROW):

We went on a trip from L.A. to Chicago. The rail car looked like a Western saloon. It was Kent and Sue, Henry and myself and Sue's cousin and her husband. Kent's birthday was one of the days during this trip. I used to write these birthday stories about people and they would be gag stories. The punch line would be some little gift.

I really didn't know Kent at that time. I wasn't around during the *Chaparral* days…But I wrote this story about him with all the presents and he was such a good sport. They were really silly gags. I remember I gave him a hat with a chicken on it and he put it on and he wore it! Just wore it all during the trip. He was like a fabulous audience for this story and all the little presents. I just found him to be so incredibly sweet because here he is, this huge guy who could be intimidating, but with us on that trip, he was just a teddy bear.

FROM DENNIS KORN

Kent, to be quite honest with you, is extremely moral and has high integrity like Michael Landon did. They taught me the way it used to be in the old days. Everything was friendly in the entertainment business, everything was done in a handshake...Kent taught me what it was like to be involved with people like Bob Hope or Lorne Greene or Dan Blocker. How everybody was just real friendly with one another and cared about one another.

FROM TOM SULLIVAN

I was doing a scene where I had to shoot baskets playing basketball. I mean, I've done that all my life with a buzzer on the basket or a bell on the basket or whatever, and I love sports. I've been an athlete all my life. Before the scene started, I probably hit six out of ten from the foul line. Now, Michael calls, "Action," and I start missing. Kent starts laughing.

Michael now starts talking. He's going, "Oh, geez. Hire a blind guy, give him a basketball and he can't hit crap." I'd shoot the next one and miss. Mike would say, "You know, it's getting dark." I missed the next one. He'd go, "We gonna be here till tomorrow morning?" He kept putting the pressure on and now the whole crew starts laughing, the cameramen start giggling, and I finally swished one after about fifteen tries..

FROM VERN LEYK

We would go on location to Sonora, California...We'd have a semi full of equipment or props. The first guy that was on the back of the big trucks to unload them was Kent McCray. He was there. First guy! He was a regular guy. He'd help us unload it or help us load it. That's the kind of man he was. He could do everything.

DOROTHY ALLEN, speaking for her husband DENNY ALLEN who suffered a stroke. (Denny and Dorothy ran the livestock outfit used by Kent and Michael):

Denny always enjoyed working with Michael and Kent and all the old crew. He really appreciated them, the job and the work. It came at a good time for us. Denny never said anything bad about anybody. He really liked everyone and got along with them really well. They're still all dear to our heart. I think Susan and Kent are wonderful people, very kind and generous and very caring.

CHAPTER THIRTY-SIX

Where Pigeons Go to Die

After *Highway* ended, we closed our office at MGM Studios and set up offices in Malibu since we weren't planning to shoot anything for a few months. Why keep going into MGM when we might as well be closer to our homes, which was better for Michael and me?

At one point, Melissa Sue Anderson brought a book to Michael called *Where Pigeons Go to Die*.[149] Michael read the book; I read the book. It was an interesting story, and Michael decided he wanted to do a movie-of-the-week. He sat down and wrote the teleplay based on the book.

The story was about a small boy and his grandfather raising homing pigeons. It could take place at any given locale, so as Michael was writing it, we talked about shooting it in the fall to get the season changes. Trevor Williams, art director John Warren and I went to Boston. Having grown up in New England, I felt that it was the best place to capture the leaves turning color in the fall.

I started out meeting with people in Boston while looking for locations there. We had a meeting with the IA Unions to be able to bring people in from Los Angeles, but we would also have to hire a lot of people from the Local in Boston.

One lady represented the associates, as they were called. They're mostly runners and people who work on productions. She asked, "How many associates are you going to have?" I said, "We don't need any." This was a small unit and we never had people/flunkies that did nothing except maybe run around to get coffee for somebody. I said, "We can get our own coffee." She said, "You have to have them." I looked at the head of the union and asked, "Is this true?" He said, "It pretty much is." I said, "This is the end of the meeting because I'm not going to be saddled with a lot of people I don't need." I got up and walked out.

That night, Trevor, John and I flew to Kansas and met some people I contacted ahead of time as an alternate locale. We went to the city of Lawrence and had a wonderful experience. We found a lot of nice locations that we showed Michael when we took him back later.

A fun story about traveling with Mike to survey the Kansas location. There were no first-class seats on the plane, which had three seats across on each side. Mike and I had two seats with an empty in the middle. We put the table down to play cards. Some lady came down the aisle and asked me, "Can I have your autograph?" I said, "Okay, but it'll cost you a dollar." I thought she was kidding. She said, "Just a minute. I'll go get one." She came back and handed me a dollar and I signed my name. She looked at it and said, "Kent McCray? I thought you were George Kennedy." I said, "No, I'm not George Kennedy. I'm Kent McCray. Here's Michael Landon. Do want his autograph?" She said, "No, I don't think so." I mean, you gotta laugh.

We shot *Where Pigeons Go to Die* in Lawrence, Kan., and we couldn't have had a better experience than we had there. The people were all friendly and helped us a great deal.

Susan cast Art Carney to be the grandfather. This was the beginning of another friendship. He was a wonderful man and he and Mike got along very well. We all did. It was great working with him; just talking to him was a great time. In later years, he lived in Connecticut. When Susan and I went back there because we were both Regents at the University of Hartford, we visited Art, sat around his kitchen table and told stories. It was a wonderful experience. Knowing him was a thrill for me. I loved Art Carney, his role on the *The Honeymooners* with Jackie Gleason. He was a gem.

One of the other things that was interesting with *Pigeons* is that we had to have an animal trainer on set. We worked with Gary Gero many times before, but this was a little different. He had to teach pigeons to fly, as silly as that may sound. A hawk or an eagle with a big wing span can soar into the wind long enough to get some great shots. We needed the pigeons to control their flight so we could get some airborne shots of them.

We had a big wind machine set up with a separate generator. For all the weeks we put this show together, Gary worked with the pigeons to fly into the wind stream made by the machine so we could capture shots of the pigeons in motion. It was quite a painstaking effort, but he did it. We also had two scissor lift hydraulic platforms. One was set higher than the other so we could get a pigeon to fly from A at a lower elevation to B, which was at a higher elevation. Back and forth so we could get the pigeons in flight.

In the story, they release the pigeons and then hope they come back to roost at the main house. It is a very heart-warming story, and if you've never seen it, you should because it's a great, great movie.[150]

I played a small part in it. I played a part in the *Highway* pilot, too. I did a few things in *Little House* as well, but that wasn't my forte. Mike said I was his Alfred Hitchcock.[151]

One story while shooting *Pigeons*. This actually happened at my brother's wedding in 1947 in Hartford. I was the best man and during the ceremony, I heard some snickering in the audience. I saw my aunt laughing and she couldn't seem to stop. She was sitting with my grandmother.

After the service was over, I asked my aunt what she was laughing at. Seems my grandmother, who was in her 80's at the time, got a little teary-eyed at the wedding and blew her nose. The only trouble was when she blew her nose, she forgot she had a veil on her face. I shared that story with Michael and he thought it was funny and wrote it into the story. Instead of a wedding, in *Pigeons*, it was a funeral we were filming.

Susan was the casting director for *Pigeons* and she had to find a gentleman to lie in the casket and play dead for the funeral scene. She went to the mall and looked around with the local casting director. They spotted somebody and asked him if he wanted to be in the film. He said, "Sure." We got him dressed and put him in the casket.

Michael rolled the camera and we shot the scene. Michael said, "Cut." The crew said, "Okay, Harry. Harry, you can breathe now. Har-ry, you can breathe now." Well, he wasn't breathing. He was still holding his breath because he didn't want to screw up anything. We had to tap him on the shoulder and tell him it was okay to breathe because he couldn't hear us in the casket.

Toward the end of *Where Pigeons Go to Die*, Art Carney had finished his part. We still had a few days of work to finish but Art was set to leave the next day. He said good-bye to everybody. When he got up the next morning to go to the airport, he noticed a piece of paper under his door. It was a letter from Michael written on a yellow pad telling Art how wonderful he was and what a great relationship they had together. Art treasured that letter. In fact, he read it after Mike passed away when I produced a film in Mike's memory.

CHAPTER THIRTY-SEVEN

Us

After we finished shooting *Pigeons*, we remained in our Malibu office. Mike came in one day and said, "I'd like to do another series." He wanted to play the character he created in *Killing Stone*. Mike would be the lead character, his father would be played by Barney Martin, and Michael's on-screen son would be played by Casey Peterson.

Mike wrote the script and took it to NBC. They said, "We don't need you anymore." After fourteen years of *Bonanza*, ten years of *Little House*, five years of *Highway to Heaven*. After twenty-nine years of quality TV shows.

That's actually what he was told. There had been a change in management[152] and different people were now in place, most of whom were lawyers. Mike's business manager Dennis Korn explains what happened:

Remember when I said Highway *in year four was going to end? Michael went to NBC and discussed it with Tartikoff and Tartikoff said, "Fine, I'll pick you up for thirteen more shows next season." That's the way things used to work.*

Then Tartikoff left; others left. Michael (who) had an affiliation with NBC...set up the meeting with NBC, but it wasn't the old timers any more. It was the young people, and they basically threw him aside and said, "We don't need you." The industry changed. It would have never happened before.

Even if NBC didn't like the concept, they trusted Michael and knew it would work out. If you think they liked the concept of Highway to Heaven, *you're nuts! When he went there, they thought it was a joke. They were cracking up. They assumed that Michael was joking with them. They said, "You, a Jew, want to play an angel talking to God?" Michael said, "Yeah." When Tartikoff realized (he wasn't joking), I believe the terminology was, "Michael, I don't understand. I don't see how it's going to work. But if you say it's going to work, we'll buy it."*

Now (Michael) goes to them with Us *and he's dealing with not entertainment people like Kent and (himself). He's dealing with business people. I'm being honest. Bottom line folks who think they know what they're doing but they don't understand what they're doing. It takes somebody like Kent or Michael to understand what the viewing audience wants to see....*

It's one thing to say, "We've read the script and we don't think it's something we want to put on the air." They could have said that. But to say, "We don't need you anymore," is one of the cruelest things they could have done. I can't remember who was in charge of what at that point, but it was the ultimate insult. It hurt Michael terribly.

Leslie Landon Matthews comments:

I don't know the politics of it all. I do know that my dad really beat to his own drum. That's why when it came to Emmy Awards and things like that, I don't think those types of awards meant too much to him because they really dealt with the politics of the entertainment field. When he received numerous People's Choice Awards? That meant a lot to him because then he knew he was dealing with the public and it was the public speaking their voice and appreciating his work.

I'm sure on some level it did (hurt), but I think he set his priorities pretty straight in terms of what was important to him. I still think at the end of the day, even though quality work was important to him, I don't think work was the thing that came first in his life... I think his greatest joy was to come home and be with family.

More from Dennis Korn:

Because NBC wouldn't do Us, *CBS did. They heard about the story; they called us up. I set up the meeting. Michael met with them and they said, "We'll buy it." They were going to do a two-hour movie-of-the-week that led into the series, like all of Mike's work. It was a really nice movie-of-the-week. In his mind, Michael had already written a hundred scripts.*

We set up offices at Sony Studios and did the pilot. We started shooting in November and finished it in December 1990. CBS gave us a twenty-two show pick-up to go ahead and do the series for the first year, but that didn't happen.

CHAPTER THIRTY-EIGHT

Us Minus One

During the filming of *Us*, I drove Mike to location. Sometimes he came by our house and sometimes I picked him up at his. At the end of the shooting day, I drove him back. On the way back, I noticed Mike starting to sit back, close his eyes and go to sleep. That was not customary of Michael's work habits. He was always very up and alert, but he seemed tired.

Many times I invited him in to have a drink. He'd talk for a while but wouldn't touch his drink. All during post-production, Michael said he was tired and he said he had pain in his stomach. He went to the doctors and they said maybe it was a hiatal hernia. Later, they said maybe he had a bleeding ulcer.

In March 1991, Mike and family went to Utah for a vacation. Mike came home early and went straight to the hospital. On April 8th, I got a call from Cindy that Mike wanted to talk to me. He informed me he had pancreatic and liver cancer. Not knowing that much about the disease, I said, "Okay, what are we going to do to correct it?" He said, "We can't do anything. It's too far gone."

I was devastated. Everybody was dumbfounded. In that era, pancreatic cancer was not as common as other cancers. Mike had gone through MRIs and doctors deemed it was too late to do anything. It tore me apart. Just unbelievable.

As soon as Michael knew he had cancer, he did not want to get lambasted by the rag magazines, *The Enquirer, The Globe* and all those. He held a press conference at his house[153] and I was there. He sat down at a table and answered all questions for a couple of hours. He told the media, "If you start doing 'rag' stuff, I'm going to come back after you because I'm giving you the opportunity to ask me anything you want, and I'll answer honestly. Don't turn around and make something out of it that it isn't. These are the facts. Let's stick with the facts." We were hopeful they would abide by that, but that didn't happen in all cases.

I thought it was smart of him and brave to hold the conference. It's tough to sit down and talk about it when you know you're going to die. He knew it. He said, "I'm not going to last. It's going to be quick." He was quick with his remarks, too. Sometimes more so than he should have been, but he was a genius in many ways. He faced it head-on.

Susan remembers:

The day of the news conference, Mike got on the floor and started doing one-arm push-ups just to make a point. He said, "I'm still capable of this. Look, guys, I called you here because I want you to hear it from me. I don't want to see wrong information leaked out. I'll do what I can. That's all I can do."

Mike never came back to the office. I canceled the preparations we made for the *Us* series and informed everybody it wasn't going to happen. I was forced to fire everyone. I had to tell them it was over.

About this time, cards and letters by the sack-full were brought in by the postal service. Letters for Mike, books on healing. I can't count how many books we received. We ended up with eight or nine cases of them that I gave to different charities. School rooms sent in class pictures with notes from the students. We got nineteen bottles of Lourdes water from France.[154] People cared, as we all did, about Michael.

Some sent articles on cancer treatments like "Swim Up the Amazon with the Dolphins," or some other crazy thing. One man wrote to Michael in a felt pen, red and black, and he quoted a little thing out of Bible Scripture. Then he wrote, "Your money could be doing this." He wrote a bit more then, "Your money could be doing this." At the bottom of the letter, the guy said, "I only want ten percent of your money," and he included a little calculator which in those days was about the size of a telephone. Morbid!

Somebody outside of Tehachapi, Calif., wanted Michael to build her a five-car garage because she had these old cars that she and her husband were restoring. She also included a shot of herself with nothing on but a fur coat. Some of the things you had to laugh at. I took those to him so he *would* laugh. I took a lot of letters out to the house. He read some of them and then said he couldn't take it anymore.

Lots of times I went out to the house to play cards to pass the time. Remember, we both had a bold sense of humor. One day when he got real sick at the end, I spent the afternoon with him. I was shuffling the cards and I said, "Mike, you suppose if I got lucky today we could play for cash?" He said, "You mercenary son of a bitch!" We both laughed. It's a line he'd have given me if circumstances were reversed.

I went out to the house while he was getting transfusions. He had a nurse with him at all times, which bothered him because he couldn't move around like he wanted to. He still wanted to know what the Studio gossip was and I tried to fill him in as best I could. I brought scripts people wanted him to read, but it was not an easy time. He didn't complain. He took it very well, but he wanted to do more.

The one thing Mike *did* want to do was go on the *Tonight Show* with Johnny Carson.[155] He'd been on the show many times and he really wanted to do one more with Johnny. They became close friends throughout the years. Carson asked Mike what he was doing for treatment. Mike said, "I take coffee enemas. Anyone out there ever heard of a coffee enema?" Some audience members said yes. There was a long pause. Michael said, "You must be fun to have breakfast with." That got a tremendous laugh.

On Saturday, late in June, we got a call from Cindy and she said it's best to come to the house. We went out and Mike was lying in bed. All the kids were there. It was a very sad moment. We were there Saturday, Sunday and Monday, the day Mike left us.[156]

Dennis Korn remembers:

I was at Michael's home when he passed away. We all had a chance to say good bye to him...I couldn't talk. All Michael was worried about was not himself. He was concerned about his family. He was concerned about abandoning his crew. Michael talked to me about watching over the family, watching over Cindy and the two youngest kids. He asked me to do whatever I could for them.

Susan was there, of course. Michael loved Susan and he always respected her. Susan remembers:

Kent and I walked in the room and the children started lighting candles. Mike looked at me and said, "I love your jacket." I said, "You do?" He said, "I just think it's really nice." I said, "Oh, Michael, come on." He said, "No, I do." He said to Kent and me, "What do you think is going to happen in Afghanistan?" He was always thinking about things and concerned. Sad. Sad ending. A sad ending to a really special life.

Susan leaned down to give him a hug in bed. But Afghanistan? It wasn't even a household word back then like it is now. Nobody even thought about it, but he did. You know, his mind was still clicking.

I gave him a hug and I said, "I'll think about you always." And I have. I know we're not to question, but why? Mike was only 54. I feel as sad today as I did then. His greatness, his love for the family and all the people he worked with. He touched us all.

It leaked out somehow that Mike might pass away. All of a sudden people lined the streets and some tried to climb the walls to look over into his property. It became a zoo. I called the Sheriff's Department. They said it was a public street and we couldn't stop them from being there, but we sure as hell could stop them from getting on the wall with ladders. The sheriffs came out in two squad cars and controlled the traffic. I was also very concerned about the helicopters that were flying overhead, trying to get a shot of Michael being put into the van.

Dennis Korn continues:

...Kent said, "Dennis, come downstairs with me." We went to the back of Michael's residence. He had a two-rail fence there. Kent said, "Let's just remove this fence." We started to remove the fence. He had the hearse drive onto the porch, we loaded Michael's body into it and the press wasn't able to take a picture when it drove off. That's how Kent got things done.

Susan continues:

Kent took such care and he said to Cindy, "Please don't run after that van because every photographer, every video camera will be going and you don't want to be seen doing that." She ran after the van. She was hysterical. It was heartbreaking.

Dennis again:

I was the business guy, so several days before he knew he was going to die, Mike pulled me aside and told me, "I don't want a big production at the funeral. I want my crew up front with my family. I don't care about anybody else."

When funeral plans were made, we were contacted by President and Mrs. Reagan and they were there, secret service and all. Michael knew President Reagan well.

Susan fills in more of the story:

When Mike was ill, he told me he loved Kent. We started to talk about people who might speak at his funeral. Mike said, "I know Kent won't be able to speak. I love him and I don't want him to get up there and start crying." It's the truth. We both cry about Michael because he was a tremendous man and very close.

Mike started talking about who he should have. Kent mentioned Melissa Gilbert. I suggested Barney Martin because Barney played his father in the Us *series. Everybody loved Mike.*

We arranged the service and called the crew. Merlin Olsen was asked to speak at Michael's service. He told me he was in a remote area with a group who were fishing and hunting and he didn't think he could get back in time. He called me the next day and said, "Kent, I'll be there."

Mike's daughter Leslie Landon Matthews spoke at the service. She read an excerpt from an episode Michael had written for *Little House:*[157] "Remember me with smiles and laughter, for that is how I will remember you all. If you can only remember me with tears, then don't remember me at all." It's almost as though he wrote it for himself.

In those days, I was petrified to get up and talk to people. I couldn't do that back then. That was a void in my skills. I didn't like it. I stuttered; I stammered. I couldn't speak well and I was embarrassed. It's only been since Mike's death that I've been asked to say things at funerals for people who worked on the crew, try to make it light and tell stories about the person because that's what Mike would do. My persona has changed a little. I've become bolder in terms of my speaking.

It's hard to put my feelings for Michael into words because it breaks me up so. It's so hard. It was such a loss. Is still a loss. He was in his prime. It's tough for me to talk about him twenty years later. I become very emotional. It's tough to speculate what we would be doing if he hadn't died. Mike said he wanted to do the *Us* series and specials or movies for television. We'll never know. Mike's passing was a blow to all of us. Michael, I just can't say enough.

CHAPTER THIRTY-NINE

With Laughter & Love

After Mike's passing, Dan Gordon, our staff writer on *Highway to Heaven,* wrote a script to honor Michael which he titled *Michael Landon: Memories with Laughter and Love.*[158] I put together four or five editing crews to work on different segments of the show: one to work on Mike's early life with movie clips from some of those early shows; a crew working on *Bonanza;* a crew working on *Little House;* a crew working on *Highway to Heaven;* and another crew to conduct interviews.

Susan remembers:

When we were using clips from Bonanza *for the tribute. I called Pernell (Roberts) and said, "We're doing this and we need your okay to release the use of the footage. We need clearance." He said, "Anything for Michael. Not a problem."*

We got support from pretty much everyone to do this. We set up the first day of shooting interviews to include all of Michael's kids as they sat around the patio and reminisced about their father. We also did an interview with Dick Van Dyke, Merlin Olsen and Leslie Landon Matthews at Mike's house. Later, we did one with Mike, Junior.

At my house, we did Melissa Sue Anderson, Matthew Laborteaux, Tom Sullivan, and Karen Grassle. At the CBS Studios, we interviewed Ossie Davis and Richard Mulligan. One night we traveled to New York with the cameramen and Buzzy

Boggs, our cinematographer and camera operator, and make-up man, Hank Edds. We flew all night to LaGuardia Airport and rented a car. Dan Gordon had gone ahead to direct the segments. We went to David Canary's house in Connecticut and then later in the day drove further up the Sound and interviewed Art Carney.

We drove back to New Jersey and spent the night. Got up the next morning. We photographed Eli Wallach, who came over from New York, and Moses Gunn, who was doing a play in Newark and got off on an extended lunch hour to do his segment. Flying home that night, we were able to finish with Melissa Gilbert the next morning. We filmed her at the Big Sky Ranch which was the *Little House* location. Fortunately the little bench around the big tree in Walnut Grove was still there. It was quite a heart-warming story.

We did a final tribute with Cindy Landon at her house to end the show.

Susan again:

Remember that Michael hosted the Michael Landon Celebrity Tennis Tournament in Tucson for over a decade. When he became ill and didn't come that year, the Tournament set up The Michael Landon Children's Cancer Research Fund, which was affiliated with the University of Arizona Medical Center.

The proceeds from the syndication of *Memories with Laughter and Love* went to Mike's cancer research fund. It was about $100,000.

CHAPTER FORTY

Bonanza Movies:
This Ain't No Music Video

After Michael passed away, I didn't work on anything at all for a while. Many months passed. I was over Michael's death by then. Let's be real. I'm still not over Michael's death more than twenty-five years later. What I mean to say is that I accepted that we had to move on. It was a conflicting time, though. I didn't want to work but I didn't want to retire, either.

In 1993, NBC called and said they wanted to do a two-hour *Bonanza.* This was in conjunction with David Dortort and Tom Sarnoff. David asked me to come back and join him for the show, which ended up being titled *Bonanza: The Return.*[159]

The story revolved around Ben Johnson as the patriarch of the Ponderosa along with three sons and a daughter of the original Cartwright boys which would make them Ben Cartwright's grandchildren. The cast included Richard Roundtree, Jack Elam, Michael Landon, Jr., Dirk Blocker and others.

By this time, General Electric owned NBC. They knew how to make light bulbs, but they had no idea how to make a film show. It became quite a challenge. I was working in the production office at NBC for at least two weeks making arrangements for equipment and support materials. Someone came in with The Book and said, "Here's The Book on the equipment you're supposed to use." I said, "What do you mean? I've already made deals." He said, "Oh, no. You have to use the vendors that are in The Book." I said, "I've been here two weeks and no one ever mentioned this Book." He said, "We've been working on it. Here it is."

I read The Book. Very exciting. The wardrobe vendor was listed as Macy's Department Store. Nothing in there about period wardrobe, nothing in their about period props or period set dressing. I turned the page. The only thing they had listed for film was Polaroid. I asked, "Are you going to shoot this show on Polaroid?" I just got a blank stare. They didn't have a clue.

It shouldn't surprise you when I say I called the company in The Book for electrical equipment and they said, "Oh, no, we don't have any equipment for NBC. We only gave them that kind of discount so we could get our name in The Book." I had already canceled the electrical equipment that I arranged, and I had to go back and re-hire those vendors.

This GE-owned NBC network also couldn't understand the transportation department. I wanted to send a driver to Lake Tahoe with some additional construction equipment. I arranged for our staff driver to get the other driver's advance travel money, meet him at four o'clock in the morning to give him the money and send him on his way. The other driver was to unload and then come back. A two-day trip. NBC said, "No, the actual driver who's using the money has to come in and get it. We can't give it to the staff driver." Therefore, I had to hire the other driver for a day to get his money, a day to drive to the location and unload, a day to drive back, and a day to turn his money and receipts in. A four-day charge instead of two. Stupid.

Then it was time to get the equipment to the location. I always gave the drivers advance money. They left on Saturday morning and drove Saturday and Sunday. We started shooting Monday and later that night, the drivers reconciled their per diem money. They turned in receipts for what was spent and returned any monies unspent per accounting office tracking.

NBC didn't like this idea. They did not like giving cash to anybody. They said, "We'll give money to one of the drivers. They'll drive in a convoy and the driver with the money will be the last one in line." I informed them that only military people drive in a convoy. You cannot put eight or nine trucks on the road and block the road with commercial equipment.

After much haggling, they said, "Okay, we'll give each driver a credit card." I said, "You're going to give each driver a credit card? That's fine. I don't care. But consider this. The drivers will be on location for maybe four weeks before coming back. You're not going to get a credit card for six weeks, and then it'll be mailed to New Jersey. How's that going to work?" They didn't like my comments. Of course not. Their policies were so stupid. We ended up doing it my way.

We left for location in June and went to Lake Tahoe to begin shooting the show. I talked to Ben Johnson before he got to location. Ben was the lead character in the show. He said he was going to drive himself and his horse from Phoenix to Tahoe. "It'll take me two days," he said. I said, "Fine. Let me know where you stay on the way and I'll reimburse you."

When we got on the set Monday morning, Ben said, "I got here early, came in Saturday night, but they didn't have any room for me." I said, "No, you were supposed to come in on Sunday." He said, "I changed my mind." I asked, "Why didn't you call me? I'd have found someplace for you." He said, "No, I slept in the stable with my horse. I've done that many times."

Ben Johnson was one of the best. He was always cordial, nice and never a word of complaint about anything. Ben was one of the most caring people you could ever encounter. When he met a lady, he tipped his hat and greeted her accordingly. One time, one of our producers started to mouth off with a lot of four-letter words.

Ben walked over to him and said, "You do that again, and you're outta here. I won't take that kind of talk."

He was originally an extra, and then he got into acting. Of course, he did almost every John Wayne picture. Wayne loved him. Ben, Susan and I were very good friends. He really was the best to work with. A true gem.

If NBC wasn't enough of a challenge, Mother Nature was, too. While we were shooting on location in June, I got up at three o'clock one morning and looked out the window. It was snowing. I turned to Susan, who was still half asleep, and said, "Honey, wake up. It's merry freakin' Christmas. We have to get the cast up here as soon as we can for the interior scenes." At three o'clock in the morning, she got up and got on the phone. By eleven o'clock we had the cast ready to shoot inside the Ponderosa set, which was our cover set in case of bad weather.

Snow at the Ponderosa!

Susan adds:

It was odd doing the two-hour Bonanzas. *Even though we were up in Tahoe and we were working on the show, it just wasn't the same. Kent was the same because he was working and he loved it. He went forward and did what he does. But the decisions weren't there like before with Michael.*

Eventually we finished the piece and it came time to edit. You got it. NBC, again. When we edited the show, they wanted to make it look like a music video. Chop. Chop. Chop. Here we are on *Bonanza*, the big open countryside of Lake Tahoe, and they wanted to cut it up in pieces. We finally convinced them the reason we went on location was to show the great scenery of Lake Tahoe. If they let it play a little longer in places we could add music. What an ordeal! But we got that one done.

Our original deal with NBC was to do two movies. However, after *The Return* they said they didn't want to do anymore. *The Return* came in at number eight in the ratings, so they had to back-track and agree to do another one.

NBC came to me and asked, "Is there any way we can reduce the cost?" I understood the question. It was expensive. A fair-sized cast. We were all on location. I said, "You might be able to save money if we do two, because we can amortize some of the sets and a lot of things over two shows rather than one." I know it was expensive to do two shows, but at least they would get more for their buck.

They liked that idea, so I laid out a whole schedule. We commissioned a story outline to be written. We had to go through three or four other programming people first. As I said, it was an outline of a script written by Denne Petitclerc who wrote the pilot for *Chaparral*. It was about nine or ten pages. The programming lady asked, "Where are the act breaks? I have to know where the commercials are going. I have to know now."

When a writer gives you an outline, he's giving you an overview of what the total story is about. He's not breaking it down scene by scene by scene. That's what she wanted in a ten-page outline. "Oh, I *have* to know it." Insisted on it. If we didn't have it, then we couldn't move forward. Denne had to go back and write more.

Once that was done, we met with the head of programming, and her first comment was, "Why do we have all these family members? Can't we get rid of some of them?" We said, "This is *Bonanza*. The Cartwright family is the essence of the show." She said, "I've never seen the show." And she's head of programming. She okayed the second script because of the ratings on the first one, but just no concept. I didn't have any respect for people like that.

At the end of the meeting, Tom Sarnoff and David Dortort asked, "Can we start the script for the second show?" She replied, "What do you mean the second show?" We said, "It's in our contract that we're going to do two back-to-back to reduce costs." She said, "No, you're not. Let me put it to you this way. Do you want to do one or none?" That was her attitude. We did one.[160]

About a year later, there was a big ad in the trade magazine *Variety:* "Ding dong, the witch is dead." Everybody despised this woman who had been let go by NBC. We never did get to do the third *Bonanza* movie.

Around the time the second *Bonanza* movie was scheduled to air, David Dortort published a letter in *Variety*. I was having coffee when I opened the daily trade paper and saw a full-page letter addressed to me from David Dortort. It thanked me for all my work. I was dumbfounded because he took out a whole-page. I found myself moved to tears. I was proud that David took the time to write a letter about me and my work and place it on a full-page for everyone else to read.

Here's what David wrote:

DAVID DORTORT
January 13, 1995
Mr. Kent McCray
Ten-K Productions
Malibu, CA 90265

Dear Kent,

On the eve of our newest *Bonanza* a two hour Movie of the Week that will air on NBC Sunday evening, I'd like you to know how much I value your work, your knowledge, your expertise, and especially your friendship.

We started this little show, together, more than 35 years ago, in September of 1959. We pioneered the use of color in television for the first time ever, together. We made 430 great, hour long episodes together. We ran for 14 beautiful years on NBC, together. We broke all sorts of records along the way, together.

The point is, my dear friend, none of this could have been accomplished without you. You encouraged and helped win the battle, and what a battle it was, to bring color to a black and white television world. You solved every difficult, impossible production problem, and in the process, you built what were acclaimed the best crews in the business. That goes for *Bonanza* and perhaps even more so for *The High Chaparral*. You became the uncrowned King of Tucson, Arizona.

And, you did all this with grace, with consistent good humor, with never-ending patience and tolerance and understanding. Our crews loved you, respected you, were fiercely loyal to you. How else can one explain bringing in 430 *Bonanzas* and 100 *High Chaparrals* on time, and on or under budget? You made friends for *Bonanza* and *High Chaparral* wherever we went, and they remain friends to this day.

You then went on with our beloved friend Michael Landon, and successfully helped bring glory to television with more decent, wholesome, family-oriented shows like *Little House on the Prairie* and *Highway to Heaven.* You, and your darling Susan, brought more new faces to television, more fresh and exciting new talent, than any husband and wife team in the industry.

You're still at it, big man. Thank heaven you're back with "Old Dad" to give us and the world, the best *Bonanza* of them all, this Sunday night. *Bonanza* and *The High Chaparral* is a testament to your handiwork, your skill, your great, wonderful heart. There's never been another like you, Kent. Those of us who have worked with you are blessed to share your beneficent presence.

With Love and Huge Respect,
David Dortort

Can't tell you how much of a surprise it was but a really nice one, for sure. The last two Bonanza movies were really where I ended my career in 1996.

CHAPTER FORTY-ONE

It's Not Where You Start;
It's Where You Finish

I graduated from the Hartt School of Music in 1951, and later it became part of the University of Hartford. Around 1995, I was contacted by the Hartford alumni office because they wanted to give me an achievement award for alumni success. I was grateful. I met with different university officials when they came out to California to visit. We went to a Sunday afternoon concert at UCLA and then attended dinner for a number of alumni I didn't know.

They gave me a nice award that we display in our home. After that, I was asked if I would consider being a Regent.[161] That's a position that acts as an advisor to the University. They felt I could offer input as an outsider and alum coming back. They had three meetings a year. I first went back in February but later on we skipped that meeting due to the cold weather.

I enjoyed it. I was on several committees including planning. I did a lot of communication over the phone when I couldn't attend meetings. Susan and I drove back because Susan doesn't like to fly. As a non-Regent, she wasn't allowed to attend the meetings so she found other activities during the day and joined me for the dinners.

University of Hartford President Dr. Walter Harrison[162] remembers meeting us early on:

Kent was incredibly proud of his experience at the Hartt School. Remembered it down to the minute detail. He could tell me about the operas he had worked on and how they were staged and who taught them. He has roots in Hartford. He was proud of those roots, and he was proud of having been at the Hartt School. Now, because it's part of the University of Hartford, he transferred that allegiance to us and was constantly asking questions about how he and Susan could help us with our mission...

...I was struck by Kent's absolute devotion to the school and also struck by Susan's analysis of what would make the University, and especially the Hartt School, better. They always acted as a team, so I never exactly knew whose idea was what, but together they suggested a number of things that we have put into place that have really helped the University and the Hartt School.

On campus property, they erected a magnet school[163] which was a children's school from kindergarten up through fifth grade. The magnet school was run, not by the university, but by a separate state corporation. President Harrison was very enthusiastic about the school. At one of the meetings, he asked me if I'd ever visited it, which I hadn't. He said, "I sure wish you'd go. It's just beautiful." That was on a Thursday and I came back to the hotel and talked to Susan. We agreed to visit it Friday after the Regents' meeting adjourned.

We met with the principal, Cheryl Kloczko. She took us on a tour from classroom to classroom. You could tell that it was well-run. The students were admitted on a lottery basis from seven different communities. They were bused in. Very well-organized. We even sat in on a few of the classes.

During one of the classes, the younger kids, maybe second or third grade, were all sitting on the floor. There was a teacher and a person from the wellness center. The wellness center gentleman asked the first student if anything was troubling her at home. She made a comment. He went to the next person, but before the next person could speak, she had to repeat what the person before her said. It made each child concentrate more because they knew they had to repeat the other person's information. They went around the whole room. They cried. I cried.

Then we went to the library. A beautiful library. No books. They ran out of money. That upset Susan and me. All the way home in the car, Susan and I kept asking what we could do to help the library.

President Harrison continues:

Susan, supported by Kent, said, "We can't accept this. We've got this great school, great principal, great idea, we're about to get these great students here and we have no books for them in the library. "Susan struck on this idea of holding a concert and magic show for the kids and the parents, charging admission. She underwrote the show. All the admissions charges would go toward buying books for the library. Plus, she went out and found publishers who were willing to donate books or provide them at very low cost, kids' books from Pre-K to the fifth grade.

We had this wonderful concert that was called, "The Magic of Reading[164] *and there were magic acts and musical acts and entertainment acts all aimed at children of all ages, up to my age.*[165] *Hugely successful. Through that show and finding sponsors and finding book publishers who were willing to donate books, we filled that library completely in the most up-to-date, wonderful way. It's still a model library.*

How many people go out and say, "I'm going to give money, but more importantly, raise money, to support a public school. Not only a public school, but a public school three thousand miles away from where I live?" It's just an incredible, incredible act of generosity.

With Susan at "The Magic of Reading"

There's a plaque in the library that has our names on it.

When we lived in Malibu, we started and ran a store called Malibu Nutcorn during a break in our film production work. We had a six-foot stuffed bear sitting in a chair in the window. Eventually we closed the business but we kept the bear. We put it in the back of the car during a trip back for a Regent's meeting and we took it to the magnet school. Principal Kloczko named him "Junior." He was a pretty stout bear. I put my clothes on him and they fit perfectly. The bear was in the lobby near the principal's office. All the kids would come by and hug Junior, who became part of their family.

Cheryl told us one time during an ordinary fire drill, the kids left the building. When they got outside, Cheryl said some of the kids were crying. "Where's Junior?" From that point on, Junior was taken out on all the fire drills.

Then there was a thing that started in Chicago, a Cow Parade they called them. They were cows made out of fiberglass, some mounted on wheels. It was a parade of all kinds of cows. They were artistically painted and some were used as business promotions. They held a Cow Parade in West Hartford near the college. At the end of the parade, they auctioned off some of the cows and we bought one. We donated that to the magnate school, too. It's still there. The plaque reads: Madam MooCray![166]

In 2005, Susan was asked to be a University of Hartford Regent, too.[167] Since she went back with me when the meetings were held, she was already involved in a lot of University projects. Now, she became even more involved.

Walt Harrison explains:

...We have an auditorium called Millard Auditorium that is a large performing arts venue within the Hartt School. It was built in 1962 and opened in '63 and really hasn't been changed very much since then. Outside in particular there was an area that was really dreary. It was built in early-1960s style, heavy wood, dark colors, and nothing really had been changed about it.

Susan...said, "Look, this is a world-class performing arts conservatory, but you would never get that impression standing in this lobby. We've got to do something to make the lobby brighter and more inviting. It'll signal to people coming to concerts and to students who are considering the school that this is one of the great performing arts schools in the country."

She said, "I have an idea. I want to find a place where I can appropriately display my father's memorabilia from his incredibly successful career. If we can find a way to incorporate that in the lobby, Kent and I will be willing to donate the money to completely refurbish and brighten the lobby so it reflects a world-class conservatory." Essentially, she helped, well, that's an understatement. She drove the design of it. She found people to do the fine work that it isn't necessarily possible for universities to do. She provided the funding and she constantly oversaw the transformation of this very important space.

Walt is right. The Harry Sukman Foyer[168] came about from Susan. We were back there for a Regents' meeting and we walked through the lobby. Dingy-looking place. You could hardly see across the room it was so dark. No warmth.

Susan took her dad's memorabilia and donated his beloved Steinway piano that came from her parents' home. There are actually nine different panels about Harry Sukman's life created by Susan from the material she collected. They're gorgeous. Now when we go back there, kids are rehearsing, they're sitting there reading and enjoying the area. The foyer is used quite regularly, even for formal receptions.

Then, I went down to the television studio they had for the students. The equipment they were using was so inadequate it was ridiculous. They just didn't have the money. I gave them a good amount of money so they could buy new equipment.

More from Walt:

...the station was built about 1988 and nothing really changed much...Kent was aware that it needed significant upgrades. They said, "Look, here are ways to upgrade both the equipment and the station and the way it looks." We re-named it the Kent McCray Television Studio[169] and it now features quite a tribute to Kent's remarkable career in television. So, it serves our student needs and it reflects a very important alumnus, maybe the most important alumnus, we have ever created for television.

**With President Walt Harrison during the dedication of the new
TV studio named after me.**

*So, pretty similar, right? They give the money; they supervise
the way it's going to be done. They have expertise in this area that
they help provide us with. Then, it's a tribute really to, in one case
her father, and in the other case Kent's life in the art or the field
that these students are studying.*

A little bit later, the university felt it needed a whole separate
area for the performing arts center which was off the main campus
a little way. I gave them money for a black box theater in my
name.

Walt Harrison continues:

*The last act of generosity is near the campus. A mile south of
the campus, there was an old Cadillac dealership that had moved
and was now an abandoned building. I came up with the idea...to
convert that into a home for the dance and theater division in the
Hartt School who up until then had been in this makeshift space in
various places around town.*

A lot of people worked on this. It took a long time to do. It was a $22-million project. We managed to do it and Kent and Susan said, "We want to be a part of this.

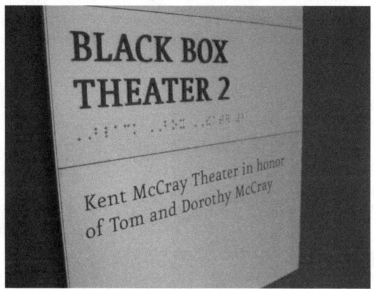

The Black Box Theater to honor my parents.

Given Kent's long-term involvement with the Hartt School and with its theater, we'd like to give the money to name one of the two black box theaters." So, we did that. It's now called The Kent McCray Theatre.[170]

Walt continues:

Since we're located on the East Coast, we've taken our students down to New York and they would do a kind of talent audition in their senior year and we invite producers and directors from the New York area in to see them, and theoretically give them a chance to see this talent and maybe approach these students individually for Broadway musicals or touring musicals or whatever they were doing.

Susan said, "Why don't you expand that to Southern California and do this for the arts industry here?" which, of course, is primarily for film and television, but also for live theater. So, she not only helped them locate a theater and find producers, but she really sort of helped them set up a West Coast version of this same talent audition for students out there, which again, has continued to this day.

I was a Regent for ten years, I think, or longer. I enjoyed it and I met a lot of nice people that I wouldn't have met. I think it's important to give back because education is important. Kids today *need* a degree, they *need* a good education. I think anything I can do to help that situation, that's where my money's going to go. There are a lot of charities out there and I'm not saying they're not worthy of it, but the bulk of any monies I have left is going to schools. My prep school, where I spent three years, and the University.

Walt concludes:

I've been here (since 1998) and they've remained active and generous supporters of the University, people whose advice and direction I count on. Their spirit, Kent's spirit and Susan's spirit, infuses this campus in so many ways, and continues to be a real source of support and joy for all of us...Kent was given an honorary doctorate from our school.[171] It was so deserved.

Susan feels the same way about education. Now, she and I are also involved with Eastern Connecticut State University.[172] She tells how that happened prior to her becoming a Regent for University of Hartford:

I met a representative from Eastern Connecticut State University while on one of our Regent trips to Hartford. During one of Kent's meetings that I wasn't allowed to attend, I called this man, a vice president, and asked him to show me around ECSU's campus. He did and as we were going around, the head of the theater department was writing her resignation. I asked why. It seems that department was on the verge of closing.

It became a project I was passionate about. I started different funds for students to go to New York to see plays. I became very involved. On April 9, 2016, they held the grand opening of the new

Fine Arts Building, with the Susan Sukman McCray foyer named after me for all my support.[173]

In 1999, Susan set up "The Susan McCray Account for The Theatre Arts" to support special initiatives within the theater arts. Susan donated "The Harry Sukman Master of Music Collection" to Eastern in 2004. It includes music scores from such composers as Franz Liszt, George Gershwin, Brahms, and Beethoven, to name a few. She was awarded an Honorary Doctorate degree from Eastern in May 2008.[174]

We think education is important and if we can contribute to make things better, that's something we will continue to do.

CHAPTER FORTY-TWO

My Work

I'm not after glory. I've had all the glory I wanted or needed from the work I did. I kept behind the scenes. Susan and I are not in the limelight. The stars are the ones the papers want to focus on. I'm not upset about that. It's just the way it is. The people I work with know me.[175]

My awards have been very gratifying. When I talk to people, they're in awe of the shows I've done which makes me feel good. When I sit back and think about the fact that many of them are historic, it makes me proud.

The early days of Skelton were great; Groucho Marx was fantastic, a very clever man who could talk for hours without looking at a script. I respected Bob Hope and liked him. My three years with him were wonderful.

I started on *Bonanza* in 1962 and it's still on the air. *High Chaparral* first aired in 1967 and it's still on the air. Getting bigger. Global. In fact, Susan and I are hosting the 50th Anniversary of *The High Chaparral*[176] and honoring all who made the show so special.

Little House is a phenomenal show. It has a bigger audience today than when it actually aired because of the technology changes. You can turn the TV set on and find *Little House* on different channels all day long. It's on in the morning here, in the afternoon there. Somewhere, you're going to find *Little House* during the day.[177] *Highway to Heaven* still offers meaningful stories that touched the heart and inspired many.

The devotion of our fans is very strong for all these shows. When I'm in public, my greatest enjoyment is talking to fans one-on-one. I tell them if they have a question, ask me. I'll answer it! Any question they ever had.

I enjoy talking to people about the shows and I think they do, too. I can give them an insight of what the actual show looked like. Most of the people have only seen the shows on television or DVDs. I can talk about what we did, where we did it. Then they'll say, "Oh, I remember that scene!" I can add that color to their memories, which I enjoy doing. Immensely.

If it hadn't been for Susan prompting me, I probably wouldn't have pursued doing my life story, but I *am* pleased with what I've done. This book is life at a different age, a different era. How many people who started in live television are still around?

Most of the books in the industry you read are about actors or people close to actors. A lot of them don't get into the nuts and bolts of what it took to do the job and that's what I've tried to relay. That's what it takes to bring the audience a well-produced television show. It doesn't happen overnight. You have to work hard. You have to know what you're doing. You have to love it with all your heart. That's how people should remember me. That's what I want to share with my grandkids and my great-grandkids.

END NOTES
(About these notes at the end. English—I just hate it!)

CHAPTER 1

[1] http://americanradiohistory.com/Archive-BC/BC-1952/BC-1952-03-17.pdf, pg 58

[2] WTIC made its first broadcast on Feb. 10, 1925. http://www.wticalumni.com/history.htm

[3] http://www.wticalumni.com/history.htm "The flood of 1936 and hurricane of 1938 set the pattern for WTIC's further development -- accurate, responsible and community-oriented reporting. The Connecticut River inundated Hartford in 1936 and WTIC became the focal point for disaster information. It served the role again in1938 when a hurricane swelled rivers all over the state. WTIC was the only station able to remain in constant operation. Ben Hawthorne and program manager Tom McCray used a makeshift shortwave setup to report live from atop the Travelers Tower."

[4] http://www.hartfordradiohistory.com/WTIC__AM_.php, Newspaper clipping entitled, "Hartford Man Takes Radio Censor's Post."

[5] By 1945, he was named National Program Manager for the entire NBC network. http://americanradiohistory.com/Archive-BC/BC-1952/BC-1952-03-17.pdf, pg 69

CHAPTER 2

[6] Nagy is pronounced Nah' Gee.

[7] The Billboard, April 1, 1950

[8] "Channel 9 signed on the air as KFI-TV on August 25, 1948…and General Tire changed its new television station's call letters to KHJ-TV in September 1951." https://en.wikipedia.org/wiki/KCAL-TV

CHAPTER 3

[9] The International Alliance of Theatrical Stage Employees, http://iatse.net/about-iatse .

[10] Around 1947, American Telephone and Telegraph (AT&T) began building what they called the Transcontinental Microwave Relay System, a series of microwave towers with coaxial cables that could boost signals across the nation, including television signals. On Sept. 4, 1951 President Truman addressed the opening session of the Japanese Peace Treaty Conference in San

Francisco…Regular television programs are scheduled to begin September 28.
http://long-lines.net/places-routes/1st_transcon_mw/Telephone_Skyway.pdf
[11] *My Favorite Year* was released Oct. 8, 1982.
http://www.imdb.com/title/tt0084370/

CHAPTER 4

[12] DuMont network aired from 1946 to 1956. http://www.dumontnetwork.com/
[13] *Colgate Comedy Hour* aired from Sep. 10, 1950 to Dec. 25, 1955.
http://www.imdb.com/title/tt0042094/
[14] *The All Star Revue* aired Oct. 4, 1950 to Dec. 26, 1953.
http://www.imdb.com/title/tt0042106/
[15] Kent remembers: "The crews that worked for NBC were the IA stage hands
from Local 33. The engineering members were part of a union called NABET,
which handled all the television technical directors, sound engineers,
cameramen and anybody who actually touched the cameras, did sound
operation as well as all the video people who controlled the sets in the booth."
http://www.ia33.org/ and http://www.nabetcwa.org/
[16] *The Red Skelton Show* aired from Sep. 30, 1951 to Mar. 15, 1971.
http://www.imdb.com/title/tt0043224/

CHAPTER 5

[17] Ralph Edwards describes this show's format:
> It didn't really have a theme. I was given carte blanche to do anything
> I wanted, try out new ideas, be a talk show, a variety show. Anything.
> We had a good musical group and a wonderful singer, Carol Richards,
> who had a big hit singing "Silver Bells" with Bing Crosby. Muscle-
> man Steve Reeves, kind of our answer to Dagmar, something for the
> female audience to look at. Steve usually just walked around the stage
> flexing his muscles, but once we gave him a line to say. 'Yes, Mr.
> Edwards.' He practiced and dramatized it very well. 'Yes, Mr.
> Edwards. Yes, Mr. Edwards. Yes, Mr. Edwards.' When he came out
> on stage, you guessed it, he forgot his line. I never knew whether to
> believe him or not. But we had surprise elements, good gestures, skits
> and so on. Kind of an experimental theater.

Ralph Edwards, Archive of American Television, interviewed by Bob Warren
on May 21, 1987 in Beverly Hills, CA.   Visit http://www.emmytvlegends.org/
for more information. (Archive of American Television, 1997)
[18] *The Johnny Dugan Show* aired May. 19, 1952 to Sep. 5, 1952.
http://www.tvtango.com/series/johnny_dugan_show/episodes
[19] *This Is Your Life* aired Dec. 10, 1952 to Aug. 24, 1961, although it reappeared
in later years as well.   http://www.imdb.com/title/tt0044296/
[20] The Victor McLaglen Episode aired Oct. 28, 1953.
http://www.thisisyourlife.com/search2.html?id_tiyl=0209TL425796

[21] The Dr. Kate Pelham Newcomb episode aired March 17, 1954.
http://www.thisisyourlife.com/search2.html?id_tiyl=0209TL425796
[22] The Billie Clevenger episode aired Nov. 19, 1952.
http://www.thisisyourlife.com/search2.html?id_tiyl=0209TL425796
[23] *Hollywood Opening Night* aired Oct. 6, 1952 to Mar. 23, 1953.
http://www.imdb.com/title/tt0043206/

CHAPTER 6

[24] Ruth Senkel McCray passed away on April 11, 2001.

CHAPTER 8

[25] *Texaco Star Theater* aired June 8, 1948 to June 5, 1956.
http://www.imdb.com/title/tt0040041/
[26] Berle became so popular, he is credited with greatly influencing television set sales. "When Milton originally went on the air, there were only 500,000 sets in the entire country. By mid-season, the number had skyrocketed to over a million, and by 1954, more than 26 million American homes had at least two television sets." (http://www.cmgww.com/stars/berle/about/biography.html)
[27] Kinescope copies were made of shows to rebroadcast for different time zones, but generally the quality was poor. Kinescopes were basically special film cameras focused on recording a monitor displaying the live performance. Find more information about kinescope recordings here:
http://www.museum.tv/eotv/kinescope.htm
[28] *The Pinky Lee Show* aired Jan. 4, 1954 to May 11, 1956.
http://www.tvrage.com/the-pinky-lee-show
[29] *Queen for a Day* aired Jan. 3, 1956 to Oct. 2, 1964 on various networks.
http://www.tv.com/shows/queen-for-a-day/
[30] *Lux Video Theatre* aired Oct. 2, 1950 to Sep. 12, 1957.
http://www.imdb.com/title/tt0042123/
[31] *You Bet Your Life* aired Oct. 05, 1950 to June 29, 1961.
http://www.imdb.com/title/tt0042171/. "Both the radio and television versions of *The Groucho Show* (as it was retitled in its final season) were somewhat pioneering in that they were recorded and edited for later broadcast...He (Groucho) could venture into risqué banter, knowing anything too blue for broadcast could be cut. Dull bits of his unrehearsed, hour-long interviews were deleted...Putting the program on film (and paying a star's salary) gave *You Bet Your Life* a higher production cost than other game shows. The investment was returned, however, by both high ratings and the ability to repeat episodes."
http://www.museum.tv/eotv/marxgroucho.htm
[32] NBC's Film Division was established on March 3, 1953. In early 1956, Kagran Corporation acquired the NBC Film Division and by mid-1956, changed its name to California National Productions, Inc. to reflect its expansion of the film and syndication arm of NBC. The network announced,

"Production staff for the California National Studios includes William Fenton Coe, former senior unit manager for NBC Film Production Facilities and Production Services as production manager...and four production supervisors: Richard A. Larsen, Kent B. McCray, Robert T. Stillman and William Tinsman...who are also former West Coast production staffers." *NBC Chimes*, July/August 1956 pp. 6-7.

[33]*Dragnet* first aired Dec. 16, 1951 to Aug. 23, 1959 and returned again in 1967 to 1970. http://www.imdb.com/title/tt0043194/

[34] *Matinee Theater* aired Oct. 31, 1955 to June 4, 1958. http://www.imdb.com/title/tt0047756/

[35](Albert McCleery) "...created the 'Cameo Theatre,' using minimal props and only the actors and dialogue as the main attraction...Successful with this new venue, he went on to produce and direct *Matinee Theatre* a daytime project which earned him an EMMY." http://www.tv.com/people/albert-mccleery/biography/

[36]Jim Buckley of the Pewter Plough Playhouse (Cambria, California) recalled: "When Al McCleery got back to the States, he originated a most ambitious theatrical TV series for NBC called *Matinee Theater* to televise five different stage plays per week live, airing around noon in order to promote color TV (which had just been developed) to the American housewife as she labored over her ironing..." https://sites.google.com/site/thunderdrumsradio/radio-shows-1/radio-shows-beginning-with-m/matinee-theater

CHAPTER 9

[37]Bob Hope was born on May 29, 1903 and died on July 27, 2003 at the age of 100. He first performed on stage around 1921 and retired in 1997. http://bobhope.org/bob-dolores-hope/bob/ "Bob Hope performed his first USO Show at California's March Field on May 6, 1941...(and he) entertained until December 1990, when he brought laughter and Christmas cheer to troops participating in Operation Desert Shield in Saudi Arabia and Bahrain on his final USO tour." http://www.uso.org/bob-hope/

[38]The 1956 show included guest stars Ginger Rogers; baseball great Mickey Mantle; Hollywood columnist Hedda Hopper; comedian Jerry Colonna; singer Peggy King; song and dance act The Del Rubio Triplets; the Purdue University Glee Club, Miss Universe Carol Morris, and Les Brown and His Band of Renown. http://www.imdb.com/title/tt0528267/fullcredits

[39]An edited version of the actual episode can be seen at the following website. Kent said he made the chicken clucks off stage in the sergeant skit at 31:12 into the video: https://www.youtube.com/watch?v=IiCiSts-S28

CHAPTER 10

[40]In between working with Mr. Hope, Kent was also doing early film production on *Boots and Saddles* (aired Sept. 19, 1957 to June 10, 1958, http://www.imdb.com/title/tt0050000/) and *The Silent Service* (aired Apr. 5,

1957 to Nov. 28, 1958, http://www.imdb.com/title/tt0050061/). Per Kent, "I did not have to go on location to Kanab, Utah—I wasn't that smart yet—but I did all the legwork here in town. Shuffled people back and forth. Made sure they got on planes and had the equipment they needed. Made sure all the film got back to the lab. I also did that on a show that was shot in Long Beach called *The Silent Service*, which was a story about submarines. Those were my first chores back in the film division."

[41]Bob's guests for the 1957 Christmas show were actress Jayne Mansfield; Jerry Colonna; Hedda Hopper; actor Peter Leeds; dancer Arthur Duncan; Jayne Mansfield's fiancé Mr. Universe Mickey Hargitay; singers Erin O'Brien and Carol Jarvis, and Les Brown & His Band of Renown. http://www.tv.com/shows/the-bob-hope-show/january-18-1958-1201394/

[42]http://www.tv.com/shows/the-bob-hope-show/january-18-1958-1201394/

CHAPTER 11

[43]*Paris Holiday* went into production in early April to late June 1957. Starring Bob Hope and Anita Ekberg, it was released in the early 1958. http://www.tcm.com/tcmdb/title/86256/Paris-Holiday/original-print-info.html

[44] Kent and wife Susan Sukman McCray live in the Westlake area.

[45]Bob's guests for the 1958 Christmas show were actress Gina Lollobrigida; comedian Jerry Colonna; Hollywood columnist Hedda Hopper; singers Molly Bee and Randy Sparks; actress Elaine Dunn-Shendal; and Les Brown & His Band of Renown.

[46]Locations included the Azores; Port Lioti, Africa; Marone and Madrid in Spain; Barona, Bajensa, and aboard the *USS Forrestal* at Naples, Italy; Frankfurt and Tempelhof in West Germany; Prestwick, Scotland; Keflavik, Iceland; and Goose Bay, Labrador. http://www.tv.com/shows/the-bob-hope-show/january-16-1959-1201580/

[47]The *USO Xmas European Bases Show.* http://www.tv.com/shows/the-bob-hope-show/january-16-1959-1201580/

CHAPTER 12

[48] *Philip Marlowe* aired Oct. 6, 1959 to March 29, 1960. http://www.imdb.com/title/tt0052501/

[49] *Perry Mason* aired Sept. 21, 1957 to May 22, 1966. http://www.imdb.com/title/tt0050051/

[50] *The Lawless Years* aired Apr. 16, 1959 to Sept 22, 1961. http://www.imdb.com/title/tt0052484/

[51] *Outlaws*, Sept 29, 1960 to May 10, 1962. http://www.imdb.com/title/tt0053527/

[52] Don Collier, b. Oct. 17, 1928. http://www.imdb.com/name/nm0171896/

[53] Robert F. (Bobby) Hoy, b. Apr. 3, 1927; d. Feb. 8, 2010. http://www.imdb.com/name/nm0398338/

[54] Interview with Don Collier on Aug. 18, 2014.
[55] This show aired under the title *The Americans*, Jan. 23, 1961 to May 5, 1961.
http://www.imdb.com/title/tt0054515/
[56] Interview with Jack Lilley on Aug 23, 2014.

CHAPTER 13

[57] *The Dinah Shore Chevy Show* aired February 5, 1961.
http://www.imdb.com/title/tt1158401/

CHAPTER 14

[58] Per Kent, 'pay or play' meant that NBC had to pay Edwards anyway whether he produced something or not.

CHAPTER 15

[59] *Bonanza*, Sep. 12, 1959 to Jan. 16, 1973.
http://www.imdb.com/title/tt0052451/
[60] Per Kent, "I was always intrigued with the hardships the pioneers had to go through. It wasn't easy living. I marveled every time we drove back East. We'd take different routes. A few times we came back through Denver and the Rocky Mountains. People got on a wagon and went over these mountains in a wagon train? They must have been out of their minds! But they did it. I've watched every kind of movie like that. I'm hooked. The Civil War movies I like. Anything that has to do with history I'll watch it. I think that's why I've always liked Westerns, because I've always liked historical stuff."
[61] David Dortort, b. Oct. 23, 1916; d. Sep. 5, 2010.
http://www.imdb.com/name/nm0234228/
[62] *The Restless Gun*, Sep. 23, 1957 to Sep. 14, 1959
http://www.imdb.com/title/tt0050055/
[63] Michael Landon, b. Oct. 2, 1936; d. July 1, 1991.
http://www.imdb.com/name/nm0001446/
[64] Dan Blocker, b. Dec. 10, 1928; d. May 13, 1972.
http://www.imdb.com/name/nm0088779/
[65] "Ponderosa Explosion," aired Jan. 1, 1967.
http://www.imdb.com/title/tt0529628/
CHAPTER 16

[66] Harry Sukman, b. Dec. 2, 1912; d. Dec. 2, 1984. Oscar-winning composer (with two other Oscar nominations) who did all the episode music for *The High Chaparral* and composed music for many episodes of *Bonanza*. He is the father of casting director Susan Sukman McCray, and Kent McCray's father-in-law. http://www.imdb.com/name/nm0006313/

[67] David Rose, b. June 15, 1910; d. Aug. 23, 1990.
http://www.imdb.com/name/nm0741328/
[68] "The Other Son" aired Oct. 3, 1965. http://www.imdb.com/title/tt0529784/
[69] Lorne Greene, b. Feb. 12, 1915; d. Sep. 11, 1987.
http://www.imdb.com/name/nm0001296
[70] According to Michael Landon, Dan Blocker, who eventually did wear a toupee, would do gags with it. "He'd sit in a restaurant and sneeze and let it fall over so that it hung in front of his eyes, but pretend that he didn't know…" The Tonight Show starring Johnny Carson, air date Jan. 19, 1990 (presumed date, although marked 1989.) https://www.youtube.com/watch?v=4x6cqtwYnTo
[71] Bonanza, "The Gamble," is the first episode giving teleplay credit to Michael Landon. It aired Apr. 1, 1962. http://www.imdb.com/title/tt0529721/
[72] Bonanza, "To Die in Darkness" is the first episode of the series directed by Michael Landon. It aired May 5, 1968. http://www.imdb.com/title/tt0529869/
[73] Sept. 1961. Brooks, Tim & Marsh, Earle (1979). The Complete Directory to Prime Time Network TV Shows (5th ed.). New York: Ballantine. ISBN: 0-345-37792-3, pg. 108.
[74] The Bonanza episode "Patchwork" is the last show to be broadcast with the character Adam. It aired May 23, 1965. http://www.imdb.com/title/tt0529626/
[75] Haskell B. "Buzzy" Boggs, b. Apr. 17, 1909; d. May 30, 2003.
http://www.imdb.com/name/nm0091772/. Per Kent, "Haskell Boggs was his name but he was called Buzzy. Carol Lombard gave him the name because he was always buzzing around. And the light meter was always in the cleavage. If he had to check a light, he placed the meter on the cleavage. He wasn't any dumbbell!"
[76] Little House on the Prairie aired Mar. 30, 1974 to Mar. 21, 1983.
http://www.imdb.com/title/tt0071007/
[77] Directors Guild of America, http://www.dga.org/

CHAPTER 17

[78] Bonanza episode "The Code" aired Feb. 13, 1966.
http://www.imdb.com/title/tt0529689/

CHAPTER 18

[79] The High Chaparral, Sep. 10, 1967 to Mar. 12, 1971.
http://www.imdb.com/title/tt0061263/
80 Mallory Furnier, archivist for the David Dortort papers at the Autry National Center, shared comments from some documents on file:

> In October 1969 the Mexican-American Opportunity Foundation awarded David Dortort and the cast of The High Chaparral a merit award for its contributions to the Mexican-American community…The show also received international recognition. A September 22, 1970 letter sent from Alejandra Páez Urquidi, Governor of the Mexican

state of Durango, to NBC headquarters noted that 'because *The High Chaparral* uses so many Mexican characters and treats them with a kind of dignity and understanding that is seldom seen in an American television show, that as a result it has become a favorite throughout Mexico and is greatly admired and loved by our people.'
http://mfurnier.weebly.com/archives.html

[81] Robert "Bob"Shelton (b. Mar. 21, 1921; d. Dec. 15, 2016) decided to create an Old West tourist attraction in 1959 and found the location at the Old Tucson film set outside of Tucson, AZ. http://www.oldtucsonblog.com/bob-shelton/

[82] Interview with Bob Shelton on June 16, 2015.

[83] Interview with Henry Darrow (b. Sep. 15, 1933) on Aug. 25, 2014.
http://www.imdb.com/name/nm0201688

CHAPTER 19

[84] Per Kent about John Gammons: "John was a BIG man. He knew every back road and he knew anybody everywhere. I always used him if I wanted to go look at locations someplace. If I drove up in the Sheriff's truck, they were going to talk with me. If I drove up in my own car, they were going to come out with a shotgun! John also had access across the border into Mexico. He had a shell on the back of his truck, and when we needed a little extra Mexican furniture, he would drive us down in his truck, and we'd load it in the back under the shell and drive home. We didn't have to stop and pay duty on it. He was a great guy."

CHAPTER 20

[85] In a letter written by Neil Summers dated May 8, 2015.
http://www.imdb.com/name/nm0838612

[86] Interview with Steve DeFrance on May 13, 2015.
http://www.imdb.com/name/nm0214567

[87] *Bonanza* episode "All Ye His Saints" aired Dec. 19, 1965.
http://www.imdb.com/title/tt0529495/

[88] *The High Chaparral* episode, "For What We Are About to Receive" aired Nov. 29, 1968. http://www.imdb.com/title/tt0601095/

[89] The scene described here is not in the final aired version.

[90] "The Buffalo Soldiers" featured about forty members from the 10th Cavalry Regiment from Los Angeles. The finale has the regiment lined up side by side as they charge the baddies. At the last minute, one half of the group wheels right while the other wheels left, circling around the bad guys who end up in front of the cavalry as they're herded to town for arrest. According to Kent, the scene was shot by a camera crew about 70 feet in the air. The episode aired Nov. 22, 1968. http://www.imdb.com/title/tt0601129/ It won a National Cowboy Museum Western Heritage Award in 1969.

http://nationalcowboymuseum.org/awards-halls-of-fame/western-heritage-awards/western-heritage-award-winners/

CHAPTER 22

[91] Per Kent the episode "The Night Virginia City Died" was produced to cover for any set differences that may have occurred from changing production locations. The episode aired Sep. 13, 1970.
http://www.imdb.com/title/tt0529782/

CHAPTER 23

[92] Interviews with Susan Sukman McCray in July 2014.
[93] Per Susan, "Burt Lancaster won his Oscar for *Elmer Gantry* the same year my father did. Jim actually brought his father's Oscar to school that next day in a paper bag for show and tell! I said, 'Jim, how could he let you do that?' Jim said, 'My dad said it was okay.' Then I came home and I told my dad, and he said, 'There's no way I'd give you my Oscar in a paper bag to take to school.'"
[94] 1961 Oscar Winners include Harry Sukman for Best Music, Scoring of a Motion Picture. http://www.imdb.com/event/ev0000003/1961
[95] Henry Mancini won for Breakfast at Tiffany's,
http://www.imdb.com/title/tt0054698/
[96] Per Susan, writing for two shows was not new to her dad. "He did that also with *Dr. Kildare* and *The Eleventh Hour* before that, also for NBC."

CHAPTER 24

[97] The last *High Chaparral* episode to air was "A Man to Match the Land" on Mar. 12, 1971. http://www.imdb.com/title/tt0601075/
[98] The last *Bonanza* episode to air was "The Hunter" on Jan. 16, 1973.
http://www.imdb.com/title/tt0529742/
[99] The last *Gunsmoke* episode to air was "The Sharecroppers" on Mar. 31, 1975.
http://www.imdb.com/title/tt0594516/0
[100] June 6, 1968
[101] June 11, 1970 http://www.blackpast.org/aah/silvera-frank-1914-1970
[102] *The High Chaparral* aired on Sunday nights at 10:00 pm EST from 1967 to 1968, then on Friday nights at 7:30 pm EST from 1968 to 1971.
[103] Dan Blocker died May 13, 1972 from a pulmonary embolism after having gall bladder surgery. He was 43. http://www.imdb.com/name/nm0088779/bio
[104] *Bonanza* episode "Forever" aired Sept. 12, 1972.
http://www.imdb.com/title/tt0529566/
[105] Kerkor "Kirk" Kerkorian (b. June 6, 1917; d. June 15, 2015) bought MGM in 1969 and "...downsized the struggling MGM and sold off massive amounts of historical memorabilia, including Dorothy's ruby slippers (from *The Wizard*

of Oz), and several acres of MGM's backlots (which were razed to build houses)." http://www.armeniapedia.org/wiki/Kirk_Kerkorian

CHAPTER 25

[106] *Barnaby Jones* aired from Jan. 28, 1973 to Sep. 4, 1980.
http://www.imdb.com/title/tt0069557/ Kent worked as production manager for about one season starting later in 1973.
[107] *Love Story* aired on NBC from Oct. 3, 1973 to Jan. 2, 1974.
http://www.imdb.com/title/tt0069604/
[108] "Love Came Laughing" aired on Oct. 3, 1973.
http://www.imdb.com/title/tt0636942/
[109] Laura Ingalls Wilder, b. Feb. 7, 1867; d. Feb. 10, 1957.
http://www.lauraingallswilderhome.com/
[110] Interview with Leslie Landon Matthews on Sep. 10, 2014.
http://www.imdb.com/name/nm0484930/

CHAPTER 27

[111] *Streets of San Francisco* aired Sep. 16, 1972 to June 9, 1977.
http://www.imdb.com/title/tt0068135/
[112] The pilot for *Movin' On* aired May 8, 1974.
http://www.imdb.com/title/tt0068135/
[113] *LaVerne & Shirley* aired Jan. 27, 1976 to May 10, 1983.
http://www.imdb.com/title/tt0074016/
[114] *Happy Days* aired Jan. 15, 1974 to Sep. 24, 1984.
http://www.imdb.com/title/tt0070992/
[115] The *Odd Couple* aired Sep. 24, 1970 to Mar. 7, 1975.
http://www.imdb.com/title/tt0065329/
[116] *Mannix* aired Sep. 16, 1967 to Apr. 13, 1975.
http://www.imdb.com/title/tt0061277/
[117] *Kung Fu* aired Feb. 22, 1972 to Apr. 26, 975.
http://www.imdb.com/title/tt0068093/
[118] *The New Land* aired Sep. 14, 1974 to Oct. 19, 1974.
http://www.imdb.com/title/tt0071023/
[119] "I'll Be Waving as You Drive Away, Part II" aired Mar. 13, 1978.
http://www.imdb.com/title/tt0633030/
[120] "The Lord Is My Shepherd, Parts I & II" aired Dec. 18, 1974.
http://www.imdb.com/title/tt0633104/ and
http://www.imdb.com/title/tt0633105/
[121] Interview with Dean Wilson on Nov. 14, 2014.
http://www.imdb.com/name/nm0933279/
[122] Interview with Clarence Tindell on Dec. 3, 2014.
http://www.imdb.com/name/nm0863890/

[123] Interview with Brad Yacobian on Nov. 23, 2014.
http://www.imdb.com/name/nm0944792/ Mr. Yacobian's other credits include *Cold Case; Star Trek: Enterprise; Star Trek: Voyager;* and *Star Trek: The Next Generation.*
[124] Interview with John Musselman on Nov. 21, 2014.
[125] Interview with Vern Leyk on Nov. 20, 2014.

CHAPTER 29

[126] Thomas McCray passed away on May 20, 1974 and Dorothy "Dode" McCray died May 9, 1975.
[127] *The Loneliest Runner* aired on Dec. 20, 1976.
http://www.imdb.com/title/tt0074814/
[128] *Carter Country* aired from Sep. 15, 1977 to June 21, 1979.
http://www.imdb.com/title/tt0075489/
[129] "The Godsister" aired on Dec. 18, 1978.
http://www.imdb.com/title/tt0633091/
[130] Stage 15 dimensions are 315' wide by 135' long.
http://www.sonypictures.com/studios/stages.php
[131] *Thirty Seconds Over Tokyo* was released in November 1944.
http://www.imdb.com/title/tt0037366/

CHAPTER 30

[132] *Killing Stone* aired May 2, 1978. http://www.imdb.com/title/tt0077802/
[133] *Father Murphy* aired from Nov. 3, 1981 to Sep. 18, 1983.
http://www.imdb.com/title/tt0081861/

CHAPTER 31

[134] Interview with Dean Butler (b. May 20, 1956) on May 19, 2015.
http://www.imdb.com/name/nm0124890/
[135] *Feherty* can be found at http://www.golfchannel.com/tv/feherty/
[136] Legacy Documentaries can be found at
http://legacydocumentaries.com/dean-butler
[137] Interview with Stan Ivar (b. Jan. 11, 1943) on Oct. 13, 2014.
http://www.imdb.com/name/nm0412177/
[138] *Little House: Look Back to Yesterday* aired Dec. 12, 1983.
http://www.imdb.com/title/tt0085855/
    Little House: Bless All the Dear Children aired Dec. 14, 1984.
http://www.imdb.com/title/tt0087630/
[139] *Little House: The Last Farewell* aired Feb. 6, 1984.
http://www.imdb.com/title/tt0087631/
[140] *Sam's Son* aired Aug. 17, 1984. http://www.imdb.com/title/tt0088034/

CHAPTER 33

[141] Kent and Susan were married on Jan. 28, 1984.
[142] ALS: amyotrophic lateral sclerosis also known as Lou Gehrig's disease.
[143] Francesca Paley Sukman died Apr.7,1990 at age 73.

CHAPTER 34

[144] *Highway to Heaven* aired from Aug. 19, 1984 to Aug. 4, 1989
[145] Per Kent, the average bonus was $5,000.
[146] Interview with Tom Sullivan (b. Mar. 27, 1947) on July 17, 2014.
http://www.imdb.com/name/nm0837945/
[147] "All the Colors of the Heart" aired Nov. 18, 1987.
http://www.imdb.com/title/tt0601524/
    "Summer Camp" aired July 14, 1989. http://www.imdb.com/title/tt0601583/
[148] http://sullivanlive.com/

CHAPTER 36

[149] *Where Pigeons Go to Die* by R. Wright Campbell, 1978, Rawson Associate Publishers.
https://books.google.com/books/about/Where_Pigeons_Go_to_Die.html?id=mbQdAAAAMAAJ
[150] *Where Pigeons Go to Die* aired Jan. 29, 1990.
http://www.imdb.com/title/tt0100923/
[151] Alfred Hitchcock was known to appear in background scenes in almost all movies he directed.
https://en.wikipedia.org/wiki/List_of_Alfred_Hitchcock_cameo_appearances

CHAPTER 37

[152] "In 1990, Tartikoff was elevated to the newly created position of chairman of NBC Entertainment. He left the network in 1991 to become chairman of Paramount Pictures, staying for only one year."
http://www.sfgate.com/news/article/TV-Programming-Genius-Brandon-Tartikoff-Dies-2829046.php

CHAPTER 38

[153] Portions of that conference can be seen in *ET*'s coverage of Michael Landon's passing. https://www.youtube.com/watch?v=2guCdRyaKm8

[154] St. Bernadette at Lourdes, http://www.medjugorjeusa.org/lourdes.htm
[155] May 9, 1991.
http://www.yourememberthat.com/media/8100/Michael_Landon_Final_Tonigh
t_Show_Appearance/#.VpuiNfkrJD8
[156] Michael Landon passed away on July 1, 1991.

[157] *Little House on the Prairie* episode entitled "Remember Me, Part 1" aired
Nov. 5, 1975. http://www.imdb.com/title/tt0633063/

CHAPTER 39

[158] *Michael Landon: Memories with Laughter and Love* aired in 1991.

CHAPTER 40

[159] *Bonanza: The Return* aired on Nov. 28, 1993.
http://www.imdb.com/title/tt0106460/
[160] *Bonanza: Under Attack* aired Jan. 15, 1995.
http://www.imdb.com/title/tt0112554

CHAPTER 41

[161] Kent became a Regent in July 1995 and served until June 2005.
[162] Interview with University of Hartford President Walter Harrison on Nov. 6,
2014. http://www.hartford.edu/aboutuofh/office_pres/biography.aspx
[163] University of Hartford Magnet School. http://www.crecschools.org/our-
schools/university-of-hartford-magnet-school
[164] "The Magic of Reading, an Evening of Fantasy and Illusion" fundraiser was
held May 10, 2003. https://www.hartford.edu/observer/files/pdf/summer-
2003/alumni-news.pdf
[165] Per Kent: "Susan and I put together—mostly Susan—she and I funded the
talent to come and perform. We brought in a gentleman we knew who used to
work in Circ du Soleil. We had a juggler that came out of Virginia and an
illusionist that came down from Boston. We had a big cocktail party before the
dinner we sponsored."
[166] See a photo of "Madam MooCray" here:
https://www.hartford.edu/observer/files/pdf/summer-2004/campaign-news.pdf
[167] Susan served as Regent from July 2005 until June 2011. She and Kent were
named Lifetime Regents in July 2011.
[168] The Harry Sukman Foyer was dedicated April 17, 2005.
https://www.hartford.edu/observer/files/pdf/winter-2005/life-music.pdf
[169] The Kent McCray Television Studio was dedicated Sep. 15, 2005.
http://unotes.hartford.edu/announcements/2005/09/2005-09-19-tv-studio-
dedicated-to-industry-pioneer.aspx

[170] The Kent McCray Black Box Theater in Honor of Tom and Dorothy McCray has approximately 100 seats. It was dedicated Sep. 12, 2008.
http://susanmccray.com/News.html
[171] Kent's Honorary Doctorate was awarded in 2007.
http://www.hartford.edu/Observer/honorary.asp
[172] http://www1.easternct.edu/performingarts/theatre/patrons/susan-and-kent-mccray/
[173]http://www.easternct.edu/universityrelations/files/2016/05/easternMagazine2016Spring.pdf p.6.
[174] http://www1.easternct.edu/newsflash/files/2014/10/20080600.pdf

CHAPTER 42

[175] Kent remembers: "One of the top production managers in the business who'd been in it for years used to join a luncheon of all us old timers. This guy had been around for years. The first time I met him, he motioned me over and said, 'I just want to say hello to you and to shake your hand.' I said, 'I want to shake *your* hand. I've heard about you for years.' He said, 'Yes, but *you're* a legend.' Wow!"
[176] Sept 15 & 16, 2017. See http://www.50thanniversarythehighchaparral.com/ or https://www.facebook.com/The-High-Chaparral-50th-Anniversary-224373281260501/ for more information.
[177] Per Dennis Korn: "*Little House on the Prairie* has been one of the highest-rated shows in television history in syndication. It's in most of the countries in different languages. The number of episodes, that's what I deal with. When you see the number of episodes on *Little House*, there are 216…and three two-hour MOWs (movies of the week). They sell like crazy. Nobody's been on television this long."

INDEX

3

38th parallel 81

6

60 Minutes 212

A

ABC 31
Akins, Claude 188
Alias Jesse James 90
All Star Revue, The 34, 36
Allen, Dorothy and Denny 249
Ancona, Ed 126
Anderson, Melissa Sue ... 178, 251, 265
Arngrim, Alison 183
Arthur, Bea 171
Autry, Gene 172
Azores 87, 89

B

Bachom, Jack ....ii, 60, 72, 74, 84, 87
Baldwin, Ralph Lyman 1, 2
Barnaby Jones 175
Batchelder, David 12
Bateman, Jason 190

Bay of Naples 88, 91
Bayonet Bowl 81, 82
Bedelia, Bonnie 188
Beethoven 286
Begley, Ed 5, 121
Berle, Milton 44, 45, 55, 56
Blocker, Dan ...116, 124, 132, 170, 171, 248
    as Hoss Cartwright 171
Blocker, Dirk 268
Blue and the Gray, The 98
Bob Hope 30, 44, 45, 51, 55, 56, 60, 63, 65, 69, 72, 73, 79, 80, 83, 85, 93, 98, 100, 164, 248, 287
Bob Hope Chevy Show, The 67
Bob Hope Far East Christmas USO Show 85
Boggs, Haskell "Buzzy" .. 127, 132, 135, 137, 185, 266
Bonanza 51, 60, 112, 113, 115, 119, 121, 123, 125, 126, 127, 128, 131, 133, 135, 144, 145, 147, 148, 152, 157, 158, 159, 160, 166, 167, 169, 170, 171, 173, 175, 183, 187, 193, 195, 207, 211, 230, 255, 265, 268, 272, 273, 274, 275, 287
    The Return 268, 272
Boomer, Linwood 190
Borgnine, Ernest 194
Boyton, Bill 12

Brahms 286
Brill, Bud 102
Brown Derby 42
Brown, Les 65, 83, 197
Buick-Berle Show, The 55
Bull, Richard 183
Burbank Studios 59
Burton, Hal 221
Butler, Dean 191, 215, 224
    Almanzo.................................. 215
    Feherty 215
    Legacy Documentaries 215

C

California
    Baldwin Lake............................ 121
    Big Bear 121, 154
    Cedar Lake 121
    City of Simi Valley 184
    Frazier Park............................... 121
    Sonora 177, 179, 181, 185, 186,
        205, 206, 222, 232, 248
    Yankee Hill 179
Canary, David 126, 171, 266
Cannon, Katherine.......................... 211
Cantor, Eddie................. 32, 36, 42, 43
Capitol Records building................... 29
Caranchini, Sil 93, 94, 101
Carey, Philip "Phil".......................... 95
Carney, Art 252, 253, 254, 266
Carson, Johnny 261
Carter Country 205
Casper, Robert............................... 190
CBS .31, 39, 40, 57, 171, 203, 223, 257,
    265
Central City Opera Association.........23
Central City, Colorado 23
Century Fox 172, 188
Channel 9 KFI-TV 25
Channel 9 KHJ-TV 25, 27
Chevrolet................................. 125, 171
Claxton, William "Bill" ... 121, 132, 135,
    137, 141, 142, 145, 183, 190
Cleopatra 172
Clevenger, Billie.......................... 43, 44
Coaxial cable............................... 28, 31
Coe, Fenton ..29, 36, 57, 59, 60, 63, 93,
    99, 105, 109, 110, 116, 135, 173,
    207

Coil, Marvin..................60, 72, 84, 85
Colby, Tony 12, 13
Colgate Comedy Hour 32, 33, 34, 36
Collier, Don 96, 97, 111, 112, 139, 146,
    147, 154
Converse, Frank 188
Cooley, Charlie 70
Cristal, Linda................................. 152

D

Darin, Bobby 164
Darrow, Henry.138, 144, 145, 152, 247
Daves, Don 121, 141
Davis, Ossie 265
DeBenning, Burr............................ 211
Dee, Sandra.................................. 164
DeFrance, Steve 146
DeMille, Cecil B. 57
Denmark 99, 100, 101, 102
    Copenhagen 100, 101, 102
Directors Guild of America 128
Doherty, Shannon 191
Don Pasquale 18
Donohue, Jack...99, 100, 103, 106, 110
Dortort, David 115, 124, 128, 131, 133,
    145, 148, 157, 166, 168, 268, 273,
    275
Dortort, Rose.................................. 166
Dragnet 59
DuMont.. 31
Durante, Jimmy.......................... 32, 33

E

Eastern Connecticut State University
    285
Ebsen, Buddy................................. 175
Edds, Hank 266
Edwards, Ralph ..39, 40, 41, 42, 43, 44,
    112
El Capitan Theater............... 29, 32, 42
Elam, Jack............................... 212, 268
Elmendorf Air Force Base................ 63
England
    London 53, 100, 101, 102, 106
Enquirer, The 260
Erickson, Leif 138, 152

F

Father Murphy............... 209, 211, 212
Fenneman, George........................... 58
Fidler, Jimmy 45
Flippin, Lucy Lee 191
Folsom Prison 210
France.............................. 41, 100, 260
    Paris 40, 41, 87, 101, 106
Francis, Melissa "Missy" 190
French, Victor 178, 180, 190, 194, 205,
    211, 235
    Mr. Edwards 179, 180, 205, 211
Friendly, Ed............. 177, 183, 184, 185

G

Gammons, John...................... 141, 142
Garson, Greer 165
Gaynor, Jock 96
General Electric 110, 268, 269
Gerard, Gil 209
Germany...87
    Frankfurt...................................... 88
Gero, Gary 253
Gershwin, George........................... 286
Gilbert, Jonathan 183
Gilbert, Melissa 178, 216, 218, 221,
    224, 264, 266
    Laura Ingalls....... 175, 178, 194, 215
Gleason, Jackie 253
Globe, The 260
God's Little Acre 223
Gold, Sylvia 188
Gordon, Dan 265, 266
Grassle, Karen...................... 178, 265
Greenbush twins 178
Greene, Lorne 122, 123, 124, 132, 171,
    172, 173, 248
    as Ben Cartwright 122, 268
Greenland................................. 63, 100
Greenlaw, Charlie 159
Greer, Dabbs 183
Guam...81
Gunga Din.............................. 11, 57
Gunn, Moses 190, 211, 266
Gunsmoke............................... 169, 183

H

Habib, George 69
Hagen, Kevin 183
Hainey, Wynn.................................... 34
Hamerman, Milt............................. 187
Hansel and Gretel..................... 18, 22
Happy Days 188
Hardy, Andy 172
Hargitay, Mickey 79, 80
Harris, Pat 188, 189
Harrison, President Walter ... 278, 279,
    281, 282, 283, 284, 285
Hartford
    hurricane 6
Hartt School 5, 7, 17, 18, 22, 29, 47,
    277, 278, 281, 284
Hawaii Five-O 223
Hawkins, John 124, 183, 206
Hayes, Helen 235
Hayward, Chuck 143
Hedrick, Earl 137
Hellzapoppin 161
Heyes, Doug 96, 97
High Chaparral, The i, 51, 60, 119, 121,
    135, 136, 137, 138, 139, 141, 143,
    144, 145, 146, 147, 148, 149, 151,
    152, 157, 159, 160, 162, 166, 167,
    169, 170, 172, 183, 187, 207, 247,
    272, 274, 275, 287
Highway to Heaven ..60, 196, 204, 229,
    235, 236, 238, 239, 240, 241, 243,
    244, 251, 253, 255, 256, 265, 275,
    288
Hitchcock, Alfred 253
Hollywood Opening Night 45
Honeymooners, The 253
Hope, Bob 56, 60, 63, 64, 65, 69, 70,
    71, 72, 77, 78, 80, 81, 82, 84, 85,
    87, 88, 89, 90, 91, 92, 93, 94, 95,
    100
Hope, Jack 56, 73, 84
Hopper, Hedda 78, 79
Housiaux, Ron 225
Hoy, Robert "Bobby"96, 138, 139, 144,
    154, 155

I

IA Union 27, 251

Iceland
  Keflavik 87
ICM Agency 188
Italy............................ 87, 88, 100, 102
  Rome 100
Ivar, Stan 190, 216, 218, 224
Ives, Burl.......................................147

J

Jackson, Anne.................................219
Johnny Dugan Show, The..................41
Johnson, Ben 268, 270, 271
Justman, Bobby 95, 96

K

Kellogg farm 3, 8, 12
Kennedy, George...........................252
Kennedy, Robert "Bobby" 169
Killing Stone.................... 209, 210, 255
Kimball Union Academy . 12, 13, 14, 18
Kleinman, Marsha 188, 189
Kloczko, Cheryl 278, 281
Korean War 27, 28
Korn, Dennis .. 240, 241, 248, 255, 257,
  262, 263
Kung Fu...188
Kwajalein 81

L

Laborteaux, Matthew............. 190, 265
Laborteaux, Patrick.........................205
Lachman, Mort 78
Lancaster, Burt 162
Landon Matthews, Leslie....... 178, 193,
  195, 223, 237, 256, 264, 265
Landon, Cindy 259, 262, 263, 266
Landon, Lynn 133, 197, 206
Landon, Michael 115, 116, 117, 124,
  125, 131, 132, 133, 134, 169, 170,
  171, 172, 173, 175, 176, 177, 178,
  179, 180, 181, 183, 184, 185, 186,
  188, 189, 190, 193, 194, 195, 196,
  197, 198, 203, 204, 205, 206, 210,
  211, 212, 215, 216, 217, 218, 219,
  221, 222, 223, 224, 225, 228, 229,
  230, 231, 235, 236, 237, 238, 239,
  240, 241, 244, 245, 248, 249, 251,
  252, 253, 254, 255, 256, 257, 259,
  260, 261, 262, 263, 264, 265, 266,
  268, 272, 274
  as Little Joe Cartwright..... 169, 171,
  216
Landon, Michael Jr. 178, 265, 268
Lane, Jimmy 122, 158, 159
Larkin, Bill..78
Larson, Richard "Dick"..... 99, 167, 175,
  176, 207
Laverne & Shirley 188
Lawless Years, The 96
Leeds, Peter 78, 79
Lester, Ketty 190
Levian, Lauren 247
Lewis, Jodie 239
Lewis, Judy 111
Leyk, Vern 197, 248
Lilley, Jack.................98, 138, 147, 153
Liszt, Franz.....................................286
Little House on the Prairie . 34, 60, 127,
  175, 176, 177, 178, 182, 186, 188,
  189, 190, 193, 196, 197, 198, 202,
  204, 205, 206, 207, 209, 211, 215,
  216, 217, 218, 223, 224, 229, 230,
  235, 245, 246, 253, 255, 264, 265,
  266, 275, 287
Loneliest Runner, The 203
Lord, Jack 223
Love Rides the Rails 14
Love Story............................... 175, 176
Lux Video Theatre 57

M

MacGregor, Katherine.................... 183
MacLane, Barton.............................. 96
Mancini, Henry............................... 165
Mann, Al... 182
Mannix 188
Mansfield, Jayne 78, 79, 80, 84
Mantle, Mickey 66
Martin & Lewis........................... 32, 35
Martin, Barney 255, 264
Martin, Dean.................................. 110
Martin, Quinn........................ 175, 188
Martin, Strother 212
Marx, Groucho 58, 287
Matheson, Tim............................... 171
Matinee Theatre 59, 60, 63, 72

Matyasi, Andy..................................221
Maude 171
McCleery, Albert...............................59
McClintock....................................209
McCray, Alden 3, 9, 10, 53
McCray, Calvin Curtis..........................4
McCray, Carolyn 49, 50
McCray, Deborah 48, 50
McCray, Dorothy "Dode" Baldwin.. 1, 5
McCray, Kent......1, 2, 96, 98, 111, 112,
    131, 136, 137, 138, 139, 145, 146,
    147, 151, 153, 154, 155, 167, 187,
    189, 195, 196, 197, 198, 199, 206,
    216, 218, 221, 224, 225, 227, 228,
    230, 231, 232, 237, 239, 240, 241,
    243, 247, 248, 249, 252, 256, 262,
    263, 264, 272, 274, 275, 278, 279,
    282, 283, 284, 285
    his father .5, 6, 8, 10, 11, 15, 17, 24,
       25, 27, 29, 49, 54, 202
    his mother .5, 6, 7, 8, 11, 12, 17, 25,
       29, 49, 54, 202
    Honorary Doctorate 285
    Letter from David Dortort 274
McCray, Kristen 48, 49, 50
McCray, Scott 48, 50
McCray, Spencer 48
McCray, Susan Sukman . 161, 163, 165,
    166, 168, 187, 188, 189, 190, 195,
    198, 203, 206, 211, 212, 218, 222,
    223, 224, 227, 229, 230, 231, 232,
    233, 237, 238, 243, 246, 247, 249,
    252, 254, 260, 262, 263, 265, 266,
    271, 272, 275, 277, 278, 279, 280,
    281, 282, 284, 285, 286, 287, 288
    Foyer at Eastern Connecticut State
       University..............................286
    her father... 163, 164, 166, 167, 230
    her mother 163, 230
    Honorary Doctorate 286
    Susan Sands 166
McCray, Thomas Chapman.................4
McLaglen, Victor................................43
McNulty, Barney...............................80
McQueen, Steve 126
Melody Ranch.................................172
Memories with Laughter and Love 265,
    266
Meriwether, Lee 175

MGM 95, 96, 97, 99, 159, 172, 197,
    202, 207, 251
    Stage 15............................ 197, 207
Middough, Miles 176, 177, 183
Minelli, Liza 162
Mitchell, Cameron 151, 152
Montgomery, George 132
Morley, Bill 73
Morocco....................................87, 89
Mulligan, Richard 265
Musselman, John 196
My Favorite Year 31

N

Nagy, Dr. Elemer 17, 18, 19, 20, 21, 22,
    23, 25
NBC .. 11, 24, 28, 29, 30, 31, 32, 33, 34,
    35, 36, 37, 39, 40, 42, 43, 45, 55,
    56, 57, 58, 59, 60, 61, 63, 67, 70,
    92, 93, 96, 98, 101, 103, 105, 109,
    110, 112, 115, 116, 117, 125, 126,
    128, 135, 136, 137, 139, 144, 153,
    157, 159, 167, 170, 172, 176, 177,
    178, 182, 184, 188, 189, 197, 202,
    205, 207, 215, 217, 235, 241, 255,
    256, 257, 268, 269, 270, 271, 272,
    273, 274
Newcomb, Dr. Kate Pelham 43
Norway.. 100

O

O'Toole, Peter 31
Odd Couple, The 188
Okinawa 77, 79
Oklahoma Crude 177
Old Tucson Movie Studios..... 136, 137,
    145, 172
Olsen, Merlin.. 191, 205, 206, 211, 264,
    265
    as Father Murphy 211
    as Jonathan Garvey 205
Opie, Jim 179, 181
Orbison, Roy..................................166
Orvis Ranch 177, 179, 181
Outlaws 95, 96, 97, 98, 99, 109, 111,
    112, 115

P

Palace Theater................................29
Parady, Hersha 191, 205
Paramount..87, 97, 111, 115, 127, 131,
    159, 162, 172, 175, 176, 177, 183,
    188, 207
Paranov, Moshe 5, 17, 20
Pardon Our French 161
Pawlek, Johnny.............. 72, 74, 77, 87
Payne, John 115
Penn, Leo.......................................190
Peterson, Casey..............................255
Petitclerc, Denne........... 135, 272, 273
Pevney, Joe....................................190
Philip Marlowe 95
Pickens, Slim..................................111
Pinky Lee Show, The 57
Pitti, Carl.......................................138
Portugal.................................. 100, 101
    Lisbon 101, 103, 104, 105

Q

Queen for a Day 57
Quiroga, Alex.......... 103, 104, 106, 126

R

Ralph Edwards Show, The 39, 41
Ramos, Rudy...................................152
RCA.............. 28, 29, 61, 112, 126, 197
Reagan, President & Mrs...............263
Red Skelton Show, The.... 36, 37, 41, 57
Reivers, The 126
Restless Gun, The............................115
Rettig, Earl....................................29
Roberston, Cliff..............................111
Roberts, Pernell...... 125, 126, 171, 265
Rogers, Ginger.......................... 64, 65
Roland, Gilbert 170
Rose Bowl........................ 44, 90, 197
Rose Bowl Parade...................44, 197
Rose, David....................................121
Rosenbloom, Carroll.......................203
Roundtree, Richard 268
Roylance, Pamela 190, 216

S

Sam's Son 219
Samuel Goldwyn Studios........ 185, 188
Sarnoff, General David 29
Sarnoff, Robert................................29
Sarnoff, Thomas 29, 110, 268, 273
Say a Prayer for Michael 166
Scandal...196
Scotland 87
    Prestwick....................................92
Senkel, Ruth 47, 48, 49, 50, 51, 52
Sharp, Florence 209
Shelton, Robert "Bob"... 136, 142, 145,
    153, 170
Shore, Dinah.......34, 99, 101, 102, 103,
    104, 105, 106, 107, 110
Silvera, Frank...................... 152, 170
Sinatra, Frank 232
Skelton, Red 36, 37, 39, 44, 57
Slade, Mark 152
Snead, Sam................................ 69, 70
Song Without End: The Story of Franz
    Liszt 163, 164
Sonntag, Jack..................................176
Sony Studios...................................257
South Korea.............................. 77, 81
    Seoul 77, 83, 84
Spain 87, 89, 100, 101, 102, 104
    Madrid...89, 90, 101, 102, 103, 104,
    105
Stanley, Jerry...................................58
Stevens, Ray 166
Stoner, Sherri 191
Streets of San Francisco, The.......... 188
Sukman, Francesca (Paley).... 161, 229,
    232, 233
Sukman, Harry 121, 161, 164, 165, 166,
    199, 232, 282, 286
Sullivan, Tom...........239, 240, 248, 265
Summers, Jerry 139
Summers, Neil.................................146
Sweden 100
Swenson, Karl.................................183

T

Tartikoff, Brandon...212, 241, 255, 256
Taylor, Dub....................................212
Telford, Frank.................................97

Texaco Star Theater...........................55
Thirty Seconds Over Tokyo 207
This is Your Life 41, 43, 61
Tindell, Clarence............. 195, 197, 225
Tonight Show..................................261
Tracy, Spencer 207
Tracy, Steve 190
Trapper John, M.D...........................126
Travelers Insurance 5
Travis Air Force Base 74
Turnbaugh twins 191

U

United Artists 87
University of Hartford 18, 224, 252,
    277, 278, 281, 285
    Kent as Regent..................277, 285
    Magic of Reading, The 279
    Susan as Regent........................281
Us 256, 257, 259, 260
USO..................... 63, 65, 72, 76, 87, 92
USO Xmas European Bases Show 92
USS Forrestal 88, 91, 92

V

Van Dyke, Dick................................265
Variety...273
Ventura, Jesse 218
Vogel, Mitch 126
Voigtlander, Ted.... 132, 177, 179, 183,
    210

W

Wake Island................................ 76, 81
Wallach, Eli............................. 219, 266
Walnut Grove.183, 185, 205, 217, 218,
    266
Wang, Gene 95
Warner Brothers 159, 171, 188
Warren, John................. 210, 251, 252
Wayne, John............139, 204, 209, 271
Webb, Jack 59
Welch, Dick 29, 32, 33, 34
West, John 28, 29, 30
Where Pigeons Go to Die251, 252, 253,
    254, 255
White Wings...................................... 19
Wilder, Laura Ingalls....................... 175
Williams, Esther 172
Williams, Trevor 177, 183, 251, 252
Wills, Henry.............138, 141, 142, 146
Wilson, Dean 195
Wizard of Oz, The 207
World War II.............................. 10, 11
WTIC....................................5, 6, 11, 17
Wynn, Ed... 32

Y

Yacobian, Brad 196, 225
Yarnell, Bruce 111
You Bet Your Life 58, 59
Young, Victor.................................. 163

Z

Zuckerman, Lee................ 99, 100, 102

LIST OF SELECTED RESOURCES

American Radio History. (1952, March 03). Retrieved from
http://americanradiohistory.com:
http://americanradiohistory.com/Archive-BC/BC-1952/BC-1952-03-
17.pdf

Archive of American Television. (1997, May 21). Retrieved 2016, from
www.emmytvlegends.org:
http://www.emmytvlegends.org/interviews/people/ralph-edwards

Bob & Dolores Hope Foundation. (2015). Retrieved 2016, from
BobHope.org: http://www.bobhope.org

Hartford Radio History. (n.d.). Retrieved 2015, from
www.hartfordradiohistory.com:
http://www.hartfordradiohistory.com/WTIC__AM_.php

IMDB. (n.d.). Retrieved 2014-2017, from imdb.com:
http://www.www.imdb.com

McCray, S. S. (2017, April). *50th Anniversary The High Chaparral.*
Retrieved March 4, 2017, from 50thanniversarythehighchapaarral.com:
http://www.50thanniversarythehighchaparral.com/

New Telephone Skyway Serves U.S.A. (1951). Retrieved from
http://long-lines.net/places-
routes/1st_transcon_mw/Telephone_Skyway.pdf: http://long-
lines.net/places-routes/1st_transcon_mw/Telephone_Skyway.pdf

TTV.com. (2017). Retrieved 2016, from TV.com: http://www.tv.com

Wikipedia Channel 9 KCAL-TV. (2011, November). Retrieved February
2017, from https://en.wikipedia.org:
https://en.wikipedia.org/wiki/KCAL-TV

WTIC Alumni. (1936). Retrieved from www.wticalumni.com:
http://www.wticalumni.com/history.htm

ABOUT THE AUTHORS

Marianne Rittner-Holmes

Marianne Rittner-Holmes, a U.S. Army veteran, retired from the corporate world after 25 years. She now pursues a freelance writing career online and in print. She has a B.A. in English from St. Francis University in Loretto, Penn., and an M.A. in Journalism from the University of Arizona.

Marianne is active in her church and volunteers in her rural community as an EMT-Intermediate. She and her husband Dave live in the desert south of Albuquerque, N.M., along with their three rescue dogs. (http://www.alphadox.us)

Kent McCray

Kent McCray is one of the most-recognized production managers/producers in the television industry. He has run production crews and produced shows for Bob Hope, Michael Landon, Ralph Edwards, Red Skelton, Groucho Marx and more. He and his wife Susan reside in the North Ranch area of Westlake Village, Calif. (http://www.kentmccray.com)